C000132916

DREAM CARS

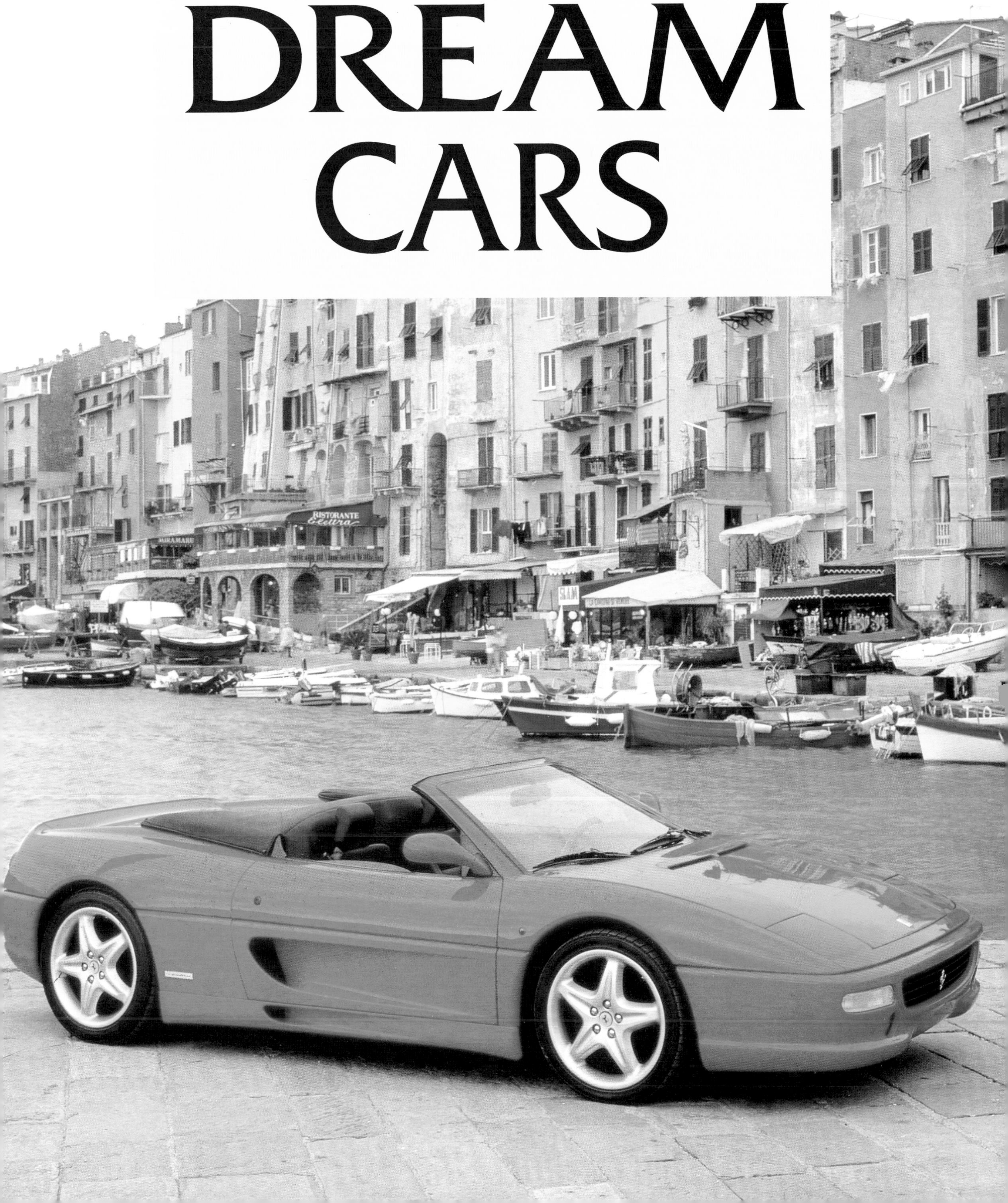

DREAM CARS

MICHAEL BOWLER • JONATHAN WOOD

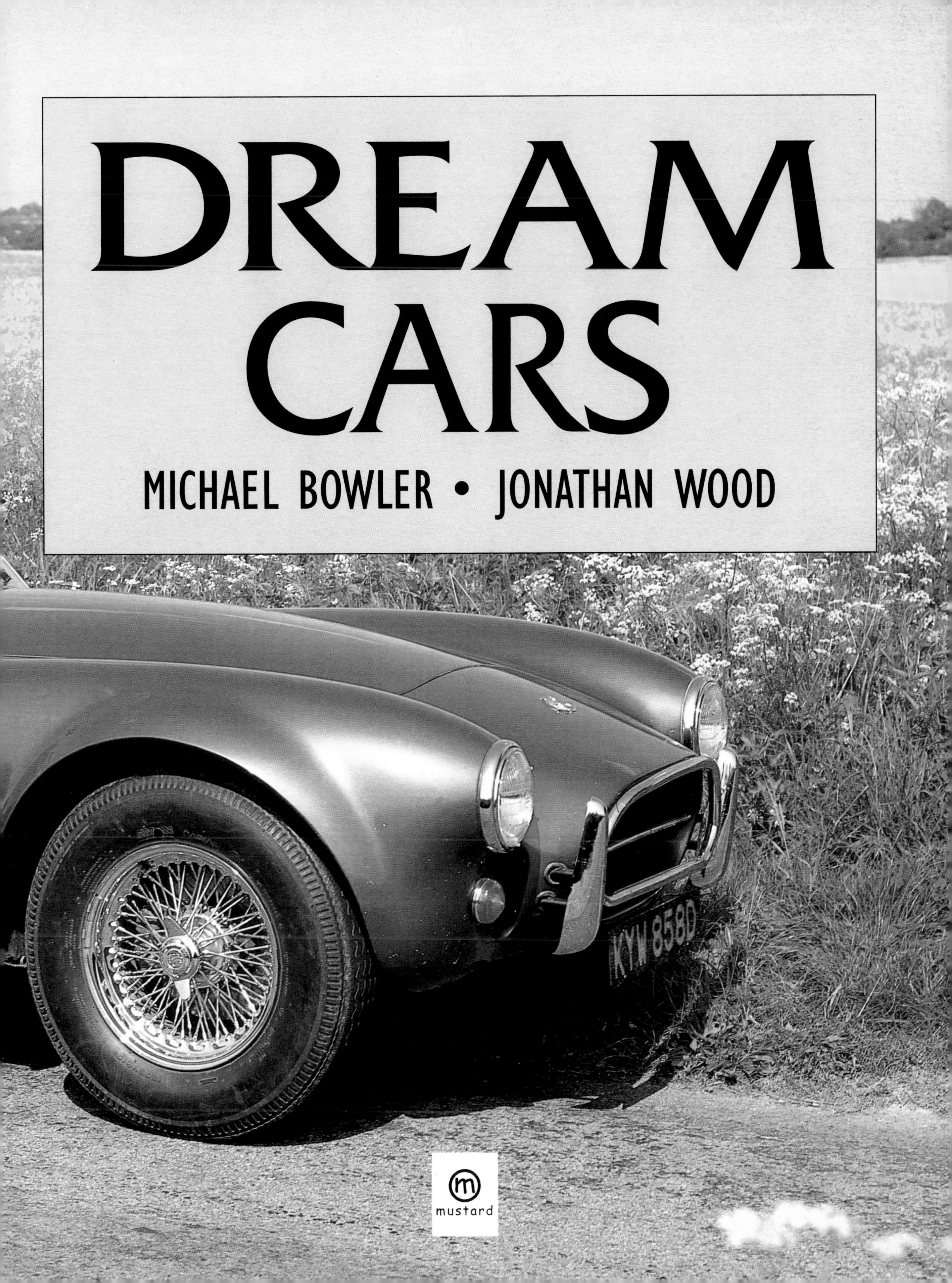

mustard

Page 1

A Ferrari is usually near the top of most Dream Car lists.

Pages 2-3

The AC Cobra 289 is the most copied classic of all-time, a tribute to the style of the original Ace of 13 years earlier than this 1966 version.

Page 6

The fabulous McLaren F1 LM, incorporating race-bred technology and capable of a stupendous 220 mph.

This edition published by Mustard, 1999
Mustard is an imprint of Parragon

The Fastest Cars From Around the World and *Classic Cars From Around the World* first published by Parragon in 1995

Parragon
Queen Street House
4 Queen Street
Bath BA1 1HE
United Kingdom

Designed and produced by
Stonecastle Graphics Limited
Old Chapel Studio, Plain Road, Marden
Tonbridge, Kent TN12 9LS United Kingdom

ISBN 1-84164-145-6

Printed in Italy

Photographic credits

All photographs by Neill Bruce Motoring Photolibrary with the exception of the following: (Abbreviations: r = right, l = left, t = top, b = below)

The Peter Roberts Collection c/o Neill Bruce: pages 24-25, 28-29, 31, 32-33, 40, 43(t), 45(b), 46, 51(t), 58-59, 66, 70, 71, 77, 78, 79, 82-83(b), 86, 88-89, 90-91, 92-93, 94-95 107(b), 115, 118, 125(t), 135(t), 145(b), 158, 167(t), 167(b), 175(t), 175(b), 182, 186, 187(b).
The National Motor Museum: pages 48-49, 114(b), 123(b), 126(l) *Nicky Wright*, 138, 139(t) *Nicky Wright*, 156-157, 168 *Nicky Wright*, 169(b) *Nicky Wright*, 176 *Nicky Wright*, 181(t), 181(b).
Andrew Morland: pages 52-53, 60-61, 62-63, 97(b), 116, 117(b), 124, 147(r), 149(t), 164, 166, 171(t), 177(b), 178, 184, 185(b).
D. Hodges: page 97(t), 97(r), 119(t), 123(t), 134-135(b), 177(t), 180.
McLaren Cars Ltd: pages 5, 74, 75(t).
Bengt Holm: page 13(b), 133(r).
Giles Chapman Library: page 1.
Trevor Legate: page 10.
Michael Bowler: page 137(b).

With grateful thanks to Neill Bruce for his kind assistance, and to all other photographers and copyright holders for their contributions.

Lister Storm photographed courtesy of Denbies Wine Estate, Dorking, Surrey, UK.

Contents

The Fastest CARS From Around the World

MICHAEL BOWLER
REVISED AND UPDATED BY JONATHAN WOOD

CONTENTS – THE FASTEST CARS

INTRODUCTION

Man is a very competitive animal, and few pastimes evoke such instincts among otherwise staid individuals as does the challenge of fast cars; ever since the first engine-driven carriages chugged down a dusty track, the same old question has always been asked . . . *'What'll she do, mister?'* This book details just what the road-going production car is capable of achieving in the hands of independent testers with accurate instruments. Not optimistic statements by manufacturers, not exaggerated claims from keen owners reading inaccurate speedometers with a following wind, down a hill – but real timed speeds, as an average of runs in opposite directions.

The traditional method of showing who had the fastest car was to organise a motor race. The first officially timed event was the 732-mile round trip from Paris to Bordeaux and back in 1895 – Levassor won in a Panhard at 15 mph. The first land speed record was established by the Count de Chasseloup's Jeanteaud electric car in 1898 at 39.3 mph, eclipsed the next year by Jenatzy's electric Jamais Contente at 65.8 mph. The last record to be taken on a closed public road was in 1924 when Ernest Eldridge recorded 146 mph in the aero-engined Fiat at Arpajon, just south of Paris; and the first to break the 150 mph barrier was Malcolm Campbell with a Sunbeam, also aero-engined, in 1926.

Ever since the arrival of the 911 over 30 years ago, Porsche have built fast cars; the data-base lists 22 different models that have exceeded 150 mph. This 1986 Carrera clocked 154 mph.

By then, the ultimate speed records could only be taken by purpose-built machines, built either by enthusiastic amateurs or factory experimental departments. Now, 70 years on, such speeds can be attained by comfortable, fast road cars which have to provide so much more than just an impressive top speed figure; in fact, both BMW and Mercedes, have given up claiming top speeds and electronically restrict their cars to 250 km/h (155 mph) despite Germany providing the last stretches of unrestricted road in the western world – for those, we have assumed a simple 'chip-change' and calculated their real maxima.

All the cars chosen are standard road cars, with the specifications as listed by their manufacturers. We have ignored any faster versions which have been prepared by special tuning companies, even when these are approved by the manufacturer. BMW approve of the work of Alpina and Schnitzer who run their touring car race-teams; Mercedes include some AMG-tuned cars in their own price-lists, and there are a number of German specialists who tune Porsche Turbos. From across the Atlantic, Callaway fits turbochargers to Corvettes; the Sledgehammer version has clocked 250 mph at Daytona Beach and it was driven there on the road.

It has always been possible to make a car go faster than the maker intended, but generally the car won't last as long and the manufacturer's warranty will be invalidated. If you want to work out how much faster a tuned car will go, a 10% power increase will give a 3.5% increase in ideal maximum speed provided the power peak has been moved to match the new top speed, or the gearing has been changed. If however, you increase the aerodynamic drag at the same time, by adding spoilers and wheel arches, you may increase stability but the maximum speed increase will be less than expected.

While maximum speed has long been used as an indication of general performance, it is

acceleration that drivers can legally use; actual driving conditions would suggest that the time taken to accelerate from 30-70 mph in an overtaking gear should be the most interesting, but few people carry such a comparison in their heads, so the time taken from 0-60 mph is generally used. Although this involves the sort of driving you shouldn't use on the road – clutch-dumping wheelspin starts – it is far easier to measure and compare 100% effort than anything less. In fact, the 0-60 mph time is very dependent on gear ratios as you lose a noticeable proportion of the overall time whenever you have to change gear; with these fast cars, a comparison of the 0-100 mph times is far more valid – gear change times and take-off techniques make less apparent difference.

While manufacturers will take such figures as part of comparison during development, there has been no world-wide standard that covers the last 40 years and some manufacturers have exaggerated more than others. Until the mid-'seventies they used to exaggerate power figures too – the American power race of the late 'fifties inflated figures well beyond those of their European counterparts. We can't go back to check what these should have been but, for performance figures, we have used those taken by independent magazines at the time. Not all magazines are as objective as each other. *Autocar* and *Motor* magazines, once separate then merged and latterly just *Autocar*, used professional recording equipment; drivers were trained to get the best out of any car. In America, *Road & Track* and *Car & Driver* have been equally objective. The vast majority of the figures here have come from these sources; where other magazines' figures have been borrowed, these have only been used after careful checking of test methods and confirmation by calculation. To all of them I am grateful for the use of their hard work; I spent many hours doing the same myself in the 'sixties at the Motor Industry Research Association track.

Nowadays, *Autocar* and other British magazines use the General Motors facility at Millbrook near Luton. While a lap round the banked track is accurate up to 150 mph, speed is scrubbed off by cornering beyond this, so some of the cars listed in the 150-175 mph bracket may be able to go 2-3 mph faster – certainly none of them is exaggerated. Faster cars will have been tested in Germany or at the high-speed Italian track in Nardo, or at American equivalents.

The Database lists 150 different production models that have reached at least 150 mph; naturally there are a large number from Ferrari and Porsche. From these we have selected 43 that have exceeded 160 mph regardless of age; but within the chapters most of the others have been mentioned as part of the development story that has led to the fastest, and usually latest, equivalent model. Some of those that have still to confirm their ability have been included in the final chapter.

'What'll she do, mister?' – Now you know.

'This book details just what the road-going production car is capable of achieving in the hands of independent testers with accurate instruments.'

Jaguar have a strong competition record but mostly just build cars that are comfortable and quick. This XJ220 was a statement that Jaguar technology is still up with the best of them; at 217 mph only two are faster.

AC COBRA 427

1965

160 mph

(257 km/h)

Carroll Shelby added muscles to the AC Ace, first with the 4.7-litre Ford V-8, then as the Cobra with the 7-litre Ford in a new, stronger chassis. The competition Cobra shown was originally raced by John Woolf.

Few cars have captured the imagination of the performance world as the Cobra did in the mid-'sixties, and the legend has lived on through the many replicas to emerge again in the Viper, its spiritual successor. It was the time-honoured recipe of getting the biggest possible engine into the lightest frame that could handle the power and clothing it in an attractive two-seater body, preferably an open top for maximum enjoyment on the open road.

While the AC marque was founded back in 1901, the Cobra story starts with the 1953 introduction of the second generation Ace. Engineer John Tojeiro had created his own sports two seater modelled on the Ferrari 166 Barchetta (little boat); Tojeiro's cars were powered by MG or Bristol. He sold the design to AC who installed their own 85 bhp 2-litre six-cylinder engine; in 1957, a Bristol 2-litre version was introduced giving another 30 bhp and a maximum around 115 mph.

A Ford 2.6-litre version followed in 1961 with anything from 100-170 bhp.

All was to change in 1962 when Carroll Shelby, impressed by the performance of the AC-Bristols in American racing, persuaded AC to drop a Ford V-8 into the spacious engine compartment. Fitting the initial 260 cu.in. (4.2-litre) lightweight engine was little problem but the suspension and drive-train needed considerable beefing up to take double the previous power output. AC were soon turning out five engine-less cars a week for Shelby to install Ford's engines and gearboxes; the 4.2-litre would soon be replaced by the 271 bhp 4.7-litre (289 cu.in.).

Not content with a mere 270-350 bhp from the small block Ford, Shelby wanted even more power, so the 7-litre Ford (427 cu.in.) was inserted, but only after the chassis had been given the Ford computer treatment. The main chassis tubes were increased in diameter to 4-inches, the car was widened and the old transverse leaf springs were

The road-going Cobra was only a little more comfortable than a racer but was still draughty and noisy by any standards.

replaced with proper wishbones and coil springs all round; the chassis was adopted for the subsequent 4.7-litre versions from 1964. It was these uprated 289s using a mixture of open and coupé bodies that gave the Cobra its World Sports Car championship victory in 1965; there weren't enough 427s built for them to race in International GT racing but they were successful in American SCCA events.

On the road they were everything that they set out to be, fast and fun but somewhat lacking in creature comforts. Although the 'fifties ACs were appropriate for the time, by the 'sixties they were feeling dated alongside more sophisticated designs like the Lotus Elan. The 289 was the pleasanter road car; with narrower tyres it was lighter to drive and didn't twitch on every white line; but it was still shatteringly fast off the line reaching 100 mph in 13.7 seconds for *Motor* magazine. *Motor* also tested a competition version of the 7-litre with 580 bhp which could reach 100 mph in under 10 seconds, accompanied by raucous bellowing from the twin side exhausts. Noise and the sheer exhilaration of the performance were abiding memories of both cars, and the shape had a timeless beauty.

Finding true performance figures for the two models is difficult as magazines seem to have tested them in a variety of different states of tune and a choice of axle ratios. American tests of the original 260 version claimed 100 mph in 10.8 seconds which was faster than many managed with the later 427; it was always difficult balancing the wheelspin for the best times. Reasonable figures for the later, wider 289 would suggest a maximum of 145 mph with the later 3.31 axle, 0-60 mph in 5.2 sec and 0-100 mph in 13.0 sec.

The standard output for the 427 was 425 bhp, but they could also be bought in Street/Competition form with 485 bhp. *Motor* magazine tried the latter and recorded 0-100 mph in 10.1 seconds, which was very fast indeed for 1965. Others observed a maximum speed of 160 mph which corresponded to a heady 7000 rpm. The Cobras were real muscle cars.

SPECIFICATION	AC COBRA 427
ENGINE	V-8 6998 cc (427 cu.in)
HORSEPOWER	485 bhp @ 6500 rpm
TRANSMISSION	Manual 4-speed
CHASSIS	Twin tube steel
BRAKES	Discs all round
TOP SPEED	160 mph (257 km/h)
ACCELERATION	**0-60 mph** 4.6 seconds **0-100 mph** 10.1 seconds

'On the road they were everything that they set out to be, fast and fun.'

ASTON MARTIN V-8 VANTAGE

1977

170 mph

(274 km/h)

'It was a much more comfortable car than its predecessors.'

With 375 bhp, Newport Pagnell's bespoke Vantage was the world's fastest four-seater in 1977.

Big but still elegant, the V-8 Vantage put Aston Martin firmly into the 'seventies supercar league and gave the company a justifiable claim as producers of the world's fastest four-seater production car. Motor racing in the 'fifties and James Bond in the 'sixties had put Aston Martin on the world map as the car you promised yourself, one day. The V-8 Vantage made sure that its performance would be in keeping with its reputation when that day arrived.

In days when most supercars weighed no more than a ton and a half, the 4000 lb Vantage needed a pretty impressive power output to keep up. The trusty 5.34-litre four-cam V-8 was worked on to produce a reliable and tractable 375 bhp thanks to four big downdraught 48 IDF Weber carburetters, bigger inlets valves and a better exhaust system; with a drag factor of 0.38, this enabled a maximum speed of 170 mph; but, even the standard V8 saloon had 300 bhp which was good for nearly 150 mph.

While James Bond had made the DB series famous – he used a 147 mph 1963 DB5 – and these continued through to the DB6 Mk II, Aston's then owner David Brown wanted to produce a genuine 4-seater which even the longer wheelbase DB6 didn't really achieve, and it had to be faster than the 4-litre cars. Accordingly work started in 1963 on a new all aluminium V-8 engine. While the new car might have been one designed by the Italian coachbuilder Touring, who had styled the DB4, the company switched to one designed in-house by William Towns; although the extra width of the V-8 engine demanded a new chassis, this was essentially just a widened DB6 with new bodywork, but there was an important change in the rear suspension which adopted a de Dion axle.

Unfortunately development on the V-8 wasn't as fast as with the rest of the car, so the new DBS had to start life in 1967 with the 6-cylinder 4-litre engine; it was a much more comfortable car than its predecessors, but inevitably it was slower. It was

1969 before the V-8 was finally ready with 315 bhp using Bosch fuel injection to give a top speed of 160 mph. That the 1977 V-8 produced less horsepower was a function of increasingly restrictive emission laws.

Between the 1969 launch of the DBS V-8 and the 1977 170 mph test, Aston Martin went through two changes of ownership and a six-month shut-down. Sir David Brown had, for a long time, run Astons at a loss, almost as the promotional arm of the David Brown Corporation; by the end of 1971 this had to come to an end and Company Developments took over the ownership, and successfully continued development of the renamed Aston Martin V-8. By the end of 1974, they were in trouble and had to put the company into receivership; although the service department continued, production stopped. New owners, American Peter Sprague and Canadian George Minden, started in July 1975, to be joined six months later by Alan Curtis. Enthusiasts all, they soon had the V-8 back in production and started development of the new razor-edge Lagonda, also styled by William Towns. The intention had been that a new Aston shape would follow as a two-door version, but that never happened. Everyone was quite happy with the old V-8 style; in 1978 this was further revised with an integrated tail spoiler, a result of the Vantage development which had reduced the drag.

With steady refinement, the Vantage was to stay in production for another 12 years from the date of this test; even now it is still a very quick car.

Filling in the grille area and allowing engine air to enter through the spoiler usefully lowered the drag factor, opposite: Middle East cars retained the V-8 grille for extra cooling.

Almost as fast were the limited run of Vantage Volantes; obvious Vantage details were supplemented by wheel arch flares and sill mouldings.

SPECIFICATION	ASTON MARTIN V-8 VANTAGE
ENGINE	Aluminium V-8 four-cam, 5340 cc
POWER	375 bhp @ 6000 rpm
TRANSMISSION	Manual 5-speed ZF
CHASSIS	Steel with aluminium body
BRAKES	Discs all round
TOP SPEED	170 mph (274 km/h)
ACCELERATION	**0-60 mph** 5.4 seconds **0-100 mph** 13.0 seconds

ASTON MARTIN VANTAGE ZAGATO

1986
186 mph
(299 km/h)

'It was to be the renewal of an old association which brought Aston Martin back, once again, among the world's fastest cars.'

Back in 1984, Aston Martin needed a new model. The same shape had been in production since 1967 when it was launched with the 6-cylinder engine, but a completely new model was too expensive. A new suit of clothes would be more affordable.

It was to be the renewal of an old association which brought Aston Martin back, once again, among the world's fastest cars. Back in 1959, the company wanted to produce a special lightweight version of the DB4GT; they went to the Italian styling house of Zagato in Milan and 19 models were built from 1962-4. Twenty-five years on, the new owners were looking for a similar extension to the Vantage range at the time of the 1984 Geneva Motor Show; they visited the Zagato stand. Founder Ugo Zagato had died, but the company was being run by his two sons, Dr. Elio and Ing. Gianni.

During the earlier Aston Zagato production, the Italian company was building a number of niche models for the various separate Italian manufacturers. By 1984, the major part of the Italian industry was controlled by Fiat and Zagato needed to find work outside Italy. The arrival of the Aston principals, Victor Gauntlett and Peter Livanos, was manna from heaven. Shortly after that motor show meeting, the general specification for a new Zagato-bodied Aston Martin was agreed – light enough to reach 60 mph in under 5 seconds and aerodynamic enough to achieve 300 km/h with 435 bhp, with just two seats and a probable production of 50 cars.

The engine to be used was the trusty V-8 which had been the company's mainstay from 1969. An aluminium 5.3-litre unit, it had twin overhead camshafts for each bank with four downdraught Weber carburetters sitting in the vee.

With 50 examples built, the 1986 Zagato-bodied Aston was more successful if less appealing than the 1961 DB4GT Zagato. Bonnet bulge, less obtrusive than prototype version, hides downdraught Weber carburetters.

As used in the V-8 saloon and Lagonda it developed around 300 bhp, and 375 bhp for the Vantage; a more powerful 435 bhp version was developed for the after market with bigger carburetters, new camshafts, higher compression and larger exhaust manifolds and this was the one fitted to the Vantage Zagato.

The Zagatos set to work and would probably have had a prototype ready for the following Geneva show had Aston Martin not imposed a 6-month delay in the middle. As it was, there was only a sketch for show visitors, but this and the Aston Martin and Zagato reputations were enough to persuade 50 buyers to place deposits over the next six months.

Finally, three prototypes were at the 1986 Geneva Show, and production of the 50 cars began shortly afterwards. Aston Martin sent a rolling chassis out to Italy, a working platform which had already been tested on the road. Zagato built a new superstructure, fitted the aluminium panels, trimmed the interior, painted the car and then sent it back to Newport Pagnell. Despite mixed feelings about the styling, there was no doubt about its appeal or its performance.

After the Vantage Zagato came 35 Volante Zagatos, here showing how flat the earlier bonnet would have been with fuel injection.

The car that was offered to the press was one of the prototypes and the French magazine *Sport Auto* was the only one to record a true maximum speed. Using a piece of unopened motorway, they achieved 299 km/h, only 1 km/h short of the target. The 0-60 mph figure came to 4.8 seconds – on target.

That prototype had a somewhat unsightly power bulge on its bonnet to clear the downdraught carburation. Originally, it had been intended to fit fuel injection to the Vantage engine, as had been developed for the less powerful V-8, but this was never completed on the two-valve engine; however Zagato designed the bonnet around the lower profile of an injection system and had to change this after the overall shape was finalised. The prototype's bulge was roughly shaped at the factory; although Zagato designed a much less obtrusive bulge for the production cars, the press never forgot and always drew attention to that bulge. How it should have looked was seen on the subsequent Volante Zagato convertibles, a limited run of 35 cars fitted with the less powerful injection engine.

Awesome in its noise and performance, the Vantage Zagato served its purpose and put Aston Martin back into the supercar league.

SPECIFICATION	ASTON MARTIN VANTAGE ZAGATO
ENGINE	Aluminium V-8 four-cam, 5340 cc
POWER	435 bhp @ 6000 rpm
TRANSMISSION	Manual 5-speed ZF
CHASSIS	Steel with aluminium body
BRAKES	Discs all round
TOP SPEED	186 mph (299 km/h)
ACCELERATION	**0-60 mph** 4.8 seconds **0-100 mph** 11.3 seconds

ASTON MARTIN VANTAGE

1993
184 mph
(296 km/h)

'But the handling is all that you expect and want from a powerful rear-wheel-drive sports car.'

Understated it is not. The latest Aston Vantage is a far more brutal version of the standard car than any Vantage has ever been since the name was coined for the DB2's more powerful engine back in 1951. Then and through the DB series, Vantage just meant more power; it wasn't until 1977 that Vantage became a separate model, recognisable at a glance with wider wheels with wheel-arch flares and a wind-cheating front with fashionable and effective front air-dam.

The standard Virage isn't slow with a maximum speed around 157 mph, but it has a fair amount of weight to get under way, so the 0-60 mph time is not really to Aston standards – at 6.8 seconds, it is slower than a Volkswagen Corrado VR6. And the Virage is designed for comfortable fast touring, so it lacks the handling tautness that the traditional Aston driver expects. The Vantage addresses these relative shortcomings in full measure.

The standard engine is a development of the original Marek-designed aluminium V-8, only it now has four-valve heads designed by the American Reeves Callaway, who had been responsible for the race engines used in the 1989 AMR-1 race programme.

In full emission form this develops 335 bhp. For some time, the traditional way of increasing power has been to use turbo-charging, but this brings with it the problem of turbo-lag – the delay in response to the throttle while the turbos build up speed; big turbos for big engines take even longer, which is why the Bugatti uses no fewer than four units. Aston Martin decided to revert to the 'thirties traditions of supercharging, where the units are directly driven by the engine and thus provide instant response; the drawback is that this consumes extra power so fuel consumption suffers. Using twin Eaton 'blowers' the 5.34-litre V-8 now produces a massive 550 bhp, but still has tremendous torque – 550 lb.ft. is more than any other production engine.

The traditional ZF 5-speed gearbox has been replaced by a 6-speed version used in the Chevrolet Corvette; five gears are used to power the Vantage up to its maximum speed with sixth an overdrive, giving a very long-legged 42 mph per 1000 rpm. *Autocar* testing saw 177 mph in fifth gear around the Millbrook bowl and there was more to come; Aston Martin say the car has recorded 191 mph, so we have settled for an average of the two at 184 mph at a red-lined 6500 rpm, which is the point at which the engine develops its maximum power. In acceleration, the new Vantage is very quick despite weighing nearly two tons; 0-60 mph in 4.6 seconds and 0-100 mph in 10.1 seconds put it into the top ten, and it is the only four-seater among them.

Heavy fuel consumption – you might get 15 mpg – is one drawback, but there are others

SPECIFICATION	ASTON MARTIN VANTAGE
ENGINE	Supercharged aluminium V-8 5340 cc
POWER	550 bhp @ 6500 rpm
TRANSMISSION	Manual 6-speed
CHASSIS	Steel with aluminium bodywork
BRAKES	Discs all round with ABS
TOP SPEED	184 mph (296 km/h)
ACCELERATION	**0-60 mph** 4.6 seconds **0-100 mph** 10.1 seconds

inevitable when you try to make that size of car handle like a two-seater sports car. The suspension has been considerably stiffened to keep roll angles down, so the ride is bouncy while wide low profile tyres add to the road noise that this generates; and the engine is far from quiet until you drop into that long-legged sixth. But the handling is all that you expect and want from a powerful rear-wheel-drive sports car; the front responds well to the steering and the back answers to the throttle.

The standard Virage was launched in the winter of 1988 after a very quick design period. The original V-8 was costly to build and many of its parts, borrowed from other manufacturers, were long obsolete; Virage thinking went back 10 years when a new V-8 was planned as a shortened version of the more modern Lagonda, only this would have its own body. The first Virage prototype was a shortened Lagonda to test all the mechanical components; and the new body came from the RCA duo, John Heffernan and Ken Greenley, echoing the past in a new modern shape. The Vantage took Astons back into the supercar league.

Steroidal Virage has 550 bhp thanks to twin super-charged V-8 with muscular bulges to match. Interior trim is to legendary Aston levels with full instrumentation.

ASTON MARTIN DB7

1994

161 mph

259 km/h

'Aston's own tests produced 165 mph.'

A convertible DB7, that was accorded the marque's traditional Volante name, appeared in 1996. Its top speed of 155 mph is slightly less than that of the coupé.

After a gap of 24 years, the DB7 has continued the range of numbers that David Brown set up when he took over the company in 1947. As Sir David Brown he had sold the company at the end of 1971 when the DBS was in production; the six-cylinder DB6 Mk II had stopped in November 1970. However Sir David was brought back into the fold as patron when new owners, Ford, started the design of the new small Aston; he was delighted to allow the use of his initials for the new car – in fact, the original DBS was nearly called a DB7.

Throughout the 'eighties, Aston's previous owners, Victor Gauntlett and Peter Livanos, had recognised that the company needed an entry level Aston 2+2 to join the Porsche 928 and Mercedes SL market. Unfortunately there just wasn't sufficient capital available to be able to embark upon the design and production of an entirely new car; to be possible it would have to borrow a number of parts from an existing higher-volume manufacturer. When Ford took over in 1987 this began to look possible, but it wasn't until Ford absorbed Jaguar in 1989, that the possibility moved to the probable; a combination of Ford engineering know-how and a Jaguar base would provide the appropriate background. While Jaguar had supplied some components for Aston Martin V-8 and Lagonda models, they weren't keen to provide too much until Ford came along to define the markets for the two former rival marques more precisely.

Jaguar had long intended to replace the XJS with the new XJ41 once the XJ40 – the 1986 XJ6 – was in production; to many this was regarded as the F-type successor to the legendary E-type. A number of XJ41 prototypes had been built when it was decided that the production cost would be too high for the numbers that could be sold as Jaguars; in a bid to rationalise the situation, Jaguar then put

the new XJ41 body design onto the existing XJS platform as Project XX. Ford axed this one too, but it was to provide an excellent basis for a small Aston Martin which could be priced at a more realistic level for lower volumes. Work started on the Aston version – Project NPX – in 1991.

Jaguar componentry offered a number of advantages, not least a well developed platform with independent rear suspension. There was also the six-cylinder Jaguar AJ-6 engine which would form a logical progression from the DB2-6 range, provided it could be Astonised. This was achieved by taking an unique 3.2-litre version of the AJ-6 engine and adding a supercharger to give 335 bhp to match the Mercedes 500SL V-8 at 320 bhp and the Porsche 928 S4 at 350 bhp. Closed circuit tests showed a maximum of 157 mph, but Aston's own tests produced 165 mph, so our quoted figure is a mean of the two.

Jaguar had, of course, continued to develop the latest XJ6 which was launched in October 1994 as an evolution of the previous model. One derivative has been the XJR, a sports saloon using a 4-litre AJ-16 development of the AJ-6, also with an Eaton supercharger; this has been tuned to produce slightly less power than the Aston's at 321 bhp, but with slightly more torque. The result is a 155 mph full four-seater only marginally less accelerative than the DB7 but £33,000 cheaper.

But the proof of the pudding is in the eating. Forgetting the mixed heritage, the new Aston does provide exactly what was required for a little sister to the Virage range, and in time it will spawn its own Vantage and convertible versions. Designed to match the DB6 in length, it is lower and wider with a body style that is evocative of its predecessors, despite that 24-year gap. It looks and behaves just as one would expect an Aston to be.

The lines of the DB6 are discernible in the 7, a tribute to stylist Ian Callam. Like its predecessor, power comes from a twin overhead camshaft, six-cylinder engine although the DB7's is supercharged. Bumpers are present but concealed beneath deformable front and rear panels.

Left: The DB7 uses the traditional ingredients of walnut veneer and leather although the combination did not feature on the earlier cars. It is the work of Neil Simpson, like Callam, a Royal College of Art graduate.

SPECIFICATION	ASTON MARTIN DB7
ENGINE	Supercharged straight-6, 3239 cc
POWER	335 bhp @ 5600 rpm
TRANSMISSION	Manual 5-speed
CHASSIS	Steel with some composite panels
BRAKES	Discs all round with ABS
TOP SPEED	162 mph (259 km/h)
ACCELERATION	**0-60 mph** 5.8 seconds **0-100 mph** 14.4 seconds

BMW M1

1979
162 mph
261 km/h

A combination of German components, Italian styling and (initially) engineering, the mid-engined, glass-fibre-bodied M1 with its miniature radiator grille was unmistakably a BMW. Created to break Porsche's dominance on the race tracks, production delays rendered this impossible. This is a 1980 road car, one of some 400 built that were required to homologate the racing versions.

Undeniably sleek and sporting, the Giugiaro-designed M1 is thus far unique in BMW history for its mid-engined layout; the six-cylinder 3.5-litre 277 bhp unit, featuring twin overhead camshafts and four valves per cylinder, sits in line behind the cockpit, driving the rear wheels through a ZF transaxle.

Its purpose was to take part in the Group 4 and Group 5 categories of International sports car racing, where Porsche had dominated with the competition 911 Turbo, the 934 and 935. For this, at least 400 examples had to be produced over a 2-year period; in competition tune the M1 engine could be made to produce 470 bhp, so it had a theoretical chance against the 934, and the mid-engined layout gave it potentially better roadholding. The turbocharged versions, with up to 850 bhp, could challenge for outright victory.

Although Giugiaro drew up the M1's shape, its origins were firmly based in the 'experimental safety vehicle' Turbo concept car that BMW displayed to celebrate the Munich Olympics in 1972; designed by BMW's Paul Bracq, this incorporated side impact bars in its gull-wing doors and soft end panels mounted on rams among many safety features, but it was the mid-engined layout that was of particular interest. The power unit was the, then familiar, four-cylinder 2-litre, mounted transversely and fitted with a turbocharger to give around 200 bhp; it was this engine that was fitted to the 2002 turbo the following year, albeit de-tuned to 170 bhp. Only two of the concept cars were built, but they gave BMW the chance to assess mid-engined handling advantages, and provided styling cues when it came to the M1; the black belt-line and the low slender nose – later to appear in similar form on the 850 – were obvious carry-overs for Giugiaro to adopt.

With the decision taken in late 1976 to produce the M1, BMW contracted Lamborghini to do the design, development and production build of the new car; low volume production of such a car wasn't possible within BMW, and Lamborghini were looking for outside work. And

Giugiaro wasn't far away to keep an eye on the lines. Design and development during 1977 went well, but Lamborghini then had financial problems and couldn't undertake the production. Eventually in late 1978, production commenced as a joint exercise between Giugiaro and Bauer in Stuttgart. Giugiaro's ItalDesign company didn't have production space, but he sub-contracted the build of the tubular chassis and glass-fibre bodywork, mated the two and trimmed the interior. Bauer installed the mechanical components and completed the trim; thus it wasn't until 1980 that the required 400 were built, by which time the racing rules were set to change for 1982 and they didn't suit the M1 which was too heavy for the new formula.

Meanwhile BMW launched the Procar series for 1979; M1s in 470 bhp form had their own races at *Grands Prix* with GP drivers like Nikki Lauda at the helm. It certainly gave the M1 instant acclaim and justified another 50 or so racing versions being built. They had some success in other races, but the loss of those two years meant that the M1 never had the chance to tackle the Porsches seriously in Group 4 racing or the faster Group 5.

Despite the fact that it couldn't achieve what it set out to do, the M1 was a superb 160 mph road car in the supercar mould and it played a useful part in promoting BMW's high performance image. It looked the part, it was well built with luxurious trim; it was a good cross between Italian design flair and German production engineering .

SPECIFICATION	**BMW M1**
ENGINE	6-cylinder, 3453 cc
HORSEPOWER	277 bhp @ 6500 rpm
TRANSMISSION	Manual 5-speed
CHASSIS	Steel frame, glass-fibre body
BRAKES	Discs all round
TOP SPEED	162 mph
ACCELERATION	**0-60 mph** 5.4 seconds **0-100 mph** 13.5 seconds

The M1 looks good from any angle. The long rear deck was necessary to accommodate the longitudinally-mounted ,3.5-litre, twin cam six, located ahead of a five-speed ZF transaxle.

The M1 was only produced in left-hand drive form and its interior borrowed components from across the BMW range. Despite this the cockpit could not relate to any other model. The speedometer reads to 280 km/h (174 mph).

'Giugiaro wasn't far away to keep an eye on the lines.'

BMW 850CSi

1994
170 mph
274 km/h

Coupés have been an intrinsic part of the BMW family for many years. The existing range is no exception and the 8 Series is stylistically outstanding and goes as well as it looks. This is a 1995 V-12 powered 850CSi although at the time of writing (1997) only the V-8 engined version is offered.

The German factory has a long history of producing high-speed coupés. In the 'thirties, the construction of the autobahns encouraged manufacturers to create ever faster cars; the BMW 327/80 was an elegant streamlined coupé that would reach over 90 mph on its 80 bhp and its design was carried over to become the post-war Bristol 400 with a style that was still modern ten years later.

In the 'fifties BMW were struggling for an identity, making big V-8 powered saloons and little motorcycle powered Isettas with nothing in between. The 507 was the two-seater sports coupé, using the running gear of the bigger saloons in a somewhat different style, the traditional twin intakes on a horizontal plane – very much a period classic.

Came the 1961 resurgence of BMW with the launch of the new generation heralded by the 4-door 1500 and the Munich firm embarked on the line that is recognisably still with us – clean, modern lines characterised by the ever-present twin radiator intakes in a variety of proportions, and always classically front-engined rear-drive. The basic single overhead camshaft engine configuration was unchanged for many years, but all except the smallest 4-cylinder engines now have twin camshaft four-valve heads. The first coupé in this range was the 2000C in 1966, the top of the range at that time.

When the 6-cylinder engine arrived for larger cars in 1968, the 2800CS came too, slightly shorter and with two doors. This became the 3.0CS in 1971 and on into the competition 3.0CSL – the

SPECIFICATION	BMW 850CSi
ENGINE	Aluminium V-12 5576 cc
HORSEPOWER	380 bhp @ 5300 rpm
TRANSMISSION	Manual 6-speed
CHASSIS	Unitary steel
BRAKES	Discs all round with ABS
TOP SPEED	170 mph
ACCELERATION	**0-60 mph** 6.5 seconds **0-100 mph** 15.4 seconds

Left: The underbonnet view is equally impressive with the twin overhead cam V-12 filling the entire engine compartment. It was originally produced in 5-litre form and then enlarged to 5.6-litres in 1993. A six-speed manual, or four-speed auto gearbox is fitted.

same, only lighter, with some aluminium body panels. By 1975 BMW had embarked on the new model designations, a type number preceding the engine size, as 525 – 5-series with 2.5-litre engine. From then on, the coupés have had their own series and more distinctive styling to set them apart from their saloon cousins; the first was the 630CS in 1976, a range enlarged two years later with a new cylinder block for the 635CSi, its 218 bhp making it a 140 mph car. When BMW introduced the M range, the 1983 M635CSi had a twin overhead camshaft 4-valve engine to give 286 bhp and over 150 mph, still a very desirable car 12 years on.

The coupés were always the top of the range and were produced in smaller numbers but, by using many body panels from the saloon series, they were not too much more expensive; the 6-series used a 7-series front end and running gear, and continued to use the old parts when the new 7-series arrived in 1986; part of this new range was the 750i using a 5-litre V-12 with 300 bhp which could obviously outperform the 635CSi, which was also looking a bit dated.

So to get the coupé back on top of the range, BMW created the 850i using the same magnificent V-12 in a style that stood well apart from the other models, still a beautiful car several years after its 1989 launch. The late 'eighties was the heyday of the very fast cars and it was appropriate that BMW should have one capable of 160 mph. Greener thoughts brought in a smaller engine, the all-new 4-valve 4-litre V-8 with 286 bhp which was added to the 7-series range in 1992. This lighter, more efficient unit made the cars almost as fast as those with the V-12, so a 5.6-litre 850CSi version was added with 380 bhp, and the 850Ci was enlarged to 5.3-litres and 326 bhp; those who wanted the looks and less power could have the 286 bhp 840Ci which was added to the range at the beginning of 1993.

Performance figures taken on the 300 bhp 850i produced a maximum speed of 159 mph. Although BMW now limit the maximum to 155 mph, another 27% of power should certainly yield 170 mph, so the acceleration figures below have also been adjusted. Some have described the 8-series as anachronistic, a car with only style, even more performance and less space to separate it from the 7-series; but it is a superb style.

'The late 'eighties was the heyday of the very fast cars.'

It goes without saying that comfort is the keynote of the 850CSi. This is enhanced by the fact that the seats and steering wheel can be adjusted to suit the driver's requirement and this information is retained electronically. The 'wheel also moves out of position to permit easy entry.

BMW M5

1994
170 mph
274 km/h

In 1972, the year that Munich was host to the Olympic Games, BMW founded their subsidiary, BMW Motorsport GmbH. While the two-door 2002 series and the four-door saloons had been raced with great success by private entrants using tuning conversions from Alpina and Schnitzer, rule changes demanded that any special competition parts be available in specified quantities, which could really only be made by a manufacturer.

So BMW had to get involved if the cars were to continue racing, even if the tuners ran the actual race teams. Setting up a competition department, separated from the production factory, was common practice among the companies that had works entries in International events. The long hours required didn't upset the factory unions and it was also a sure way for lessons learnt in racing to be transferred back to the factory engineers.

The mid-'seventies was a good period for touring car racing in Europe and America; BMW had their share of success with the 3.0CSLs against the Ford Capris, and special versions even took on the Porsches. BMW were also to the fore in Formula 2 racing. By the end of the decade, touring car interest was waning and BMW wanted to join Porsche in GT racing, so the Motorsport department arranged to produce the mid-engined M1 (see separate story) in 1978; that it wasn't a racing success wasn't the fault of BMW – the rules had changed again, so they joined the *Grand Prix* world instead, using a turbocharged version of the original 4-cylinder BMW engine with the Brabham team, netting a 1983 championship with

Understated wolf, the M5's six-cylinder engine is stretched to 3.8-litres and tuned to 340 bhp – more than the 4-litre V-8 540i – and will reach 170 mph.

Nelson Piquet. Although there were subsequent *Grand Prix* victories in this 1000 bhp turbocharged era, BMW withdrew from Formula 1 at the end of 1986, by which time the name of BMW M-power was well established.

By now the Motorsport division's name was being used for high performance versions of regular road cars, the first to bear the name being the 1983 M635 CSi which used the four-valve engine that had been developed for the M1; with a later fuel injection system, this had 286 bhp. When the new 5-series saloon came along in 1984, this same engine was put into the top version early the next year to create the M5, the first time that BMW used this new model system.

SPECIFICATION	BMW M5
ENGINE	6-cylinder, 3795 cc
HORSEPOWER	340 bhp @ 6900 rpm
TRANSMISSION	Manual 6-speed
CHASSIS	Unitary steel
BRAKES	Discs all round with ABS
TOP SPEED	170 mph
ACCELERATION	**0-60 mph** 5.4 seconds **0-100 mph** 13.6 seconds

The 2-door 3-series had been introduced in 1982, but the M3 appeared after the M5. This used the four-cylinder engine as a 2.3-litre with four-valve heads to develop 200 bhp. While M-power was the point of the exercise, the cars had to be completely reworked as they were handling more than double the power of the base models – wider wheels, firmer suspension, bigger brakes and aerodynamic appendages combined to produce sports car behaviour in family saloons.

While the M5 was just a fast road car, the M3 was the basis of a very effective touring car racer and won many championships; it has continued to do so with the latest 162 mph M3 following its mid-1992 launch – now with a 286 bhp 3-litre six-cylinder engine. The new 5-series came in 1988, the latest M5 equipped with a 3.5-litre six with 315 bhp; this was enlarged to 3.8-litres in 1992 with 340 bhp and given a sixth gear and even lower profile tyres in 1994. It was in this final form that it clocked 170 mph, albeit in its 5th gear as 6th is very much a cruising overdrive.

The M-series have produced some remarkable cars and they are not just racing saloons; you can have the same specifications for an M3 convertible or the M5 estate car.

There is little outward evidence of the changes wrought by the Motorsport division; bigger wheels, deeper spoiler and a little M on the tail hide a comprehensive rework of suspension and engine.

'It was in this final form that it clocked 170 mph.'

BUGATTI EB110

1993

218 mph

351 km/h

'It may not be everyone's idea of beauty, but it is undeniably dramatic.'

Parked neatly on the Bugatti stand at the 1995 Geneva Show were three examples of the EB110, each proclaiming a world record. The EB110 Supersport laid claim to being the fastest production car with a maximum speed of 351 km/h (218 mph) which was achieved during its official ministry testing at the Nardo test-track in southern Italy; the McLaren has clocked 231 mph there but not as an officially observed run. The second record was for the fastest car using methane gas as a fuel – 344.7 km/h (214.2 mph). And the third was the fastest speed ever recorded on ice – 296.3 km/h (184.1 mph) achieved on a stretch of frozen sea somewhere in the arctic circle region. Impressive. However you look at it, the Bugatti EB110 is a very fast car of exceptional stability.

The Bugatti name has a long history with a big break in the middle before its recent restart. Italian-born Ettore Bugatti set up his factory in Molsheim in 1909; over the next thirty years he produced a selection of delectable motor cars for competition and road use. Sometimes they were advanced, latterly they were technically dated, but they always had style whether they were purely for racing – like the GP types 35, 51 and 59 – or such road cars as the glorious Royale or the design pinnacle of the type 57 on which son Jean Bugatti created such wonderful forms. After World War II, with Ettore's health failing, the company struggled to regain its former glories, but failed; it was finally taken over by Messier, the last real Bugatti having emerged in 1952. While there were several attempts to revive the name with the *Grand Prix* type 251 in 1956 and a sports car in 1960, the name passed into history for nearly 30 years.

Its revival has been due to a consortium of businessmen led by Romano Artioli, with Bugatti's son Michel (by his second marriage) on the board as the family connection. In 1988, a new factory

Ettore Bugatti was born in 1881; the new Bugatti was launched 110 years later, an engineering jewel with a shrink-wrapped skin.

Remarkably compact, the EB110 is only 14ft.8in long but 6ft.5in.wide. The rear wing can be lowered into the body.

was set up in Italy at Campogalliano near Modena, supercar land inhabited also by Ferrari and Lamborghini. The first car would be the EB110, announced in 1991, 110 years after the birth of Ettore, and it would be a technical masterpiece worthy of the best of Bugatti.

The new car embodied all that was state of the art at the time. The carbon fibre chassis was built by Aerospatiale; the racing-style suspension was developed by Messier Bugatti, specialists in aircraft undercarriages; transmission was provided to all four wheels through a six-speed gearbox adjacent to the mid-engine; and the engine itself is a 60-valve V-12 3.5-litre (then the *Grand Prix* size) with four small turbochargers to deliver an impressive 550 bhp at 8000 rpm. Aerodynamic control comes from underbody venturis and a tail wing that rises on stilts.

The style of its aluminium bodywork – the material of true craftsmen – is attributed to Lamborghini shaper Marcello Gandini with adjustments by Benedini. It may not be everyone's idea of beauty, but it is undeniably dramatic and contains some original Bugatti styling cues like the little horseshoe intake set within the grille. Following its extravagant series of launches in September 1991 in Paris and Molsheim, it moved into slow production. It is now available in two forms, the EB110GT with 550 bhp, and the EB110S with a massive 611 bhp at 8250 rpm; despite all that technology under its skin it weighs just 1600Kg. Small wonder, then, that it is very fast; one magazine has recorded a 0-60 mph time under 4 seconds; *Road & Track* and *Autocar* recorded 4.5, with the former recording a maximum speed of 213 mph on a shorter straight than Nardo's banked track.

The EB110 is certainly a technical masterpiece. Those who have built such supercars can only marvel at how such a technology showcase can be produced for under £300,000 when every part has been designed from a clean sheet of paper.

SPECIFICATION	BUGATTI EB110S
ENGINE	Quad-turbo V-12 3499 cc
HORSEPOWER	611 bhp @ 8250 rpm
TRANSMISSION	Manual 6-speed with 4WD
CHASSIS	Carbon fibre with aluminium body
BRAKES	Discs all round with ABS
TOP SPEED	218 mph
ACCELERATION	**0-60 mph** 4.3 seconds **0-100 mph** 9.2 seconds

The car shown is the 25th produced and is the personal car of the chairman, Romano Artioli.

CHEVROLET CORVETTE

1996
170 mph
273 km/h

'The result is an almost completely new car.'

A '97 Corvette, with headlamps ablaze, that is wider and longer than its predecessor and is also improved aerodynamically. Brakes are excellent, a combination of big discs and calipers and wide tyres. As previously, it is only available in left-hand drive form.

Chevrolet's seemingly evergreen Corvette sports car was radically revised for the 1997 season and this fifth generation model looks all set for a long production run. It is also noticeably faster than its predecessor that in stock form had a top speed nudging 160 mph. The new car is capable of 170 mph and is accordingly quicker off the mark.

The 'Vette has been around since 1953. Created by General Motors in response to the British sports cars that were finding favour among young Americans, the original version was powered by Chevrolet's six-cylinder 3.8-litre engine and was capable of a rather unpredictable 100 mph. The open two-seater roadster body was made of glass-fibre and this material has been a feature of the Corvette ever since.

The original six was replaced by a V-8 engine, of 4.3 litres, in 1955 and all versions have thereafter been so equipped. Top speed was approaching 120 mph.

In 1962 the Corvette was greatly enhanced by the appearance of a new body, the work of GM's newly appointed styling supremo, William Mitchell. The assured lines of what was allotted the Sting Ray name betrayed a strong European influence and the open car was joined, from the outset, by a coupé version. Mechanical refinements included the creation of a new chassis and introduction of independent rear suspension.

By the time the car ceased production in 1967 it was available with a choice of V-8 engines, with a top of the range 7-litre unit capable of endowing the model with a flat-out speed of 135 mph.

The next Corvette of 1967, which arrived at the time of the Muscle Car era in America, perpetuated the top line V-8 with no less than 560 bhp on tap. This David Holls-styled car, the Stingray name spelled as one word and revived in 1969, was capable of 160 mph in its most powerful guise and endured until 1982.

By this time the roadster version had been discontinued in 1975, and from thereafter only coupés with a Targa-style roof were built. Its successor of 1983 was destined for a record 13-year production life and incorporated a hatchback. The backbone chassis was new and there was a birdcage tubular structure to which the glass-fibre panels were bonded. To European eyes, the all-independent suspension was curious in that the

Left: Like all its predecessors, the current 'Vette is glass-fibre bodied. The circular rear lights have been a feature of the model since 1961. The ducts in the front wings have been designed to allow hot air to escape from the brakes.

medium utilised was glass-fibre transverse leaf springs. At the front this was used in conjunction with wishbones although at the rear the driveshaft served as an upper link.

Although this 5.7-litre model was a 160 mph car, 1989 saw the arrival of a potent variant, the 180 mph ZR-1, with aluminium rather than cast iron V-8, a 32 valve engine developed by in-house Lotus. The mainstream model also benefited, in 1991, from a new power unit, the 5.7-litre V-8 replacing an original that dated back to 1955.

The current car was announced late in 1996 for the 1997 season. It has been a long time a-coming, work on the project having begun in 1990, only to be jeopardised when Chevrolet's cash strapped parent, General Motors, nearly axed the model.

But the glass-fibre-bodied Corvette, with its long established lineage, survived and the result is an almost completely new car, although one that is visually related to its predecessor.

The two-seater coupé, with a similar detachable Targa-style hardtop, has been stylistically and aerodynamically refined so that it possesses a drag coefficient of 0.29 which is one of the lowest in the business. Its reliance on a simple but well proportioned shape with a minimum of external decoration, suggests that it is intended for a long manufacturing run.

The new car is wider and longer and, although the front mounted V-8 engine retains the same 5.7-litre capacity, dimensions and pushrod activated valves of its predecessor, it is a new design with an alloy block rather than a cast iron one and develops 345 bhp, as opposed to 300.

A further departure from previous practice is the introduction of a rear-mounted, Borg-Warner six-speed manual gearbox although a four-speed automatic is an optional offering.

The tubular steel perimeter chassis is also new which GM claims is four-and-a-half times stronger, and 36 kg lighter, than the frame it replaces.

The transverse-leaf, independent double-wishbone suspension – a combination that had hitherto been exclusive to the front – has been extended to the rear.

A further innovative feature is the fitment of Goodyear Extended Mobility Tyres. These EMT covers are so called because they can run flat for up to 200 miles and obviate the need to carry a spare wheel, so saving valuable boot space and weight. An indicator on the dashboard immediately registers any drop in tyre pressure.

SPECIFICATION	CHEVROLET CORVETTE
ENGINE	Aluminium 4-cam V-8, 5680 cc
HORSEPOWER	345 bhp @ 5600 rpm
TRANSMISSION	Manual 6-speed
CHASSIS	Steel perimeter
BRAKES	Discs all round with ABS
TOP SPEED	170 mph (273 km/h)
ACCELERATION	**0-60 mph** 4.7 seconds **0-100 mph** 13.3 seconds

The 'Vette feels very much like its predecessor although with a strong emphasis on refinement. This is a much more comfortable car and suspension can be set according to road conditions, namely Tour, Sport and Performance, while the claimed 0-60 mph figure of 4.7 seconds is 2.3 seconds faster.

Nowadays the Corvette has competition from the home grown Dodge Viper, the Japanese and the Europeans in the form of the Porsche Boxster and BMW Z3. But if past experience is anything to go by, this version should run and run . . .

The last Corvette roadster was built in 1975 and since then it has only been made with a Targa-style detachable roof. The latest version is no exception and the car in the foreground has its roof panel detached. This is stowed in the big boot, there being no spare wheel, made possible by the use of run-flat tyres.

CHRYSLER VIPER VENOM

1995
187 mph
301 km/h

The Dodge Viper is marketed in Britain under the name of its Chrysler parent although without right-hand drive and this is the original version of 1993 vintage. Selling for £55,000, it had stupendous, if raucous, performance and a top speed of 167 mph. The brakes were accordingly large but, by all accounts, fade free.

The Viper sets out to be an anachronism and even more so in its 550 bhp Venom form. It has been created around the old-fashioned concept of enjoyable open motoring, raw fun on four wheels. But there it is, in the maximum speed table, up amongst the finest examples of supercar engineering, the Venom proving usefully quicker than the standard car and particularly with its hard top. Old fashioned it may look, but there is some new technology under that skin.

There are other cars with some of the same retro appeal, like the TVR Griffith, but the Viper has more in common with a 1965 Shelby Cobra than with Blackpool's best. What sets it apart from this decade is the big lazy engine – an 8-litre V-10 – and the studied lack of creature comforts; you didn't expect a quiet ride in a Cobra, or a snug-fitting roof, but you did expect raucous high performance in any gear, just like the Viper. Against the Cobra it is 7 inches wider and 5 inches lower, a Cobra with a modern stance.

The common denominator is indeed Carroll Shelby – Shelby who put Ford V-8s into AC's very British sports car and won a World Championship, the same Shelby who then worked over Chrysler saloons to transform their performance. And Shelby has been in the background of the Viper development. But the concept was Chrysler's, spurred on by President Bob Lutz, an arch enthusiast for the sheer fun of driving anything that challenges the driver.

The Viper was first shown as an eye catcher on the Dodge stand at the 1989 Detroit Motor Show, a fully-engineered eye-catcher that was there to gauge public reaction to retro-styling in general and the Viper in particular. Either way it was well received and, three years later, it reappeared ready for production which can reach up to 5000 units a year should the demand be there.

Its chassis is built up in sheet steel stiffened by large box-sections in the sills and central tunnel, and substantial bulkheads each side of the cockpit.

The Viper GTS is the coupé version, better equipped and its performance enhanced by the use of aerodynamic aids. Created as a one-off in 1993, it entered production in 1996 and its body and engine are lighter than the roadster's.

'The body is 'sixties curvaceous but made from a modern acrylic plastic.'

All independent suspension uses double wishbones at each corner, and the steering is power assisted; it needs to be with that big engine weight coupled with massive tyres – the front wheels are ten inches wide and the rears thirteen. The grip generated is prodigious.

That front-mounted engine started life as a cast-iron truck unit, but has been re-engineered with aluminium block and heads by Lamborghini, who were owned by Chrysler at the time. The standard Viper 7990 cc V-10 develops 406 bhp and the Venom version gets 550 bhp thanks to straightforward head, manifold and cam improvements. Even the Venom unit has a low specific output, so both versions should last. Mated to them is a six-speed Borg Warner gearbox with an axle ratio giving such high gearing that it only needs 1400 rpm to cruise at 70 mph in sixth. The most sophisticated part of the car is the engine/transmission management system which controls the fuel injection and also inserts a detent to prevent selection of second and third gears when accelerating gently, thereby saving fuel during emission testing.

The body is 'sixties curvaceous but made from a modern acrylic plastic. The overall style follows the rounded sports car themes of Mazda MX-5 and Suzuki Cappuccino, but the squat proportions and the sheer size make it a very impressive beast. And standard Viper performance is a match for its ancestor; the 7-litre Cobra, too, would achieve over 160 mph given the right gearing and reach 100 mph in around 10 seconds. The Venom is usefully faster. But the charm of both is the ability to accelerate so quickly in any gear; accompanied by an explosive roar, you can blast past anything in whatever gear you happen to be. It is an exhilarating but tiring drive, a big toy built for driving pleasure rather than practical commuting.

SPECIFICATION	CHRYSLER VIPER VENOM
ENGINE	Aluminium V-10, 7990 cc
HORSEPOWER	550 bhp @ 6000 rpm
TRANSMISSION	Manual 6-speed
CHASSIS	Steel with acrylic panels
BRAKES	Discs all round
TOP SPEED	187 mph (301 km/h)
ACCELERATION	**0-60 mph** 4.4 seconds **0-100 mph** 9.7 seconds

The more potent Venom 600 of 1997 with 635 bhp on tap. Like the mainstream model it uses a Targa-type roof although the no-frills Viper is an uncompromising two-seater with the anti rollover bar just ahead of the rear window surround.

DE TOMASO PANTERA GT5-S

1986
160 mph
257 km/h

'The 200 denotes 200 mph, but no one has yet put this to the test.'

After early forays into building single-seaters for Formula Junior and Formula 2, Alejandro de Tomaso joined the ranks of Italian sports car builders back in 1963.

The first offering was the mid-engined Vallelunga which used a backbone chassis to which was bolted a 1600 cc Ford Cortina engine; this took all the rear suspension loads via arms on the transaxle bell-housing. The theme was extended at the 1965 Turin Show with a sports-racing car using a bigger backbone which carried a 271 bhp Ford Mustang engine; never raced, this formed the basis of the Mangusta using body styling by Giugiaro while he was working at Ghia. Production started in 1967, the year that de Tomaso acquired Ghia – Ghia built the bodies in Turin and de Tomaso fitted the power train in Modena. The same year saw Ghia in production with the Giugiaro-designed Maserati Ghibli.

Meanwhile, Ford of America, having tried to buy Ferrari in the early 'sixties, were still on the look-out for an Italian supercar to add to the Lincoln range. They liked the Ghibli and came to look at the Mangusta in 1969, at which time Tom Tjaada had just completed a scale model of a new Ford-powered sports car. Ford didn't like the Mangusta, largely because it wouldn't pass the forthcoming stricter American safety standards, but they saw a better future for the Tjaada car and signed an agreement in September 1969 for technical cooperation between Ford of America, Ghia and de Tomaso who would build concept cars and niche vehicles for Ford. The first of these would be the Pantera, to be built at the rate of 10,000 a year with de Tomaso retaining the right to non-American sales.

Dallara came from Lamborghini to redesign the chassis which followed contemporary racing practice with a sheet steel monocoque centre section with strong sills; Ford's latest 351 cu.in (5752 cc) V-8 was attached to the rear and mated to a ZF transaxle. Ghia didn't have enough space to assemble the cars in the required quantity so de Tomaso acquired the Vignale factory in late 1969. Less than a year later, Ford had acquired 84% of de Tomaso's Ghia/Vignale/Pantera operation.

Nearly 300 Panteras were sold in Europe in 1970, but American approval didn't come until 1971 after a certain amount of Ford 'productionisation'. US sales were slower than anticipated, with 1550 in 1972 and 2030 in 1973; and then came the energy crisis. This coupled with even stricter emission laws coming for 1975, forced Ford to stop importing the Pantera and close the Vignale plant in late 1974, by which time they had taken over de Tomaso's minority shareholding and had become owners of Ghia and Vignale. De Tomaso continued to build the Pantera in Modena

While the original shape Pantera is the fastest recorded, this Gandini-restyled version should be faster still in its twin turbo form.

Latest de Tomaso is the Guara which employs a composite chassis with a mid-mounted 4-litre BMW V-8, which should give it a 160 mph maximum. Guara comes in coupé or roadster forms.

and has continued to update it ever since with more power, wider wheels and aerodynamic appendages.

Where the original 300 bhp Pantera would reach nearly 150 mph on the right gearing, the 1985 GT5-S clocked 160 mph. In 1990, the bodywork was restyled by Gandini and the engine had changed to the Ford 302 cu.in V-8 using fuel injection to give 305 bhp. You can still buy one in this form, or as the Pantera 200 with twin turbos and 530 bhp; the 200 denotes 200 mph, but no one has yet put this to the test.

Meanwhile de Tomaso launched the Guara in 1993, now available in open, coupé or Targa forms. Once again, it has a backbone chassis but this time in aluminium honeycomb and composites; 304 bhp comes from a 4.0-litre BMW V-8, which should give it a maximum speed around 160 mph.

SPECIFICATION	DE TOMASO PANTERA GT5-S
ENGINE	Ford V-8, 5752 cc
HORSEPOWER	350 bhp @ 6000 rpm
TRANSMISSION	Manual 5-speed
CHASSIS	Steel with glass-fibre bodywork
BRAKES	Discs all round
TOP SPEED	160 mph
ACCELERATION	**0-60 mph** 5.4 seconds **0-100 mph** 13.1 seconds

Throughout its long career, the Pantera displayed the virtues of Italian flair with old-fashioned, but economical, American muscle. It was fast, stylish, easy to maintain and established the de Tomaso name in the sports-car world. With the company now being run by the founder's son, Santiago, the Guara should keep the flag flying.

New style gave the old car a new lease of life with smoothed flanks and F40-style rear wing. It will continue to be available to special order.

FERRARI 365GTB4 DAYTONA

1971
174 mph
280 km/h

For ever known as the Daytona, the 365GTB4 was Ferrari's final fling for the front-engined two-seater; four-seaters would continue with front-mounted engines, but two-seater sports Ferraris would be mid-engined after this. But what a finale. It was a bold statement of sheer power and shameless aggression, from the sharp front end to the wide fastback that had lost any semblance of its predecessor's narrow cabin, inset from a curvaceous waist-line. It was a big car too, heavy and bulky, but a muscle car designed to appeal to the American market; its performance and maximum speed would leave all of those and the Europeans standing – it was king of the road in its day.

SPECIFICATION	FERRARI 365GTB4 DAYTONA
ENGINE	Aluminium V-12, 4390 cc
HORSEPOWER	352 bhp @ 7500 rpm
TRANSMISSION	Manual 5-speed
CHASSIS	Steel frame
BRAKES	Discs all round
TOP SPEED	174 mph
ACCELERATION	**0-60 mph** 5.4 seconds **0-100 mph** 12.6 seconds

Its predecessor had been the 275GTB4. The 250GT series, running from 1954-64, had marked the transition from race-cars adapted for the road to purpose-built road cars; the 275s were the first Ferraris to be designed and developed from the outset as road cars. As ever, the type number referred to the capacity of a single cylinder; last of the original small-block engines, the 275 was a V-12 3.3-litre mounted in the front. Unlike previous road cars, it had the gearbox, now with five speeds, mounted in the rear – a transaxle – to keep the weight distribution more even. The chassis followed the familiar tubular frame principles but finally moved with the times and had independent rear suspension.

Announced at the 1964 Paris Show it was available in two body forms, the open 275GTS and the coupé 275GTB with 250-275 bhp. It was at the 1966 Paris Show that the final version was launched, the 275GTB4 for four overhead camshafts, two per bank of six cylinders; with 300 bhp at 8000 rpm it would run to 160 mph. It was a fast and agile car with an almost comfortable ride.

But while the 4-cam was launched in October 1966, extending the life of the 275, the new 330 range had been presented in March of that year. With the traditional V-12 single-cam stretched with a new longer block, the 300 bhp 4-litre was used to power the 330GTC and GTS. The chassis remained similar to that of the 275, but the drive-line incorporated a torque tube. The new body style featured a lower waistline with deeper windows, a notchback tail treatment and an oval

Last of Ferrari's front-engined two-seater coupés, the Daytona was a magnificent charger in the right hands.

grille more reminiscent of the superamerica series. The same engine had been used in the mid-engined sports-racing 330P in 1964; the factory continued to develop the 4-litre engine but produced a 4.4-litre 365P for the non-works teams for 1965. The ultimate factory development came with the 1967 330P4 which had twin cams per bank with each cylinder having three valves and twin plugs plus fuel injection to generate 450 bhp at 8200 rpm; privateers made do with 380 bhp at 7300 rpm with carburetters and single-cam 365s. Ferrari won the world championship three times in those four years, including victory at Daytona for the 330P and 330P4.

First production car to use the 4.4-litre single-cam V-12 was the 365GT 2+2, an extremely elegant Pininfarina stretch of the 330GTC with an extra 25 cm in the wheelbase but 58 cm more in overall length to provide more luggage space as well as the extra seats; it also had self-levelling rear suspension. The 330GTC and GTS had to wait until late 1968 to be uprated to 365-series.

However, the big event of that year was the arrival of the ultimate two-seater coupé; Ferrari had profited from the racing experience in selecting its engine specification – the 4.4-litre with twin-cams per bank but only two valves, six carburetters and dry sump lubrication to produce a remarkable 352 bhp, 30 more than the single-cam cars. The chassis was basically that of the 330/365GTC. And the style set it off to perfection; early cars had the headlights visible behind a band of clear plastic running across the nose, but later cars had this replaced by body-colour metal and the headlamps became pop-ups. Other variants included a convertible – 100 only – and the 365GTC4, a 2+2 Daytona with less horsepower and a revised front end which was available in 1971/2 following the phasing out of the previous 2+2. But the Daytona stayed in production until 1974; over 1300 were built in that six-year period.

Just over 100 Spiders were made by the factory, but some Daytonas have since been decapitated to capture the same open elegance.

'It was a bold statement of sheer power and shameless aggression.'

FERRARI 288GTO

1986
189 mph
304 km/h

Smaller and a little more powerful than the flagship Testarossa, the 288GTO was the fastest Ferrari in its day. It should have been – it was designed as a racer. GTO? Gran Turismo Omologato or, in somewhat less evocative terms, Homologated GT. Homologation is the process of certifying that a number of identical units have been made; road cars are homologated by transport ministries when they conform to regulations; road-based race cars are homologated for competition by the FIA, the ruling body of motor sport, once a specified number have been built.

Over 1959-61, Ferrari had been building the short-wheelbase 250GT for road and competition use; when the FIA announced a GT championship for 1962, Ferrari needed something lower and lighter. The rules of the day stated that 100 identical cars should be built in 12 consecutive months, but that special bodied versions could be made once the 100 had been completed; the 250GT had already been accepted as a GT car, so the new car was submitted for approval with the revised bodywork. When the form came back stamped GT – Omologato, the name stuck. The 3-litre V-12 250GTO with 280+ bhp went on to win the new championship in 1962-4; while around 160 250GTs were built there were only 35 250GTOs. As most of these were road registered at some time in their lives, it is fair to record their figures as production cars but hard to establish representative ones as there is considerable variation in axle ratio and states of tune; factory cars may have achieved over 170 mph at Le Mans, but 165 mph is about right for 280 bhp.

Twenty years on and the FIA again introduced rules to encourage road-going GT cars to take part in racing and rallying with effect from 1982. This time the minimum quantity was 200 in a year for Group B. Ferrari had racing in mind, Porsche planned to race and rally the 959 while the rest of the competitive manufacturers built outrageous four-wheel-drive rally specials. In the event, Group B racing failed to capture any following and Group B rallying stopped in 1986 when the cars became too fast for their own – and spectator – safety. However Ferrari introduced the 288GTO at the 1984 Geneva Show as a Limited Edition of 200 and started taking deposits there and then.

While there was no homologation-inspired need to develop a previous design, Ferrari started with the 308GTB as the basis. Turbocharging small engines had become the fashion for ultimate power to weight ratios and Ferrari already made a 208 Turbo for the Italian market to avoid the heavy luxury tax on cars over 2-litres; so the

The latter-day GTO's rear wing vents are the only styling cue carried forward from the original 250GTO.

engine chosen was the V-8, set at 2.85-litres such that, like Porsche, the car would fit into the 4-litre category once the FIA's turbo correction factor of 1.4 was applied. With twin IHI turbochargers it would develop 400 bhp at 7000 rpm, but much more for racing, simply by adjusting turbo pressures. To allow a conventional racing gearbox behind the axle line, the engine was sited fore and aft which necessitated an extra 4 inches in the wheelbase. What had been the 308GTB's 225/50 x 16 rear tyres were used on the front of the GTO, with 265/50 x 16 tyres on the rear – so the body was flared out to accommodate them and any later increase, to the tune of an extra 7 inches. The chassis was just a stretched version of the 308's tubular frame, but the body was a mixture of materials using glass-fibre, Kevlar for the bonnet, and carbon/Kevlar for the roof. The car's weight was quoted at 1160 Kg; although production ones with full interior trim were nearer 1300 Kg they were still 50 kg lighter than the 308GTB.

All mod cons are shown inside this genuine road car.

SPECIFICATION	FERRARI 288GTO
ENGINE	Aluminium V-8, twin turbos, 2855 cc
HORSEPOWER	400 bhp @ 7000 rpm
TRANSMISSION	Manual 5-speed
CHASSIS	Steel frame, composite body
BRAKES	Discs all round
TOP SPEED	189 mph
ACCELERATION	**0-60 mph** 5.0 seconds **0-100 mph** 11.0 seconds

In looks the GTO was very similar to the 308, just longer and wider, until you came to the rear; the two or three near vertical slots, cut into the 250GTO's flanks behind the front wheels, became three similar cut-outs behind the 288GTO's rear wheels, and the tail spoiler, too, carried overtones of 20 years earlier. While the earlier car was designed for competition and won, the 288GTO was designed for competition but never ran – that hasn't stopped it from being another instant classic Ferrari.

'The 288GTO was the fastest Ferrari in its day.'

Recognisably a longer, wider 308GTB, the 288GTO uses some carbon fibre panels in unstressed areas; the turbocharged 2.85-litre V-8 sits fore-and-aft.

FERRARI F512M

1995

191 mph

307 km/h

'The design has tried to move with the times, but the times have now overtaken the design.'

Below and below right: F512M has a revised front end with exposed lamps and a 'happier' intake; it is also a little faster than the otherwise similar TR.

Maybe the 512 is neither the most practical nor the nimblest of Ferraris, but it still has an almighty presence that shouts Ferrari; 78 inches wide, 44 inches low it still manages to be graceful in its Pininfarina clothes; and with 440 bhp from its flat-12 (boxer) 5-litre midships engine, it is also very fast but user-friendly with it. If Ferrari didn't keep producing even more exciting, but considerably less practical, devices like the 288GTO and the F40/50, the 'Berlinetta Boxer' would have attracted the stronger following which its all-round ability deserves; those that can afford them don't usually buy a big Ferrari for its practicality, and the others offer more short-term exhilaration.

The Boxer genre started life back in 1973 when the Daytona was still in production. Ferrari was never one to leap into new technologies, although the company has always been good at perfecting them once proven – a sound small-company philosophy. Thus Ferrari was beaten to the mid-engined road car draw by Lamborghini; such was caution that both the mid-engined Ferraris were to be shown as styling exercises well ahead of possible production as a means of sampling public opinion before taking the plunge. Its first public airing was at the 1971 Turin Show, two years before the production launch.

At the time the *Grand Prix* and Sports-prototype racing cars were using a 3-litre flat-12 which gave a usefully low centre of gravity. It was a good configuration for a road car, too, giving a low rear deck height for better visibility but it dictated quite a wide car; however Ferrari preferred to keep the masses between the wheelbase and lifted the engine to put the gearbox within the rear of the sump – practicality ruled over the last word in handling and the model has lived with that ever since. While the engine followed the layout of the 3-litre, its dimensions and many of its components came from the 365 V-12 Daytona unit, although its camshafts were belt driven; with 344 bhp, it was slightly less powerful than the Daytona with a lower compression ratio but would pull similar speeds – *Motor* recorded 172 mph. Its style was unique, neither a big Dino nor a preview of the 308, with matt black below a line from the sharp nose to the rear bumper, set under the short stubby tail. Its title was a mouthful – 365GT4BB, Berlinetta Boxer denoting the different layout from that of the 365GTB4 Daytona. That first model was usually known as the Boxer, even though all subsequent models used a boxer engine.

The first update came in 1976; in response to restrictive emission legislation the capacity was increased to 5-litres for no power increase, the engine was fitted with a dry sump, and the rear tyre size was increased – these had been the same size front and rear on the first car – adding also to body width; a front spoiler helped to keep the nose down at high speeds. This became the 512, following the new numbering system of capacity followed by number of cylinders; the fuel injection 512i followed in 1981, again with no power increase. The first major change came in 1984 with a dramatically revised shape whose major feature was the side-strakes leading to intakes for the radiators which had been moved from the front to

just ahead of the rear wheels; the front intake stayed as a feed for brake cooling ducts. The 5-litre engine adopted 4 valves per cylinder to recover emission strangled outputs and generated 390 bhp; its heads were painted red to justify the revived Testarossa name. These changes, plus bigger rear tyres, widened the car by six inches, put another two inches in the wheelbase and increased the overall length by five inches – it had become a big car. It was faster, too, with a maximum around 182 mph.

Since then it has had minor styling changes with small power increases. For 1992 the 512TR had 428 bhp and anti-lock brakes, and the front showed a family identity that would be carried across to the 355. Only two years later came the F512M, recalling the 'Modificata' version of the 1970 racing GT car, with 440 bhp in slightly less weight, new wheels and a revised front with headlights now visible behind clear plastic; on the road, it should be fractionally faster than the earlier car, an estimated 191 mph against 188 mph. The overall shape, though, is unchanged from the 512TR. The design has tried to move with the times, but the times have now overtaken the design; the F355 is more agile and almost as fast and Ferrari are replacing the Big Boxer with a modern Daytona, a two-seater version of the front-engined 456GT labelled F555.

SPECIFICATION	FERRARI F512M
ENGINE	Aluminium flat-12, 4942 cc
HORSEPOWER	440 bhp @ 6750 rpm
TRANSMISSION	Manual 5-speed
CHASSIS	Steel frame, aluminium body
BRAKES	Discs all round
TOP SPEED	191 mph (307 km/h)
ACCELERATION	**0-60 mph** 4.8 seconds **0-100 mph** 10.2 seconds

When the Testarossa replaced the 512BB, those memorable side-strakes changed the styling from the bland to the exotic; the 512TR (above) and M have kept them.

FERRARI F50

1995
202 mph
325 km/h

'It is a real racer for the road, not a grand tourer.'

To the world of motoring, Ferrari means fast. Having someone else build the fastest road car doesn't go down too well in the corridors of power at Maranello, even if the racing heritage of the prancing horse transcends all other contenders. While the Ferrari 288GTO had topped the fastest Countach, the mid-'eighties saw the Porsche 959 at the head of the field. Ferrari responded with the F40 in 1988 with all but 200 mph. All were to be engulfed by the rash of supercars that flooded a diminishing market – Jaguar, Bugatti and McLaren cleared 200 mph comfortably. Ferrari has returned to the fray with the F50, but not to challenge the rest for maximum speed; the new car is an unashamed *Grand Prix* car for the road. They plan to build just 349 in three years; there were only 270 GTOs but over 1300 F40s.

The dramatic success of the limited edition 288GTO had suggested that the market would still absorb a large number of even faster cars bearing the prancing horse. With the GTO Evolution still-born by the lack of anywhere to race Group B cars, Ferrari had a sound base for the car that would celebrate 40 years of production. The chassis followed the tubular space-frame principles of the GTO but bonded carbon-fibre replaced the welded sheet steel boxing to give a lighter, stronger structure; body panelling and interior trims also benefited from modern composites. While the suspension was similar to that of the GTO, it was modified for Pirelli's latest P Zeros which were considerably wider; so track and car-width increased too. Power was also greater; using the same basic 308 unit but with larger bore, shorter stroke and higher turbo pressures, the output rose to 478 bhp at 7000 rpm from the 2936 cc V-8.

With all the weight reduction and near 20% power increase, it was not surprising that the F40 was very much quicker off the mark with 0-100 mph in 7.6 seconds against the GTO's 11.0 seconds; the top speed too rose from 189 to around 200 mph. On the road the F40 was tremendously fast and responsive with levels of roadholding that could only be explored on the track.

But take the new F50 to the Ferrari test track at Fiorano and it is 4 seconds a lap faster. That is what the new car is all about – a little faster in acceleration with similar top speed, but with *Grand Prix* technology to give real race-car roadholding.

The chassis is a carbon-fibre monocoque to which the engine is solidly bolted, acting as a stressed member to carry the rear suspension loads

The Ferrari F50 is an out-and-out racer for the road, not a developed road car. The new V-12 engine is bolted direct to the carbon-fibre composite chassis. Despite more power than the F40, maximum speed will be no greater – ground effect is more important.

through the final drive casing, which doubles as an oil tank, between engine and the new six-speed gearbox. Like a GP car, the springs are laid across the top of the casing and operated by push-rods. The front suspension also uses push-rod operated transverse springs and is mounted directly onto the monocoque via aluminium inserts. Both front and rear damping is electronically controlled according to speed and dynamic forces. While the V-12 engine uses the same 65 degree angle between the banks as the 456, it is based more on the normally-aspirated 1993 *Grand Prix* engine with 5 valves per cylinder operated by chain-driven camshafts. Developing 513 bhp from 4.7-litres, its output per litre is even higher than that of the F355.

Carbon-fibre, Kevlar and honeycomb are used for the bodywork, which is wind-tunnel developed to provide a downforce balancing that from the underbody venturis; the full width rear wing and the high-lighted panel-joint line are features that link the F50 to the F40. Inside, there is naked carbon-fibre with just a little soft trim while LCD instrumentation panel gives bar graphs for minor displays but needles for rev counter and a speedometer which reads to 360 km/h! The car comes in two forms, closed with an integrated roll-bar, or open with roll-hoops emerging from the twin head-fairings. It is a real racer for the road, not a grand tourer.

The F50 comes in two forms; the coupé and the sports-racing spider. The picture above shows the cabin of the spider.

Below: Based on the Evolution (competition) version of the GTO, the F40 was produced in greater numbers than its predecessor.

SPECIFICATION	FERRARI F40	FERRARI F50
ENGINE	Twin turbo V-8, 2936 cc	V-12, 4698 cc
HORSEPOWER	478 bhp @ 7000 rpm	513 bhp @ 8000 rpm
TRANSMISSION	Manual 5-speed	Manual 6 speed
CHASSIS	Steel and composites	Carbon-fibre
BRAKES	Discs all round	Discs all round
TOP SPEED	198 mph (319 km/h)	202 mph (325 km/h)
ACCELERATION	**0-60 mph** 4.1 seconds **0-100 mph** 7.6 seconds	3.9 seconds 7.2 seconds

FERRARI F355

1994
178 mph
286 km/h

'The F355 became an altogether different car from its predecessors.'

It often happens. Small cars get bigger with each model change until finally the former top of the range gets pushed out of the list. We still have the Ferrari F512M, but the latest F355 is very little slower than the bigger car, quicker in the 0-60 mph dash and a lot more agile on the road. It is a supercar in its own right, not just a little relation lurking in the shadows.

That was certainly how its ancestor started; the little Dino 246 wasn't even called a Ferrari, although it was named after Enzo's son. Its concept was first shown as a Pininfarina styling exercise on a mid-engined 2-litre racing chassis in 1965; three years later it finally went into production as the 206GT using an aluminium twin ohc 2-litre V-6 designed by Ferrari, but built by Fiat, as 500 were required for it to be used as a Formula 2 engine. Fiat were to install it in the two front-engined Fiat Dinos, a Pininfarina open two seater and a Bertone 2+2, but Ferrari decided to use it as well for the new entry-level Ferrari for the Porsche market – the first mid-engined road Ferrari. For this, the engine was set transversely with the gearbox contained in the rear of the sump. When the required numbers had been completed – they won two F2 races in 1968 – Fiat increased the capacity to 2.4-litres using a cast-iron block which was adopted for both the Fiat and Ferrari Dinos. Ferrari's Dino 246 was a great success – an agile little jewel capable of around 145 mph.

This 1995 F355GTS features a removable roof panel.

Seeking a necessarily heavier four-seater version for 1973, Ferrari chose an aluminium 3-litre V-8, dimensionally two-thirds of a 365 V-12, but with its twin overhead cams driven by toothed belts; this was installed in the first Bertone-designed production Ferrari, the 308 GT4 with 8 inches extra in the wheelbase. Unlike the unitary 246GT chassis, the 308GT4 had a steel frame with glass-fibre bodywork; although never as acclaimed as the two-seaters, the GT4 stayed in production until 1980. Meanwhile, as Porsche continued to increase their engine sizes, the two-seater 246GT, which had been joined by the Targa-top GTS in 1972, was replaced by the 308GTB and GTS in 1975 using the same 255 bhp V-8 which propelled all models into the 150+ mph category – early models used glass-fibre bodywork but switched back to steel in 1977. Pininfarina's 308GTB took some cues from the big mid-engined 365GTBB and has long been rated as one of his best ever styles.

Fuel injection replaced carburetters in 1980 in the search for lower emission levels; the resultant power loss was to some extent mitigated by the 1982 adoption of 4-valve heads, although power was still 15 bhp down on the original. Meanwhile the GT4 had been replaced by the

more spacious, Pininfarina designed, Mondial in 1980 with a cabriolet coming in 1984. Power was more than restored with the 1985 change to 3.2-litres for the 328 range with changes to body and interior within a similar overall shape. In 1989 the capacity was further enlarged to 3.4-litres with new castings and the engine was mounted fore-and-aft, which also allowed it to sit lower so the 348 tb and ts thus had a 10 cm longer wheelbase; the new body style used Testa Rossa side strakes and a more pronounced intake grille shape. With the 3.4-litre engine initially producing 300 bhp, increased to 320 in 1993 shortly after the open-top Spider 348 was introduced, the new range could comfortably clear 160 mph – the Dino name had been dropped mid-way through the 308 series.

Good though the 348 was, the Honda NSX and Porsches had also benefited from considerable development, so Ferrari moved on several stages with the next car, the F355 which came in mid-1994. Taking the engine out to 3.5-litres and adding 5-valve heads pushed the power up to 380 bhp at 8250 rpm, 1000 rpm higher than the 348 needed for its 320 bhp, and then, the highest output per litre of any non-turbo engine; it thus needed a six-speed gearbox to make the best use of the higher rev range. The chassis, too, had changes with electronic damping control and a *Grand Prix* style underbody venturi. The F355 became an altogether different car from its predecessors, a supercar in any model range except Ferrari.

SPECIFICATION	FERRARI F355
ENGINE	Aluminium V-8, 3496 cc
HORSEPOWER	380 bhp @ 8250 rpm
TRANSMISSION	Manual 6-speed
CHASSIS	Unitary steel
BRAKES	Discs all round with ABS
TOP SPEED	178 mph (286 km/h)
ACCELERATION	**0-60 mph** 4.6 seconds **0-100 mph** 10.6 seconds

Above: Open F355 adds pose appeal to this remarkable small Ferrari.

Diverging from recent Ferrari numerology, what should have been the F355 as 3.5-litre 5-valve. With 380 bhp the little Ferrari is almost as fast as the flat-12 512TR.

FERRARI 456GT

1994
187 mph
301 km/h

'Inside is all the luxury you expect from the target class.'

Fast-back shape recaptures the Daytona, but the 456GT is a thoroughly modern Grand Tourer capable of covering long distances in quiet comfort.

Four-seater Ferraris are a rarity. The name is so bound up with racing and ultimate road-cars that a family Ferrari is almost a contradiction in terms. But, with the latest 456GT, the company has managed to create a genuine four-seater that behaves like a sports car – it was the last project in which Enzo Ferrari had direct involvement before his death in 1988. It is much more a direct descendant of the Daytona – or the matching 365GTC4 – than a development of the 400 series which came to a halt in 1989; there was a three year gap before the 456GT was launched.

Emphasising the commitment to provide a genuine on-going front-engined range, a new engine was developed; once more a V-12 with 456 cc per cylinder – using the old-style numbering for the model name – this has a 65 degree angle between the banks which carry four-valve heads with toothed belt cam drive; a dry sump system has been retained to keep the engine low. A new 6-speed transaxle was designed too. Pininfarina's new shape follows the fastback contours of the Daytona rather than the square-rigged 400 and it must have a very low drag-factor as the 442 bhp unit propels the car to over 300 km/h, only a little slower than the factory claim for the mid-engined 512M. In keeping with the fast tourer aspect, the suspension is electronically adjustable for ride firmness, and road noise has been well subdued. Inside is all the luxury you expect from the target class, traditional light leather but no wooden fillets; to assist getting into the rear seats, you tilt the front seats and they move forward automatically on their runners. And there is a deep luggage boot which comes with its own fitted luggage. It's a really *grand* tourer.

Not that the previous series were wrong in their time, but they were more like stretched sports coupés than purpose-built comfortable fast tourers. Between the 400s and the long sleek 365GT 2+2 came the 365GT4 2+2; the 4 denoted the adoption of the twin-cam heads, albeit for fashion rather than performance. But the body was an all-new more modern clean-cut shape without the sinuous curves of its predecessor; slightly shorter in overall length, it nevertheless had a longer wheelbase to provide a little more rear seat room. That stayed in production from 1972-75 before the 400 arrived as a 4.8-litre – a longer stroke – in a revised version of the previous body; what made it more remarkable, though, was that it was the first Ferrari to be offered with automatic transmission and most were equipped with the General Motors unit. The previous model hadn't been certified for the American market, but this was designed for it.

Fuel injection was added to make the 400i in 1979 in the interests of refinement and emission control and at the expense of a power drop from 340 to 315 bhp, but the basic 400 had a ten year run through to 1985. The 4.9-litre 412 followed on with further body and interior refinements for a further four years; by then it had become a genuinely comfortable fast tourer for those who had grown out of the two-seaters, but, after 17 years of the same basic design and shape, it wasn't going to bring in fresh Ferrari owners – a fresh approach was needed to put a four-seater Ferrari into a market that had such effective cars as the Mercedes 600SL and BMW 850 at its bottom end or the Bentley Continental R at the top. In 1987 it was a difficult time to make such a decision, as the supercar market was at its height and Ferrari didn't want to be lured into producing significantly more than 3000 cars a year should demand continue; in the event, the investment-led market crashed and Ferrari made the right decision to continue with a broad range. The reception given to the 456GT has proved the point; all it needs now is automatic transmission for the US market and this would be likely to take the form of an electronic clutch with matching engine management like the 1993 *Grand Prix* cars. Racing always improves Ferrari's breed.

Little changed in style from the 1975 400, this 412 was the forerunner of the 456 with similar rear seat space.

Light Italian leather is tastefully used throughout the car. Rear seats have enough headroom for adults so the 456GT is better than most of its rivals.

SPECIFICATION	FERRARI 456GT
ENGINE	Aluminium V-12, 5474 cc
HORSEPOWER	442 bhp @ 6250 rpm
TRANSMISSION	Manual 6-speed
CHASSIS	Steel frame, aluminium body
BRAKES	Discs all round with ABS
TOP SPEED	187 mph
ACCELERATION	**0-60 mph** 5.1 seconds **0-100 mph** 11.6 seconds

FERRARI 550 MARANELLO

1996
199 mph
320 km/h

An exercise of refined traditionalism, the front-engine/rear-drive V-12 engined 550 Maranello benefits from state-of-the-art mechanicals as well as electronics. The aluminium bodywork is, as ever, by Pininfarina but there is only room for two seats.Beneath is a tubular steel frame.

Practicality is the keynote of the 550 Maranello coupé of 1996, that is Ferrari's first front-engined two-seater for close on 30 years. But there's nothing conservative about the model's top speed which is claimed to be 199 mph.

This car is very much the brainchild of Ferrari's president, Luca di Montezemolo, and to place the 550 in context it is necessary to retrace our steps to the time of his 1992 appointment.

Then the company's range included two mid-engined two-seaters; the flat-12-powered 512 TR and its cheaper 348 stablemate which employed a V-8 unit. Both cars were very similar in concept with the only differences being price and performance.

Such a race-bred engine location offers its driver a better handling car than a front-engined one but this is at the expense of loss of interior accommodation and luggage capacity with an attendant rise in noise levels.

The 550 was intended to address these limitations to provide a more conventional and usable product than the 512M it replaced. The result is a superlative grand tourer rather than an uncompromising sports car.

Ferrari has been wedded to the V-12 engine since its 1947 inception. The 5.5-litre aluminium unit – the capacity is reflected in the model's name – with its twin overhead-camshafts per bank and attendant four valves per cylinder, is shared with its four-seater 465GT stablemate that is also front-engined.

However, the internal mechanicals are peculiar to the new model, most significantly the lighter pistons and titanium connecting rods to permit higher revolutions.

A further refinement is provided by the presence of hydraulic tappets, an innovation for Ferrari, that are both quieter and more efficient from an emissions standpoint.

There is also a variable-intake manifold, that is peculiar to the 550, which gives the model its own very distinctive characteristics, when compared with the 456. The purpose-designed intake system incorporates no less than 12 throttle valves actuated by electro-pneumatic servos controlled by a Bosch computerised brain.

Since 1964 Ferraris have featured a rear-mounted gearbox and the 550 similarly has a transaxle that incorporates a 456-derived six-speed unit.

The two-door aluminium body is, inevitably, by Pininfarina with retro elements, not perhaps the most memorable of designs to spring from this respected styling house but one with a sculpted bonnet and strong wing line to emphasise the

Left: The 5.5-litre, dry sump, V-12 engine has twin overhead camshafts per cylinder bank and, accordingly, four valves per cylinder. Based on the 456 model, further refinement is provided by hydraulic tappets. A Bosch M 5.2 electronic management system is employed.

hidden mechanicals. The use of composites is confined to the bumpers and wheel arches liners. Drag coefficient is a creditable 0.33.

This finely-honed shape conceals a chassis of chrome-moly tubular steel which is similar to that used on the 456. Suspension is by the customary all-round, unequal length wishbones with massive Brembo drilled disc brakes.

These have benefited from Formula 1 technology which means that the 550's progress is arrested by four-pot aluminium calipers with special heat insulating pistons that prevents the fluid from boiling, even after extreme applications.

There is an electrically-controlled traction system and the driver has a choice of two settings: Normal and a firmer Sport. This, along with the front-engine/rear-drive configuration, makes a significant contribution to the 550's handling, which is outstanding.

No Ferrari would be complete without being fitted with handsome magnesium wheels and the 550's five-spoked ones are shod with big, beefy 18-inch tyres.

The Ferrari owner and passenger can get in and out of this two-seater with ease, which is significant because some of the visually stunning, but lower slung, mid-engined models have represented something of a challenge in this respect!

Interior trim is restrained but luxurious with finely upholstered natural-hued leather seats and matching carpeting, black-faced instruments and fascia. Steering is, of course, power assisted and a little over two turns from lock to lock.

The gear lever operates in Ferrari's traditional exposed gate although, for the 1998 season, the model will be available with the company's Formula 1-related Selespeed gearbox.

The clutch pedal will accordingly disappear and gear changes will be effected by the driver operating two paddles positioned behind, and either side of, the rim of the steering wheel – just like on Ferrari's racing cars.

There are no rear seats, but luggage (secured by a pair of leather straps) can be carried on a carpeted shelf that sits above the 114-litre petrol tank which also takes up most of the boot space. This is necessary because the 550 gulps down fuel at an average rate of 7.9 mpg when being used around town although this figure improves to an overall 13 when motorway journeys are taken into account.

Turning the scales at 1960 kg, according to Ferrari the 550 can reach 60 mph in a formidable 4.3 seconds which is half a second less than the 512. Its official blistering 199 mph top speed is an eight miles per hour improvement on that of its mid-engined predecessor.

Priced on its announcement at £143,685, the 550 is over £50,000 more than the V-8-powered 355 but the top line Formula 1-related F50 is well over twice the price . . .

The Maranello also marks the arrival of names for Ferrari models, which in the past had often simply featured a number. The choice is most appropriate in this case because Maranello is the model's birthplace and the name of the small town in northern Italy where the factory is located. But Ferraris are for the fortunate few: just 3000 or so cars leave the works every year.

Purposeful and restrained, the 550's interior is upholstered in the finest leather. The front engine location ensures this is a spacious two-seater. Note the traditional Ferrari gearchange gate. A rear-mounted, six-speed 'box is used with an automatic version in the offing.

'According to Ferrari the 550 can reach 60 mph in a formidable 4.3 seconds.'

SPECIFICATION	FERRARI 550 MARANELLO
ENGINE	Aluminium V-12, 5474 cc
HORSEPOWER	479 bhp @ 7000 rpm
TRANSMISSION	Manual 6-speed
CHASSIS	High tensile moly-tubular
BRAKES	Discs all round with ABS
TOP SPEED	199 mph (320 km/h)
ACCELERATION	**0-60 mph** 4.6 seconds **0-100 mph** 10.1 seconds

FORD GT40 MK III

1966
164 mph
264 km/h

'A handful of Mk IIIs were made to provide proper street-legal motoring.'

Arguably the first of the mid-engined supercars, the Ford GT40 was designed as a racer but racing rules forced it to spawn a road-going derivative. Single-seater racing car design had changed over from the traditional front-engined layout in the late 'fifties, led by Cooper and confirmed by Lotus. The racing sports cars followed from 1960, but these were racers not road cars; putting an engine immediately behind the driver wasn't considered practical for a road car with poor visibility and nowhere to put the luggage, noisy too – with little space within the engine compartment for silencers. By the time they came to produce a real road version, Ford quietened the car considerably, made its lighting road-legal, and created a luggage box in the engine compartment – anything in there was going to get hot, a problem for the occupants too.

The Ford GT40 – 40-inches high – was a product of the merged interests of Ford of America and Lola Cars to produce an endurance race winner – Le Mans in particular. Eric Broadley's Lola GT ran with Ford power in the 1963 season at which time Ford had been working on their own GT car since mid-1962, having been thwarted in a bid to buy Ferrari. The GT40 arrived for the 1964 season; built at a new British subsidiary, Ford Advanced Vehicles, its glass-fibre body concealed a stiff sheet steel chassis carrying a 4.2-litre Ford V-8 mated to an Italian Colotti gearbox and all the suspension used race-style double wishbones. The first year wasn't a great success until Ford handed over the development and racing to Carroll Shelby's Shelby American while Ford continued work on the Mark II.

SPECIFICATION	FORD GT40 Mk III
ENGINE	Cast-iron V-8, 4727 cc
HORSEPOWER	306 bhp @ 6000 rpm
TRANSMISSION	Manual 5-speed ZF transaxle
CHASSIS	Steel frame, glass-fibre bodywork
BRAKES	Discs all round
TOP SPEED	164 mph
ACCELERATION	**0-60 mph** 5.3 seconds **0-100 mph** 11.8 seconds

A Slough-built roadgoing Mark III GT40 of 1966 identified by its reprofiled nose, modified headlights and front overriders. The mid-located, 4.7-litre V-8 was detuned to provide 306 bhp but was still able to reach 100 mph in under 12 seconds. Luggage was carried in a special container above the gearbox.

For 1965, the GT40 adopted the 4727 cc Ford V-8 tuned to around 380 bhp and used a German ZF gearbox. While the cars had some success, they failed at Le Mans as did the Mk IIs which had 485 bhp 7-litre engines. With a new sports car category scheduled for 1966, FAV had begun to build the necessary 50 GT40s while work continued in America on the Mk II cars as contenders for outright victory; the big cars went on to win Le Mans and the championship in 1966. The Mk IV development won the French race again in 1967. Ford's first target was achieved within just three years of racing; after the second victory the company retired from this form of racing, leaving others to campaign the GT40 in sports car racing until 1969 when the rules changed again and the car became outdated. However the GT40 was to win Le Mans in 1968 and 1969 as a final fling.

Ford Advanced Vehicles had completed the necessary 50 in mid-1966 but went on to build

another 57. Some 30 were built as road cars, just quieter racers on narrower tyres, but a handful of Mk IIIs were made to provide proper street-legal motoring. These had 306 bhp engines and different bodywork – new nose with four headlights, and a longer tail to allow the luggage space. Inside, the trim was somewhat more luxurious with some carpet and a radio, but it has to be said that even a racing GT40 was more comfortable than any other racer – Ford appreciated that uncomfortable cars are tiring to drive in endurance races.

With just 7 Mk IIIs produced but many racing cars converted to road use, it is not easy to find the performance figures for genuine Holley-carburetted 306 bhp cars. Given the right gearing, the 380 bhp cars with four Weber carburettors were able to reach nearly 200 mph at Le Mans; with 300 bhp they could be expected to reach 175 mph. However the road cars were available with a choice of axle ratios and most were sold with gearing more suited to everyday motoring, which limited the possible top speed to around 164 mph but gave very good acceleration. These figures came from *Motor* who tested a short-tailed Holley-carburettor car in 1968, but they are fast enough and it was a very enjoyable road car.

GT40s won Le Mans on four successive occasions, from 1966 to 1969. The latter year marked the end of GT40 production and this roadgoing example dates from then. Many drivers caught a glimpse of this rear view!

HONDA NSX

1990
160 mph
256 km/h

'The NSX is a superbly engineered driver's car with very safe handling and enough performance for most.'

Honda only began to produce four-wheelers in 1964, starting with mini-cars. Since then they have gradually built up to the level of a large-scale manufacturer with a full range of models that have also been produced in factories in America and England, where their contribution to Rover has been invaluable. But they wanted a flag-ship above the Legend range. They had the required technology, so why not produce a Japanese answer to Ferrari and Porsche?

Supercars of the mid-'eighties were essentially European and mostly Italian; most came from companies that had strong track records. Honda's own track record was as good as any on two wheels, while four-wheeled prowess encompassed a pair of *Grands Prix* victories with their own cars in 1965 (Mexican GP) and 1967 (Italian GP), the 1966 domination of Formula Two with the Brabham team plus the more recent manufacture of successful *Grands Prix* engines from 1983. If that isn't enough heritage, the NSX is out to create its own track record in GT racing – three were entered for the 1994 Le Mans as a trial run, and all finished. They will be back.

The new car had to be a practical technology showcase, a sensible pointer to the future; aluminium was used wherever possible – chassis, body, suspension were all aluminium via an appropriate process whether pressing, forging or casting. It had to be mid-engined but the V-6 was mounted transversely with the gearbox on the end, thus saving cockpit intrusion and allowing a decent amount of luggage to be carried behind. The engine is an all-aluminium four-cam V-6 3-litre which uses Honda's V-TEC variable valve timing and the VVIS variable intake volume systems, both of which allow good low speed torque and high power, 270 bhp at 7100 rpm in this case. Given that Honda joined the GP world in the turbo era, they might have used that technology to generate even more power, but 280 bhp was enough for Japanese legislation and the light weight ensured that acceleration was up to market standard – 1340 Kg.

Traction control and ABS were a necessary part of a high-tech chassis design, with speed-sensitive electrically operated assistance for the power steering; this was initially only available when the car was fitted with automatic transmission but became a no-cost option for manual transmission cars in 1994. At the same time, the wheels grew an inch in diameter and half an inch in width to take lower profile tyres.

Clothing all this mechanical sophistication is a pleasing enough shape that borrows cues from no-one, not even from Honda itself as there is little marque identity in the rest of the range. It scores against many mid-engined cars by having a compact enough engine to allow a flat rear deck for good visibility. It scores too in luggage space, at

3-litre V-6 sits transversely and there is room for luggage behind it.

the expense of an extended tail which carries a rear wing integrated with the body sides; the resulting deep and slightly detached rear section upsets the overall balance. But the shape obviously works, as the car achieves 160 mph on its 270 bhp.

However the proof of any pudding is in the eating and the NSX is a superbly engineered driver's car with very safe handling and enough performance for most. It is also very quiet and comfortable and has shown every evidence of being thoroughly reliable as an everyday car; that is now to be expected from any car in the Porsche, Mercedes market. Further appeal was added with the 1995 introduction of the T-Roof, a removable top panel to match the Porsches and Ferraris.

A T-roof version became available in 1995 to give a boost to sales.

SPECIFICATION	HONDA NSX
ENGINE	Aluminium V-6, 2977 cc
HORSEPOWER	270 bhp @ 7100 rpm
TRANSMISSION	Manual 5-speed
CHASSIS	Unitary aluminium
BRAKES	Discs all round with ABS
TOP SPEED	160 mph
ACCELERATION	**0-60 mph** 5.3 seconds **0-100 mph** 12.6 seconds

Japan's only mid-engined supercar makes extensive use of aluminium in its chassis and body.

ISO GRIFO GL365

1966
161 mph
259 km/h

'It had plenty of effortless performance and a remarkable top speed.'

Styled by Giugiaro while at Bertone, the Bizzarrini-designed Grifo was one of the best-looking cars of its day; with 365 bhp from a Chevrolet V-8 it also went very well.

Even now, over 30 years after its first appearance at the 1963 Turin Show, the Iso Grifo A3L is a strikingly beautiful car. Low, wide and undeniably sleek, it was one of Giugiaro's creations while he worked with Bertone. Powered by a 365 bhp version of Chevrolet's 327 cu.in (5360 cc) V-8, it had plenty of effortless performance and a remarkable top speed, 10-15 mph faster than Astons and Jaguar E-types could manage with their highly tuned six-cylinder engines. American power had become fashionable with a number of the smaller specialist manufacturers – Facel Vega, Bristol and Jensen used Chrysler units, AC used Ford as would de Tomaso, and Gordon Keeble also used a Chevrolet 327.

In fact the Gordon-Keeble had preceded the first Iso by two years; in its original Gordon GT form it was shown at Geneva in 1960 with a nice four-seater body which was Giugiaro's first work for Bertone. Financial problems delayed its production for four years by which time it used a glass-fibre body. Meanwhile Count Renzo Rivolta was seeking to take Milan-based Iso back into motor manufacture after the Isetta bubble-car period; aiming at the luxury GT market, he approached Bertone and the result was shown at the 1962 Geneva Show – the Iso-Rivolta followed Giugiaro's earlier design remarkably closely, apart from a revised front and higher boot section.

Not only that, but the boxed tubular chassis design was very similar, right down to the de Dion rear suspension. This was developed by Giotto Bizzarrini who had established his own prototype-building company in 1962; project director of the Ferrari 250GTO he was also designing Lamborghini's first V-12 engine, all three projects in 1962. So let's just say . . . drawing inspiration from John Gordon's earlier prototype, Bizzarrini, Rivolta and Bertone brought the high-style Iso Rivolta 4-seater into production for 1963; using the softer 327 engine with 300 bhp coupled to the Borg Warner 4-speed manual box it would do 0-100 mph in 19 seconds and reach 135 mph. It was a fine car.

For the 1963 Turin Show, Bizzarrini shortened the chassis by 20 cm for Giugiaro to create the Iso Grifo 2-seater in two forms, the road going Luxury A3L and the sleeker more aerodynamic Competition A3C, similar in form but without a single interchangeable panel – it was the homologation special derivative as the Ferrari 250GTO was to the GT and Aston Martin Project 214 cars were to the DB4GT. Subsequently

The large rear window gave excellent visibility to this Italian muscle car.

Bizzarrini was to reverse the process and make a road-going A3C as the Bizzarrini Strada 5300 in coupé and convertible forms. However, solo A3C models competed at Le Mans in 1964 (14th) and 1965 (9th) and the 1964 car clocked 172 mph down the straight using over 400 bhp from a competition 327 fitted with Weber carburetters.

SPECIFICATION	ISO GRIFO GL365
ENGINE	Cast-iron V-8, 5360 cc
HORSEPOWER	365 bhp @ 6200 rpm
TRANSMISSION	Manual 4-speed
CHASSIS	Steel frame
BRAKES	Discs all round
TOP SPEED	161 mph
ACCELERATION	**0-60 mph** 7.4 seconds **0-100 mph** 16.6 seconds

These cars ran in the prototype category as the required number had not been made by then; the first production A3L Grifos were built in 1965.

Although the 300 bhp Rivolta engine was an option, the standard A3L used the 365 bhp version with solid valve lifters for more revs and power – it would become known as the GL365. Further refinement with power was created for 1969 when the Corvette's 7-litre 427 cu.in engine was inserted with just over 400 bhp, hence the new model's Grifo GL400 designation.

While Iso replaced the Rivolta with the two-door Lele (Bertone) and the four-door Fidia (Giugiaro on behalf of Ghia) in 1969, the Grifo continued until 1974 by which time Bertone had built 411 of those stunning bodies. In that year the Rivolta family sold out to American interests which shortly collapsed. The Grifo was the car that ensures the name will be remembered.

Like the four-seater Iso Rivolta, the Grifo was designed around big Chevrolet power.

JAGUAR D-TYPE

1956
162 mph
261 km/h

'For maximum speed they let it run through to 6600 rpm to clock 162 mph.'

Jaguar's Le Mans winning race-car may not be everyone's idea of a production road car but it qualifies on two counts. First, 45 were built for private customers for general competition; they were mostly registered for use on the road at the time and some never raced. And secondly, the XKSS was sold as a road-equipped version of the standard D-type competition car with identical performance. More than the 16 XKSS would have been built had not Jaguar suffered from that notorious factory fire of 1957; as it was, 61 customer cars were built over the period 1955-7 and the works used a further 17.

Generally, race cars are improved during their careers but customer D-types were rarely subjected to modifications of which the factory didn't approve; the one tested by the American *Road & Track* magazine in 1956 was a normal 260 bhp 3.4-litre D with a slightly shorter final drive than standard countered by oversize tyres to match the Jaguar fitment of a 3.54:1 axle ratio. Owned by Continental Motors of California, XKD528 was being raced by Pearce Woods, who seemed quite happy to ignore the factory rev limit of 5800 rpm for the tests; using 6200 rpm they were able to reach 60 mph in 4.7 sec still in first gear, and go on to 100 mph in 12.1 sec. For maximum speed they let it run through to 6600 rpm to clock 162 mph. This confirmed the 164 mph run which Phil Walters had made at Daytona Beach the year before in XKD406, shortly before he and Mike Hawthorn won the Sebring 12-hour race – a Le Mans type 2.79:1 axle ratio was used for that which dropped the revs to 5500 rpm. *Road & Track's* later test of an XKSS showed 149 mph and 0-100 mph in 13.6 sec. The highest speed ever recorded for a D-type was 185.5 mph at Bonneville in 1960 with a 3.8-litre engine and a 2.53:1 axle.

Racer's cockpit. D-types had central division to mount a metal passenger-side cover. This was removed for the road-going XKSS which had full-width screen.

Although pre-war SS cars had been used in competitions, the works only seriously started competing with the XK120, launched in 1948. The XK120C came in 1951 as a purpose-built sports-racer using the same 3.4-litre twin ohc six-cylinder engine in a very different chassis under a new body. Le Mans victory then was the main goal and the C-type obliged in 1951 and 1953, among other victories. The D-type came in 1954 as another all-new car around the famous XK engine; this used an aeroplane-style central monocoque to which were attached sub-frames. Front and rear suspension followed C-type principles but with better location for the live rear axle. What set the D-type apart from any other period racer was the beautiful stream-lined body designed by aerodynamicist Malcolm Sayer; it combined proven function with elegance of form giving the high speed necessary for the Le Mans straights without seeming to suffer from high speed lift.

All the customer cars would retain the first style which would become known as 'short-nose' after the front of the 1955 factory cars was extended 7.5 inches for

even better aerodynamics; these also had the famous tail-fins fared into the standard headrest. Le Mans victories came in 1955, 1956 and 1957 with many more besides; Jaguar had stopped running their own team but continued to provide engines and assistance to the Ecurie Ecosse and Cunningham teams as well as to the cars that used Jaguar engines, notably Lister.

While the D-type engine was basically that of the original 3442 cc XK120, it featured dry sump lubrication, special camshafts, bigger valves and triple Weber carburetters to produce 250 bhp at 5750 rpm in its production form whereas the XK140 – introduced in 1954 – had 190 bhp. The limitation was in the size of inlet valves that could be fitted; accordingly the wide-angle head was introduced with the inlet at 40 degrees to the vertical rather than 35, but this was not fitted to the production cars. Works engines produced up to 280 bhp on carburetters. When the 3.8-litre engine became available in 1957, many earlier Ds were converted.

Following the 1960 Le Mans appearance of a modernised D-type labelled E2A, the famous E-type was launched in 1961 carrying many of the lessons learnt in the D-type's racing years. The ultimate 3.8-litre XK engine was that prepared for the Lindner-Nocker coupé with 344 bhp at 6500 rpm using Lucas fuel injection, some 40 bhp more than a D-type had ever used, and 37 per cent more than the production cars.

D-types came in two styles. This is a works long-nose as used by the 1955-7 Le Mans winners, complete with tail-fin head faring for high speed stability.

SPECIFICATION	**JAGUAR D-TYPE**
ENGINE	Straight 6, 3442 cc
HORSEPOWER	250 bhp @ 5750 rpm
TRANSMISSION	Manual 4-speed
CHASSIS	Central monocoque
BRAKES	Discs all round
TOP SPEED	162 mph
ACCELERATION	**0-60 mph** 4.7 seconds **0-100 mph** 12.1 seconds

The XKSS was modelled on the short-nose D-types. This is XKD527 which was sold through the same American dealership as XKD528 which clocked 162 mph.

JAGUAR XJ220

1993
217 mph
349 km/h

'The XJ220 is an electrifying road car.'

Sensation of the 1988 Birmingham Motor Show, the XJ220 aimed to set new standards of road-going performance with a 500bhp V-12 Jaguar engine mounted amidships and mated to a complex 5-speed four-wheel-drive transmission; and it looked like a Jaguar, too, with more than a hint of the still-born XJ13 sports-racer from the mid-'sixties. Conceived over the winter of 1984/5 by Engineering Director Jim Randle it was designed for International Group B racing. At that time Porsche had announced the 959 but hadn't built any, Ferrari had started building the 288GTO and Jaguar had made a tentative return to racing via the American Group 44 team competing in the American IMSA version of Group C; they would enter Group C in 1985 with Tom Walkinshaw Racing (TWR). The XJ220 would embody all that was necessary for successful Group B competition and add all the necessary road refinements too.

The original prototype was built behind the scenes, away from normal Jaguar work, with a few dedicated employees and a lot of help from the suppliers around Coventry, most notably FF Developments who supplied the transmission and the secret assembly area. That it was to take three years was due to the fact that work on it had to be fitted around normal Jaguar development. Jaguar's then chairman, John Egan, hadn't even seen the car until a week before that 1988 show.

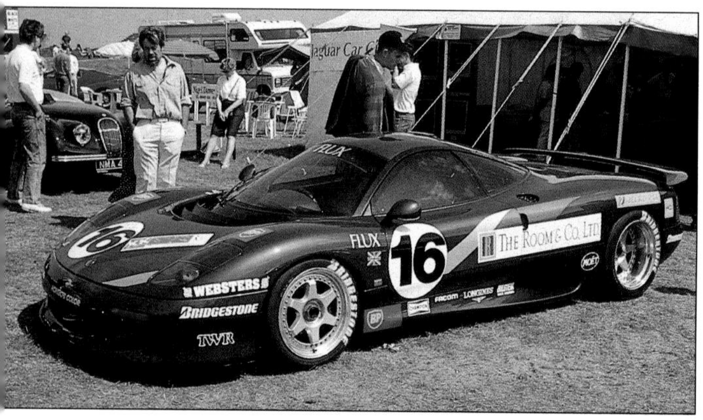

JaguarSport developed the XJR-15 as a potentially road-legal version of the Le Mans winning XJR-9 V-12 for use in a limited race series.

Announced as a prototype of which perhaps two hundred and twenty could be built, the car soon had a flock of people trying to place orders with £50,000 deposits. Jaguar couldn't possibly build it among the production lines, so the project was handed over to JaguarSport, the joint Jaguar-TWR operation set up for niche variants and motor racing. By now Group B was going nowhere, so the last word in racing technology was less important; TWR simplified the design, removing the 4WD, but sadly dropped the Jaguar V-12 in favour of the turbocharged 3.5-litre V-6 which would become the chosen unit for Group C racing for 1989/90. Having started life as the power unit for the MG Metro 6RV rally car, it just wasn't a Jaguar engine to the true enthusiast, and its racing life was to be short-lived. Other conceptual changes included shortening the car and using a chassis of aluminium honeycomb rather than sheet aluminium, but it still looked broadly the same, had even more power at 550 bhp and was 275 Kg lighter than the original.

A little over a year after its first showing, the heavily revised car was launched at £290,000 with a production quantity of 200-350. Three months later, in February 1990 this was confirmed at 350 with delivery to start two years later. Meanwhile, TWR had been gently developing a road-going version of the XJR-9 which had won the 1988 Group C championship powered by Jaguar V-12; this XJR9-R was running during 1989 and was finally announced as the XJR-15 in November 1990. While it was almost road-legal, it was launched for a one-make racing series, accompanying selected *Grand Prix* meetings, and

The original XJ220 prototype (left) was longer and heavier due to V-12 engine and four-wheel-drive system; there was little style adjustment between the two.

only 20 or so were to be built. There is no doubt that some of the potential XJ220 owners would have preferred a road-going version of a real Jaguar racer than even the ultimate road-car, but they had committed to their XJ220 purchase knowing it was powered by the turbo V-6 and the XJR-15 was not technically a road car. In fact, the racing career of the XJR-15 was not particularly notable, while the XJ220 is now embarking on its own racing as the international racing rules have changed again and the car is suited to them; a Le Mans win would change attitudes.

Meanwhile the XJ220 is an electrifying road car. When originally announced, it was claimed to be able to exceed 200 mph, reach 60 mph in 3.6 seconds and 100 mph in 8 seconds. In its final form it has clocked nearly 220 mph, and returned 3.5 and 7.9 seconds for 0-60 mph and 0-100 mph. It doesn't have four-wheel-drive, although FF also built the new gearbox, but it doesn't need it; thanks to aerodynamic down-force. While no longer such a technical *tour de force*, the XJ220 has delivered its promise to be the fastest ever Jaguar.

SPECIFICATION	JAGUAR XJ220
ENGINE	Turbo V-6, 3498 cc
HORSEPOWER	549 bhp @ 7000 rpm
TRANSMISSION	Manual 5-speed
CHASSIS	Aluminium honeycomb, ali body
BRAKES	Discs all round
TOP SPEED	217 mph
ACCELERATION	**0-60 mph** 3.6 seconds **0-100 mph** 7.9 seconds

As finally developed XJ220 had a turbocharged V-6 engine and two-wheel drive but met its performance targets.

JAGUAR XK8

1996

158 mph

254 km/h

'It is the E-type that the market wants to remember and the style reflects this.'

Like its E-type spiritual forebear, the XK8 is produced in both open and closed forms. Although this is a right-hand drive example, the majority will be sold in America.

It has been a long wait but Jaguar have finally produced the spiritual successor to the much revered, legendary E-type. The new XK8 may not develop its own track record, but it exactly matches the enthusiast's perception of a thoroughly modern version of the 'sixties sporting icon.

When Jaguar launched the E-type in 1961, it was quite obviously the production version of the racing D-type; the engine was almost the same, the monocoque chassis used the same principle and it looked very similar. Racing had improved Jaguar's road-going breed and development had made it a little more comfortable with independent rear suspension.

Adding a V-12 version in 1971 did not detract from the E-type's race-derived appeal although the design was getting a little long in the tooth. Others were more comfortable and had better road-holding. But when the XJS arrived, it was far from the F-type that enthusiasts were awaiting; they wanted an evolution E-type, not a short wheelbase XJ12 with funny headlights and curious rear sail panels.

However the XJS became a niche model in its own right and lasted 21 years. It wasn't a sports car in the E-type mould but it was a very comfortable, and very quiet, fast tourer. Latterly, JaguarSport had marketed some engine conversions and body kits that considerably altered the car's character for those still yearning for the modern E-type, while the factory came up with the 6.0-litre XJR-S capable of nearly 160 mph. Such developments removed some of the urgency for an XJS replacement but this was becoming increasingly overdue; in fact, Jaguar had planned to replace it around 1988 with XJ41 once the XJ40 – the 1986 XJ6 – was in production.

A number of XJ41 prototypes had been built, but it was finally decided that the cost of getting that car into production would be too great to amortize over the numbers that could be sold. To try and keep the project alive, Jaguar then put the new XJ41 body design onto the existing XJS platform. Initially it seemed that new owners, Ford, had stopped this one, too, as the concept was turned into a new small Aston Martin.

But Ford obviously had second Jaguar

The XK8, styled by Jaguar's Geoff Lawson, replaced the long running XJS and is the first new model to appear under Ford's stewardship of the respected British company.

thoughts as sporting cars became fashionable again. If some of the production costs could be shared with Aston Martin, then the XJ41-cum-XJS could rise again as X100. However Aston Martin had been given the six-cylinder option, albeit supercharged, so Jaguar's version needed a new engine; exhaust emissions, fuel thirst and weight were against the V-12, so the choice fell on a new, modern V-8 designed specifically for Jaguar – not just another version of an American quad-cam. Initial work started on Project X100 in January 1992, the green light came in October and the new car was unveiled at the Geneva Show in March 1996.

Although the official launch was scheduled for NEC 1996, Geneva was chosen for a preview because that was where the E-type had made its first appearance 35 years earlier. Although the car owes much of its chassis engineering to the XJS, it is the E-type that the market wants to remember and the style reflects this. The name too. The long 'bonnet' with the rounded intake is very much like the E-type, and the profile is similar to that of the fixed head coupés; it is a modern integrated design with retro appeal.

SPECIFICATION	JAGUAR XK8
ENGINE	V-8, 3996 cc
HORSEPOWER	285 bhp @ 5800 rpm
TRANSMISSION	Automatic 5-speed
CHASSIS	Uniary steel
BRAKES	Discs all round with ABS
TOP SPEED	158 mph (254 km/h)
ACCELERATION	**0-60 mph** 6.2 seconds **0-100 mph** 16.1 seconds

The new V-8 engine is a 4-litre with 4-valves per cylinder; with variable inlet cam timing it produces some 285 bhp with very good low speed pulling power. This is enough to give it a maximum speed around 158 mph; with the five-speed automatic fitted to all, the acceleration from rest is good enough but not as good as the Aston which is helped by manual transmission. It is a little faster than the original E-type but a lot more comfortable and faster versions can be expected to follow.

The all new AJ-V8 engine was designed by Jaguar and, as such, shares no components with any of its Ford counterparts, apart from a Woodruff key and its sump plug!

Just a month after the Geneva coupé launch, Jaguar displayed the convertible at the New York Show, as important a market for the XK8 as it was for the XKE.

LAMBORGHINI MIURA P400S

1970
172 mph
277 km/h

'The reception was fantastic and many orders were placed for the new car.'

Lamborghini's name became world-famous on the back of the Miura. Mid-engined with a transverse V-12, and clad in beautiful Bertone bodywork, it was the ultimate road-racer which generated ecstatic acclaim when it appeared at the 1966 Geneva Show. What is also remarkable about the Lamborghini operation is that a brand new company, started in 1962, should have been able to create two new and widely diverse cars – the front-engined 350GT being the first – in the space of just four years, including designing and developing a new V-12 engine, and building and equipping a new factory.

Tractor magnate Ferruccio Lamborghini was a perfectionist who wanted to create the ideal GT car; he had tried all the others and believed he could do better. Setting up in Sant'Agata Bolognese, not far from Ferrari and Maserati, was not a gibe at the establishment; it was just a good area for getting engineering work done well and quickly as well as providing the right kind of people. A nucleus was formed around ex-Maserati people, Paolo Stanzani, Giampaolo Dallara with New Zealander Bob Wallace joining in as development engineer. The engine was designed by Giotto Bizzarrini; a 3.5-litre V-12 with twin cams per bank, the prototype gave over 350 bhp at 8000 rpm, subsequently tamed by Dallara to a still respectable 270 bhp at 6500 rpm. A new tubular chassis carried all independent wishbone suspension and the first body style came from Scaglione; shown in October 1963, it was rejected in favour of a new body from Touring which found approval at Geneva in March 1964 and production started shortly after – development had been very quick.

A year later, this became the 400GT with the V-12 now at 4-litres and 320 bhp. For 1966 a 2+2 was added. Front-engined Lamborghinis were to continue through Islero, Jarama and Espada until 1978. Meanwhile, once the GT was under way in 1964, designers were looking to produce a race-style Lamborghini even though the boss would never race; race-style meant mid-engined but the normal longitudinal layout with the gearbox behind was going to make for a very long car with a V-12. Setting the engine across the frame was not a new idea – the Mini had done it in 1959 – but the execution, with an integral gearbox just behind, was quite brilliant; the complex crankcase casting was something that could only have been conceived in that area of Italy. Like the Mini, engine and gearbox shared the same oil, although this was to change in the later SV when a limited slip differential was fitted.

For the chassis, Dallara followed the air-craft monocoque principle using a sheet steel frame incorporating the roof and with extensions to carry the front suspension and cradle the engine and rear suspension, double wishbones all-round, of course. When the rolling chassis was displayed at the Turin Show in November 1965 – once again a very quick gestation – the reception was fantastic and many orders were placed for the new car, as yet un-named and un-styled. By the Geneva Show in March 1966, this had all been rectified. Bertone had been commissioned and 25-year-old Marcello Gandini

First of the genuine production supercars, the Miura was everyone's ideal at its 1966 launch.

Horizontal slats allowed some rearward visibility; they also covered the engine but still allowed fresh air to reach the carburetters.

drew up the design with perhaps a little inspiration from Bertone's other star employee, Giorgio Giugiaro; it was so right that little was to be changed during the Miura's sadly short six-year run – it was killed to make way for the Countach. And the name? Born under the sign of Taurus, hence the marque's badge, Lamborghini chose the name of a Spanish fighting bull. But at that point, there was no tooling and development hadn't even started; a rush programme saw the first production car delivered just nine months later, still a steel chassis but with aluminium bodywork. The 4-litre engine finally gave 350 bhp at 7000 rpm

Performance was all that it was expected to be with a maximum around 170 mph and Wallace had done a very good job in developing the chassis in such a short time. Inevitably there was a certain amount of further development by both customer and factory before the new derivative arrived in 1969, the P400S. The chassis was stiffened and suspension modified to cope with wider, grippier tyres and the engine uprated to 370 bhp. The final version was the 1971 SV with further engine work to produce 385 bhp and redesigned suspension around even wider rear tyres, requiring slight flaring of the bodywork. All told, 762 Miuras were built taking Lamborghini firmly into the lead in the supercar fold.

SPECIFICATION	LAMBORGHINI MIURA P400S
ENGINE	Aluminium V-12, 3929 cc
HORSEPOWER	370 bhp @ 7500 rpm
TRANSMISSION	Manual 5-speed
CHASSIS	Steel with aluminium body
BRAKES	Discs all round
TOP SPEED	172 mph
ACCELERATION	**0-60 mph** 6.7 seconds **0-100 mph** 15.1 seconds

Fish-like headlights came from the Bertone Testudo and were subsequently copied for the Porsche 928; they are still the least appealing part of the design.

LAMBORGHINI COUNTACH

1986
190 mph
306 km/h

'The Countach design started with a clean sheet of paper.'

They say that *Countach* is the dialect word used when a beautiful woman slinks into view in the Piedmont area, the home of Bertone, who styled and made the body for the prototype of the Miura's replacement. In its original uncluttered form, the new car certainly deserved a verbal wolf-whistle when it emerged for the first time on its way to the public launch at the 1971 Geneva Show. Not that it was ready for production at that time; it was 1974 before the first one was ready for sale, by which time Automobili Ferruccio Lamborghini had been sold to Swiss partners. It was to be sold again before the Countach had been finished; Chrysler took over in 1987.

Although it was a replacement for the Miura and aimed at exactly the same market, the Countach design started with a clean sheet of paper embodying all the lessons that had been learnt from that first mid-engined supercar. Where the Miura had its V-12 mounted transversely, the Countach had the same engine mounted fore and aft with the gearbox in front; having a smaller unit nearest the cockpit meant less intrusion into that space and the gear linkage run was very short and direct. Drive was taken from drop-down gears through the sump to a crown wheel and pinion within the engine's sump casting; while this raised the overall centre of gravity, the other benefits outweighed this and the weight distribution was the same 42/58 as the Miura.

The original intention had been to give the Countach a 5-litre engine and the prototype was called the LP500 to match, but the familiar 4-litre was retained in 375 bhp form after the first prototype, and the model was renamed LP400 for production. In fact, the Countach didn't start out with great volume in mind; it was conceived as a limited run supercar to promote Lamborghini technology, so the prototype was built in a labour-intensive fashion with a welded-up space-frame and a steel body adding strength. When the enthusiastic reception showed that there was a surprising demand, the space-frame was redesigned to be very stiff in its own right, and the body was made in aluminium.

While such features as the beetle-wing doors and their inset half-windows carried through to production, the original slender purity of Gandini's lines was somewhat lost during development. Aerodynamic tests deepened the nose and lost the sill-top feature crease. The rear mounted radiators were to be fed through slats behind the side

Almost a mono-volume shape, the Gandini-designed Countach lost its purity of line with radiator scoops and wheel-arch extensions.

windows, the air exiting through grilles into the hollow behind the rear window; not only did this give inadequate air throughput, but rearward visibility required windows where the slats had been, so air was supplied from a mixture of large NACA ducts on the flanks and a box-like scoop on top and went out through slats on the wing tops. Finally the car was in production and testers could see if the performance matched the looks and the hype. Lamborghini's testers had seen over 180 mph but *Motor* put down an estimated 175 mph for the maximum with 0-100 mph in 13.1 seconds – it was fast enough for most.

Original tyre testing had been with low profile Pirelli tyres, but these were slow to get into production and the LP400 used 70% profile Michelins. Finally the low and wide P7 became available; to accommodate these, the Countach grew unsightly glassfibre wheel-arch extensions

Radiator air emerges from the louvres. Wheel arches had to accommodate ever wider tyres during the near-20 years of the Countach existence.

SPECIFICATION	LAMBORGHINI COUNTACH LP5000S QV
ENGINE	Aluminium V-12, 5167 cc
HORSEPOWER	455 bhp @ 7000 rpm
TRANSMISSION	Manual 5-speed
CHASSIS	Steel frame, aluminium body
BRAKES	Discs all round
TOP SPEED	190 mph
ACCELERATION	**0-60 mph** 4.9 seconds **0-100 mph** 11.0 seconds

with the front ones blended into a chin spoiler and, with revised suspension, the P400S came out in 1978, still with the same power.

Not until 1982 did the Countach finally get its 5-litre engine, actually a 4.75-litre, but the car was labelled LP500S. Emission laws had brought this on, so there was no power increase, just a drop in the revs at which it was developed from 8000 rpm to 7000 rpm. The first performance increase came in 1985 with the engine up to 5167 cc and four-valve cylinder heads combining to produce 455 bhp, still on carburetters while the catalytic version had fuel injection and 425 bhp. Magazine top speed tests of the LP5000S QV varied between 180 and 190 mph, but the latter figure was achieved by a Lamborghini tester with a brave journalist alongside so we'll accept it as representative of what the long-reigning king of the supercars could do in its final form.

Squat and purposeful, the final Countach 5000S QV had 455 bhp to propel it up to 190 mph.

LAMBORGHINI DIABLO SE30

1995
207 mph
333 km/h

Lamborghini revived the SV (Sport Veloce) name for a lightweight version of the Diablo, introduced in 1996. Acceleration is better but lower gearing and greater aerodynamic drag meant a reduction in top speed to 183 mph.

Following the Countach was no easy task; it had been king of the supercars for 16 years. During that time the company had two owners which slowed progress on a replacement; however Chrysler's take-over in 1987 did much to help the Diablo on its way towards membership of the 200 mph club. Its new body shape was the work of Marcello Gandini, who had penned the original Countach during his time with Bertone. As with most designs, the Diablo was the ultimate evolution of its forerunner – retaining the same overall design, lengthened by six inches to leave space for a four-wheel-drive system.

The Countach power-train layout was ideal for four-wheel-drive; most mid-engined systems have the gearbox behind the engine, making a connection to the front wheels very difficult. The Countach put the gearbox ahead of the V-12 engine – it was a normal front-engine/gearbox swung through 180 degrees – and drove the rear wheels via step down gears and a shaft running under the engine through the sump. For the four-wheel-drive Diablo VT that transfer gear sends drive to the front wheels as well, albeit via a torque splitting centre differential.

While the Countach grew scoops and air-ducts during development, the Diablo's exterior is clean and functional, a thing of aggressive beauty, but still a single volume shape with hardly a break in profile at the base of the screen. Wind tunnel work had removed the need for a rear wing, although these are often fitted. In standard form the Lambo engine is now 5.7-litres, up from the Countach's 5.17-litre to allow cleaner emissions, but still produces 492 bhp, which is enough to power the better shape to 205 mph recorded at Nardo's test track; the VT, introduced in 1991, loses a little power through its extra transmission gears and stops at 202 mph, while extra weight robs a few tenths from the acceleration times.

Since then there have been several niche models. For 1993, the year Chrysler sold the company to Indonesian MegaTech, the Special Edition marked the 30th anniversary of

The Diablo roadster appeared in 1996. It is seen here with the detachable roof panel stored externally. Much of the bodywork is new, about half the panels have been recontoured.

'Given the power increase, it is not surprising that the manufacturer claimed 207 mph.'

Lamborghini production; for this two-wheel-drive car a traction control system has been added to cope with a power increase to 525 bhp, and the weight has been reduced from the Diablo's 1575 Kg to 1460 Kg by strategic use of magnesium castings and carbon-fibre composites – the all-composite McLaren weighs in at 1150 Kg. Outwardly, the main differences are a mildly reshaped nose, a slatted carbon-fibre engine cover filling the hollow behind the rear window and an adjuster flap in the middle of the fitted rear wing. Given the power increase, it is not surprising that the manufacturer claimed 207 mph; the 0-100 mph time came down from the Diablo's already impressive 9.7 seconds to 9.3 seconds.

The Jota was faster still. In general, Lamborghinis have never officially raced, although the company's engineering division produced *Grand Prix* engines in the early 'nineties, but the return of interest in GT racing prompted the 1995 launch of the Jota as the racing Diablo for privateers; for this, the same 5.7-litre V-12 was further developed with variable length inlet tracts and exhaust system valves to produce an astonishing 590 bhp. Although the Jota was conceived as a racer, it could be used on the road and its uprating features would fit any SE30. A standard road-going SE30 was plenty fast enough but production was limited to that 30th anniversary year.

No one went racing with a Jota, so that model gave way to the SV (Sport Veloce) for 1996. Less extreme than the SE30, this received a 508 bhp version of the 5.7-litre, together with lower gearing for faster acceleration and more downforce from a bigger rear wing – a better track specification. The final version has been the VT-based Roadster with a Targa top, whose roof panel can be stored by straddling the valley behind the rear window; its performance will be similar to that of the hard-top Diablo VT.

The SE30 in its original coupé form, glorious, costly and wildly impractical. The aerofoil is visually impressive but reduces rear visibility somewhat and the factory prefers not to fit it.

SPECIFICATION	LAMBORGHINI DIABLO SE30	LAMBORGHINI DIABLO
ENGINE	Aluminium V-12, 5707 cc	Aluminium V-12, 5707 cc
HORSEPOWER	525 bhp @ 7100 rpm	492 bhp @ 7000 rpm
TRANSMISSION	Manual 5-speed	Manual 5-speed
CHASSIS	Steel frame, ali-carbon body	Steel frame, ali-carbon body
BRAKES	Discs all round	Discs all round
TOP SPEED	207 mph (333 km/h)	205 mph (330 km/h)
ACCELERATION	**0-60 mph** 4.2 seconds **0-100 mph** 9.3 seconds	4.4 seconds 9.7 seconds

LISTER STORM GTL

1997
200 mph
321 km/h

'The press speculated that it was capable of speeds approaching 240 mph.'

The Storm GTL of 1997, which retains the substructure of the original car graced with a new body. Its is claimed to increase downforce and so improve cornering. The lightened version has a similar top speed to the original.

To anyone who followed sports racing in the 1950s, mention of the Lister-Jaguar name will produce a misty eyed but, above all, positive response. Some 40 years on, in 1993, Lister was effectively reborn with the arrival of the chunky 200 mph Storm supercar and the latest version of the design, the GTL, is a head turner if ever there was one.

Although the Cambridge-based light engineering company of George Lister and Sons withdrew from competition in 1960, in 1984 it launched a club racing series for XJ-S owners. One of the entrants drove a car prepared by Laurence Pearce, son of Warren, noted Jaguar club racer of the 1960s, and, in the best traditions, it won first time out. A link was thus forged between Pearce and the Lister company.

In 1986 Pearce established W.P. Automotive in Leatherhead, Surrey to build and market modified versions of the Jaguar XJ-S coupé under the Lister Le Mans and Mark III names.

But although he undertook extensive work on the model and produced what he regarded as 'the ultimate XJ-S', Laurence Pearce recognised that any further development would require the proverbial clean sheet of paper. The eventual result was the Lister Storm, a sensational coupé powered, appropriately, by a 7-litre Jaguar-based XJ-S V-12 engine.

By February 1991 Laurence had obtained sufficient capital to begin work and, from the outset, he was aiming to produce a design that embodied what he called the 'front-mid-engined concept.'

As such the power unit was mounted as far back in the monocoque as practical. Such a location meant that four occupants could be accommodated and there was no noisy intrusive mid-located engine that is a feature of the overwhelming majority of supercars.

Attention was also paid to the car's underside which was flat so that it could benefit from the 'ground effect' developed for racing cars to achieve the most efficient roadholding.

Two-door coupé bodywork, that stylistically resembled a mid-engined model, was the work of Mike Hughes. It was made mostly of carbon-fibre with aluminium-faced steel doors which cloaked a chassis constructed of honeycomb-sandwich aluminium alloy and Kevlar. The drag coefficient was a respectable 0.32.

The Storm, the product of Pearce's Lister Cars, certainly made waves when it was unveiled at the 1993 London Motor Show. Costing no less than £219,725, the press speculated that it was capable of speeds approaching 240 mph although the true figure was probably nearer the 195 mark.

Having said that, no magazine has tested the Storm flat out although *Autocar* recorded a 0 to 60 mph time of 4.7 seconds whilst 0 to 100 mph was achieved in a mere 11 seconds.

Such performance was only possible because the output of the engine, which in its original 6-litre form developed 308 bhp, was upped to a

SPECIFICATION	LISTER STORM GTL
ENGINE	Aluminium V-12, 6996 cc
HORSEPOWER	450 bhp @ 6100 rpm
TRANSMISSION	Manual 6-speed
CHASSIS	Aluminium honeycomb
BRAKES	Discs all round with ABS
TOP SPEED	200 mph plus (321 km/h)
ACCELERATION	**0-60 mph** 4 seconds **0-100 mph** 8 seconds

formidable 594. It comes as little surprise to find that only the Jaguar block and cylinder heads were retained, the remainder of parts were unique to the Storm.

The increase in capacity, to 7-litres, was achieved by increasing the engine's bore and stroke which required the use of Cosworth cylinder liners and pistons and a purpose-created crankshaft. Flowed cylinder heads, reprofiled camshafts, revised inlet system and, above all, two belt-driven radial superchargers, blowing at 10 psi, did the rest.

The respected Ricardo engineering consultancy was responsible for analysing the engine's porting and combustion systems and advised on the emissions and catalytic legislation.

A six-speed Getrag gearbox was attached directly to the engine and drive conveyed, via a stubby propeller shaft, to a ZF differential.

The well appointed, leather-trimmed interior was enhanced by the fitment of purpose built air conditioning whilst the Kenwood stereo system was also made especially for the Storm. The power assisted steering operated at just two-and-a-half turns lock to lock.

Since its announcement, some 20 Storms have been sold and Lister ran an example at Le Mans in 1995. This unsupercharged car, with output boosted to 640 bhp, touched 202 mph down the Mulsanne Straight. Subsequently, in the 1996 event, one of these distinctive coupés finished in a creditable 19th position, despite experiencing engine problems on the last lap.

Now the concept has evolved and the result is the rebodied Storm GTL (for Lightweight) which appeared in the spring of 1997, that retains the essentials of the Storm's substructure. Although the V-12 has been shorn of its superchargers, engine efficiency has been boosted so that output remains the same at 594 bhp.

Bodywork, essayed by Geoff Kingston, aims to increase downforce and so improve the car's cornering. The weight saving is significant for, at 1150 kg, the GTL is 288 kg lighter than its predecessor. Distinctive body features are the fins ahead of the front wheels to improve brake cooling, while a similar function is performed by vents mounted ahead of the rear wheels.

At the time of writing the GTL had not been road tested by a motoring magazine but Lister claim a 200 mph top speed, with 60 mph coming up in a mere four seconds and 100 mph whistling by in just eight.

Orders have already been taken for five cars and, as in the past, Lister has set its sights on Le Mans. Drivers Tiff Needell and Geoff Lees have been signed to drive in the 1997 GT racing season although competition from both Porsche and McLaren is formidable. What is not is dispute is that the GTL is going to be well worth watching.

The original Lister Storm, a front-engined supercar with a claimed top speed of 200 mph. As such, four people could be accommodated. Powered by a supercharged Jaguar-based V-12 engine, it has now been succeeded by the GTL version.

The Storm's supercharged 7-litre, Jaguar- based, V-12 engine sat well back in the chassis. Its internals were specially designed for the model and output was a massive 450 bhp. This was conveyed via a six-speed Getrag gearbox.

LOTUS ESPRIT V8

1996
172 mph
277 km/h

'The Esprit has managed to retain its driver appeal.'

There is remarkably little externally to indicate the presence of the V-8 engine although the Esprit's front valance is new! Brakes and air conditioning have also been improved.

At last, Britain's only affordable mid-engined supercar has gained the power unit it has so long deserved. Lotus have designed an all-new 3.5-litre V-8 producing 350 bhp in unstressed twin-turbo form. Ultra-compact, it slots into the tail of the Esprit with no difficulty and will push the top speed up to over 170 mph, while the extra torque will make the car even faster off the line.

The major reason for the new unit was that the turbo-four was no longer acceptable for American emissions legislation. However the investment in a new engine will not be recovered solely on Lotus production volumes, so expect to see others using it. Meanwhile, the 2.2-litre S4 series will continue to be available in the short term, with the recall of the 2-litre turbo adding an entry-level GT3 to the range.

Although the design concept of the Lotus Esprit is still that of the 1972 Turin Show car, it has undergone so many developments in every area that almost nothing physical remains of the original; it still has a backbone chassis carrying a mid-mounted engine in a striking body with a similar silhouette, but that is about it. Its origins go back before 1972. Lotus had used their twin-cam version of the Ford engine for the Elan and the Europa Twin-Cam, but the engine was not going to meet the stricter emission regulations of the mid-'seventies. The new engine for the next generation of cars was based on the 2-litre Vauxhall slant-four; with a Lotus 16-valve head, this LV220 would power the new Elite, Eclat and Esprit range. Progress on the new cars was slow, so the engine first saw production service in the Jensen Healey from 1972.

Meanwhile Lotus' founder, Colin Chapman, had let ItalDesign have a prototype mid-engined chassis in 1971; when the resultant Esprit was highly praised at the 1972 Turin Show, Chapman pushed the design through as fast as possible alongside the two front-engined cars. All would use a backbone chassis, of the type used on the Elan or Europa, with glass-fibre bodies built on Lotus' patent Vacuum Assisted Resin Injection process. While the front-engined cars retained the Elan's later 5-speed box, the Esprit borrowed the Citroen transaxle that had been built for the SM and the Maserati Merak. The 4-seater hatch-back Lotus Elite finally came in mid-1974, with the cheaper fast-back Eclat and the mid-engined Esprit

following in October 1975; tooling delays then deferred the Esprit's production start until mid-1976.

With 160 bhp, the Esprit was capable of 135 mph, a considerable improvement over the 105 bhp Europa Twin-Cam's 117 mph. An S2 version arrived for 1978 with minor cosmetic changes and a torquier camshaft, but the major change was to come in 1980 with the arrival of the Turbo and engine capacity increased to 2.2-litres, a size which had been developed for the Sunbeam-Lotus and was to span the Lotus range. Body changes saw a full-width chin spoiler blending into side-skirts and a rear spoiler denoting the 210 bhp Turbo, the first 100 of which were sold in the racing Essex Lotus colours – suspension changes adjusted to the wider wheels. The new maximum was near 150 mph.

The next major change came with the subtle, but effective, 1987 restyle by Peter Stevens; Giugiaro's original origami creases were smoothly rounded while front and rear bumpers were integrated to give a much more modern appearance. By now the power was up to 218 bhp, with the US version using fuel injection for the same figure.

The 1989 model year saw non-turbo units phased out as fuel injection versions were increased to 231 bhp, but the Special Equipment model used higher boost pressure with an intercooler to generate 268 bhp and had a rear wing to prove it; this became the S4 in 1993. Meanwhile Birmingham 1992 had seen the Sport 300 with a bigger turbocharger, stiffer suspension and fatter wheels. Two years later the S4S arrived with a slightly smaller turbo to give better low down response at the expense of a minor power drop to 285 bhp; a clever compromise, it retained most of the 300's race-proven roadholding but with the S4's comfort.

With some 20 years of steady refinement behind it, the Esprit has managed to retain its driver appeal despite the lack of engine sophistication. With its new, more powerful and much quieter V-8, the latest Esprit will please a much wider market.

SPECIFICATION	LOTUS ESPRIT V8
ENGINE	Twin-turbo V-8, 3506 cc
HORSEPOWER	350 bhp @ 6250 rpm
TRANSMISSION	Manual 5-speed
CHASSIS	Steel backbone
BRAKES	Discs all round with ABS
TOP SPEED	172 mph (277 km/h)
ACCELERATION	**0-60 mph** 4.5 seconds **0-100 mph** 11.3 seconds

The presence of the new V-8 is more apparent from the car's rear with a badge on the back panel and twin exhaust pipes as the give-aways. Inside there's a V8 motif on the rev counter . . .

Installed longitudinally, the twin turbocharged 3.5-litre aluminium V-8 was created in a little over two years and although it develops 350 bhp it seems likely that there's plenty in reserve for enlargements in capacity.

MARCOS MANTIS

1997
170 mph
274 km/h

Marcos is one of the handful of car companies that continues to constitute the British-owned motor industry. The 1997 Mantis, that revives a corporate model name, is a distinctive and potent two-seater capable of speeds approaching the 170 mph mark.

The Marcos make dates from 1959 and is so called because its founders, Jem Marsh and Frank Costin, allotted the first three letters of their respective surnames to the company. Racing driver Marsh contributed an all-important competition ingredient which the marque still maintains.

SPECIFICATION	MARCOS MANTIS
ENGINE	Aluminium V-8, 4601 cc
HORSEPOWER	352 bhp @ 6000 rpm
TRANSMISSION	Manual 5-speed
CHASSIS	Square section tubular steel
BRAKES	Discs all round with ABS
TOP SPEED	Around 170 mph (274 km/h)
ACCELERATION	**0-60 mph** 4.1 seconds **0-100 mph** – no figures available

Frank Costin, with an aviation background, was an aerodynamicist of note who had essayed the lines of the Formula 1 Vanwall, and was responsible for the Marcos' ungainly but windcheating silhouette and its unique light and robust wooden chassis. Power came from a variety of Ford engines.

Costin left the firm in 1961, at which point brothers Dennis and Peter Adams took over development. In 1963 came a move to Bradford on Avon, Wiltshire and, later the same year, the arrival of the 115 mph Volvo-powered 1800, a low and distinctive glass-fibre coupé, styled by Dennis Adams. Originally intended as a stop gap measure, and also available as a kit car, its timeless lines form the inspiration for the current Marcos range.

Later, in 1969, the idiosyncratic, but labour intensive, marine ply chassis was dispensed with and was replaced by a more conventional square tubular spaceframe which reduced the overall manufacturing process by a substantial 15 hours.

The company had, in 1966, introduced the Mini Marcos coupé, a stumpy glass-fibre bodied kit car, to which the buyer contributed Mini or Mini Cooper mechanicals. Creditably an example entered for that year's Le Mans event finished 15th and was the only British car to complete the race.

In 1970 Marcos unveiled the Triumph TR6-engined Mantis, a controversially styled two-plus-two-seater coupé which failed to catch on – just 33 were built. Soon afterwards, in 1972, a combination of circumstances, including a move to new premises at nearby Westbury, forced the firm's closure.

Jem Marsh, however, continued to supply owners with spare parts. In 1976 he re-acquired the Marcos name and body moulds and in 1981 revived the Adams-styled coupé, now dubbed the 3-litre on account of its Ford V-6 power unit. In

The Mantis' aerodynamically refined body looks both back and forwards, to the classic 1960s shape but also reflects the company's experience on the race track with its GT car. The tubular steel spaceframe chassis has similarly benefited from competition. Power is courtesy of Ford America's twin cam V-8, also used in the Mustang, tweaked to produce 352 bhp.

1984 it was revised as the Mantula with a 3.5-litre Rover V-8 engine and from 1986 was also built in Spyder (open) form with Ford-based independent rear suspension following three years later.

The present generation of Marcos dates from the revised Mantara of 1993 which perpetuated the closed and open options. On this model the original Triumph Herald front suspension was replaced by Ford Sierra-sourced MacPherson struts and attendant rack and pinion steering gear. This necessitated revisions to the chassis and body panels and the introduction of flared wheel arches front and rear.

Produced in 3.9-litre 400 and uprated 4.5-litre 450 forms, the company claimed that the latter had a top speed in excess of 150 mph with 0 to 60 mph spirited up in just 4.7 seconds.

This model was the first in which Jem Marsh's son, Chris had an involvement having returned from America after a successful career there as a crew chief and test driver.

Marcos unveiled the Mantara's Le Mans racing derivative at the 1993 London Motor Show with a new (although clearly related) coupé body designed, once again, by Dennis Adams. Powered by an enlarged 5-litre V-8 engine, and intended for use on both road and track, the LM, as it subsequently became, was followed in 1995 by the supplementary LM600 with a 6.1-litre Chevrolet V-8.

This brought Team Marcos the 1995 UK GT title in the hands of Chris Hodgetts. The 600 is now actively campaigning in GT events the world over.

In 1995 Marcos returned to Le Mans, which it had last entered in 1967, when an LM 600 driven by Cor Euser and Tommy Erdos, succeeded in finishing the 24 hour race.

The following year's British Motor Show saw the announcement of the Mantis powered by Ford's 4.6-litre V-8, with twin overhead-camshafts per cylinder bank, courtesy of its Mustang Cobra, where it developed 310 bhp. But ministrations by the still Westbury-based Marcos team pushed this figure up to 352 bhp. These have taken the form of a new exhaust layout and revised engine management system.

The glass-fibre composite body, styled by Leigh Adams, draws on Marcos' experience on the circuits with its Chevrolet-engined GT racers whilst the spaceframe chassis has similarly benefited.

A prospective Marcos owner usually chooses his or her own interior, in which seats can be upholstered in leather that complements a veneered dashboard of natural elm. Air conditioning and power steering are standard fitments. The Mantis is priced at almost £44,000 and there are a host of extra goodies available.

The spring of 1997 saw the appearance of the S Mantis, an even more exciting 452bhp supercharged version which, says Marcos, is capable of 184 mph . . .

Although this is the Spyder (open) version, the Mantis is also available in coupé form. The distinctive lines, the work of Leigh Adams, have been refined in a wind tunnel for low drag. As a result the shape generates downforce that aids high speed handling and safety. Like all Marcos cars, the model is handbuilt by a small team of craftsman at the firm's Wiltshire factory. Advanced projector lighting is featured.

'Seats can be upholstered in leather that complements a veneered dashboard of natural elm.'

MASERATI BORA

1973
160 mph
257 km/h

'Finding reliable Maserati top speed figures is still difficult.'

With a race-bred 4.7-litre V-8 turning out some 310 bhp, the mid-engined Bora was a sensational car when it was first shown in 1971. Although there were faster front-engined cars, only the Lamborghini Miura was in the same mid-engined ball-park. The specification was interesting enough, but the body had been designed by Giugiaro at the height of his classical period, when sports cars were designed, and often built, by coachbuilders, and practical family ware had only just begun to show styling influence; the Bora – a strong wind – suggested the coiled energy of a greyhound poised to leave the trap. Nearly 500 would leave the Modena factory over the next seven years, the later ones with 4.9-litre engines.

Finding reliable Maserati top speed figures is still difficult; the factory claims were never accurate and speedometers even less so. *Motor's* 1973 test estimated 160 mph, others believed the factory 168 mph at 6000 rpm; but acceleration figures were taken and were usually slightly better than those for the Miura. It was certainly a fast car and reasonably practical for touring with a good-sized front boot but detail failings let it down in the eyes of period observers – poor heating and ventilation, inadequate room for tall drivers and less for passengers – but its drivability was always highly rated.

Comprehensive instrumentation is provided in the Bora. The brake pedal is part of a Citroen system and thus has almost zero travel.

The Bora was a product of the Citroen period of ownership from 1969-75; although most of the design was pure Maserati, including the traditional tubular frame, there was some Citroen influence, notably in the power braking system. More obviously Citroen-inspired was the Merak which arrived a year and a half later; this shared most of the Bora's chassis and bodywork with a different rear deck treatment but was powered by an enlarged version of the four-cam V-6 which Maserati had designed for the Citroen SM – the SM had 170 bhp from 2670 cc, the Merak 190 bhp from 2965 cc. As the V-6 with a Citroen gearbox was somewhat shorter than the V-8 installation, Maserati fitted a pair of small rear seats within the same wheelbase, so the Merak was a little more practical but slower with a 140 mph maximum.

Citroen retreated from Modena in 1975 and Maserati was taken over by de Tomaso. While Merak SS (220 bhp), with the Khamsin and Quattroporte, were to continue in production into the 'eighties, De Tomaso was changing the company's direction to capitalise on the name with greater volume; the result was launched in 1982 as the Biturbo, a 2-door sports-saloon with a 2-litre V-6 using three valves per cylinder and twin-turboed to produce 180 bhp. Italian taxes favour 2-litre units, so it pays to get the best from that size. Technically it was worthy of the Maserati name, but the style was uninspiring. Subsequent model names juggled with numbers of doors and engine sizes on varying wheelbases to produce 228,

425, 430 with a short-wheelbase open Spyder having appeared in 1984.

In 1990 names came back and the Shamal was introduced with a new 32-valve 3.2-litre V-8 still with twin turbos to produce 325 bhp within a hardtop version of the short spyder; with bulging flanks to cover wide wheels, the old Biturbo shape has taken on a new lease of life. It's quick, too, with a six-speed Getrag gearbox to help; 0-100 mph should come up in under 13 seconds. The Ghibli name was brought back in 1992 for the normal 2-door model to be fitted with either the 284 bhp 2.8-litre V-6 or the Italian special 2-litre boosted to 306 bhp, both forms capable of over 150 mph. The following year saw Fiat take over from de Tomaso, hopefully to ensure that the historic name continues to be attached to the fast sporting cars that were its life-blood for so long.

SPECIFICATION	MASERATI BORA
ENGINE	Aluminium V-8, 4719 cc
HORSEPOWER	310 bhp @ 6000 rpm
TRANSMISSION	Manual 5-speed
CHASSIS	Steel frame and body
BRAKES	Discs all round
TOP SPEED	160 mph
ACCELERATION	**0-60 mph** 6.5 seconds **0-100 mph** 14.7 seconds

Large rear window gives some rearward visibility; but there is a surprising amount of luggage space available in the front.

Styled by Giugiaro from his own company, ItalDesign, the Bora looks coiled and ready to go.

McLaren F1

1993

231 mph

372 km/h

'It is geared to reach 'only' 220 mph.'

This is the limited edition LM (for Le Mans) version of the F1, note the initials on the sill ahead of the rear wheel. It used the revised front and wing of the GTR track car to improve downforce. The Peter Stevens-styled body imbues the car with a sense of movement even when stationary.

It was August 8, 1993 at the Nardo test track in southern Italy. McLaren's tester, former *Grand Prix* driver Jonathan Palmer, was doing routine high-speed testing with prototype XP3. On the last outing of the day, he kept his foot flat over the whole of a standing start lap of the 7.8-mile banked circuit; for two heady miles it clocked 231 mph. It was the fastest ever recorded for a road-going car, faster even than the racing McLarens were going to achieve.

Although its design is full of *Grand Prix* technology and the name has been synonymous with *Grand Prix* success, the McLaren F1 was not created to go racing; it was just meant to be the ultimate road car of *Grand Prix* car designer, Gordon Murray. Lightweight carbon-fibre chassis and bodywork, sophisticated shock-absorbing suspension sub-frames, race-style 1+2 seating, transverse 6-speed gearbox and a purpose built 6.1-litre BMW V-12 engine were just a few of the design highlights.

While the McLaren was in the latter stages of development, the FIA's World Sports Car championship had fallen on difficult times and the regulations were heading towards production GT racing, hoping to bring all those supercars to the tracks. Being the newest, and the most race-orientated in its design, the F1 suddenly seemed the ideal car for the new championship.

Launched on the downside of the supercar boom in May 1992, the McLaren F1 had not had an easy time. The plan had been to make 350 at a rate of four cars per month, selling at £530,000 plus taxes. By the time the first car was delivered in January 1994, 350 seemed an impossible target in a vanishing market and it was only possible to build three cars a month. Despite the avowed intention not to go racing with the F1, McLaren could not pass up the opportunity to give the car its own track record and create a few more cars.

The 1994 production numbers were sufficient to homologate the car for racing, so McLaren needed little persuasion to engineer a competition version. Good though the F1 was for road use, it didn't need shock-absorbing rubber in its engine mounts or suspension sub-frames, and it certainly didn't need the weight of air-conditioning or the hi-fi system. It also needed more downforce and a stronger gearbox for track use. So the changes were considerable, but seven GTRs were built in time for the 1995 racing season; they ran away with the Global GT Endurance Series, and won the Le Mans 24-hours at the first attempt.

To celebrate five Le Mans finishers (1st, 3rd,

This is the F1 GT, the ultimate 1997 version of the car, and the roadgoing equivalent of the sports racing GTR. Still basically F1 under the skin, apart from the fitment of a six-speed sequential gearbox, it is both longer and wider than its predecessor, the latter dimension being necessary to accommodate the GTR's rear wing.

4th, 5th, 13th), McLaren produced a limited edition of just five F1 LMs, road-going versions of the GTR, and finished in the old McLaren orange from the days when Bruce McLaren and Denny Hulme dominated Can-Am racing. The standard F1 produced 627 bhp, the 1995 GTR with regulation restrictors gave 636 bhp, but the unrestricted LM has 668 bhp to play with; however, like the GTR it generates significant downforce which increases the aerodynamic drag and it is geared to reach 'only' 220 mph. In theory, with a more free-revving power unit and closer ratio gears, it should accelerate even faster than the F1; that reaches 100 mph in just 6.3 seconds while in third gear. The LM will reach the same speed in second gear, so 5.9 seconds is entirely believable. As both will reach 60 mph in 1st gear, the improvement is nominal.

The LM is likely to remain the most accelerative of the F1s as the 1996 GT regulations asked for even more restriction in a bid to equalise the power outputs of the contenders. The 1996 GTR develops a 'mere' 600 bhp, but many other changes ensured it was even faster around the circuits; eight of those have been built.

Maybe the F1 wasn't planned as a racer, but racing success has given it the credibility it had never quite achieved as just a road-going supercar. F1 production is being stopped before even 100 have been built; without the racing versions, it would have been 20 fewer. It may not have been a financial success but it has been a superb flagship for McLaren's engineering ability.

A 1994 F1 pictured outside the firm's factory in Woking, Surrey. Unusually the steering wheel is in the centre of the cockpit.

SPECIFICATION	McLAREN F1	McLAREN F1 LM
ENGINE	Aluminium V-12 6064 cc	Aluminium V-12 6064 cc
HORSEPOWER	627 bhp @ 7400 rpm	668 bhp @ 7800 rpm
TRANSMISSION	Manual 6-speed, transverse	Manual 6-speed, transverse
CHASSIS	Carbon-fibre composite	Carbon-fibre composite
BRAKES	Discs all round	Discs all round
TOP SPEED	231 mph (372 km/h)	220 mph (354 km/h)
ACCELERATION	**0-60 mph** 3.2 seconds **0-100 mph** 6.3 seconds	3.0 seconds 5.9 seconds

MERCEDES-BENZ 600SL

1992

168 mph
(see text)

270 km/h

'It is rare to see a Mercedes listed among the fastest production cars.'

The latest generation of SL are technical marvels; they include a roll-bar that erects automatically if roll-over is imminent.

Ever since Mercedes returned to racing in 1952 and won Le Mans with the 300SL coupé, SL (Sport Light) has denoted the sporting Mercedes. Then, as now, type numbers refer to the capacity minus a zero. That first racer used all the mechanical components of the 300-series announced a year earlier, but fitted them into a new space-frame chassis with an aerodynamic body featuring gull-wing doors. Under pressure from the American importer, the factory then developed a production equivalent, still with a space-frame chassis, which was announced in early 1954. It was the supercar of its day with 150 mph performance given the highest optional ratio; with the standard ratio the maximum was 140 mph with 0-60 mph in 7.0 sec and 0-100 mph in 16.2 seconds – amazing figures for 1954. Alongside it came the smaller engined 190SL, and the Roadster 300SL came in 1957 to replace the coupé; both were phased out in 1963 to make way for the new 230SL, no longer a road-going racer but a short wheelbase, higher powered derivative of the saloon range, the pattern of years to come – future SLs would be neither Sport nor Light until the arrival of the little SLK.

The 230/250/280SL series, with six-cylinder engines, ran through to 1971. Although 280 and 300SL models would arrive with six-cylinder engines, the new range was mostly V-8 powered from 3.5 litre 350SL to the American market 5.6-litre 560SL and also included longer 2+2 versions as 350 and 450SLC. The latest series started in 1989 with a 300SL six as well as the V-8 500SL; since then, the sixes are split into two models, 280 and 320, with a 6-litre V-12 as the flagship arriving in 1992 – now an SL600 as Mercedes decided to put the class before the capacity in 1994. These are wonderful pieces of engineering for fast comfortable travel in style; the roll-over bar which pops up in the event of an accident is just one example of the design sophistication. The body shape is also very good aerodynamically with a drag factor of 0.31, but this is more for fuel economy than sheer speed.

It is rare to see a Mercedes listed among the fastest production cars, particularly since they, along with BMW, have decided to limit top speeds electronically to 250 km/h (155 mph); however, sometimes the limiter allows a little more and *Autocar* clocked the the 600SL and the 600SEL at

159 mph. At Mercedes, outright performance is less important than longevity, so the engines have always been relatively unstressed with low bhp/litre figures and maximum speeds have not been as high as the equivalent model BMWs of unlimited days. Even if the limiter is deleted, the cars are unlikely to go much faster as the gearing is now generally chosen for the engine to peak near 250 km/h, which is better for acceleration.

Working out how fast they should go isn't difficult if you start with the 230 bhp SL320 which has been timed at a non-limited 144 mph. Give the same car the 5-litre V-8 with 320 bhp and the theoretical maximum goes to 162 mph. Use the 6-litre V-12 with 394 bhp and theory gives 174 mph which, on present gearing, would ask the engine to do over 6000 rpm. For comparison's sake we have settled for 168 mph as a true indication of the SL600's potential without artificial restriction. The SL500 would be slower in top speed but actually returns very similar acceleration figures as the V-12 version is 10 percent (180 Kg) heavier than the V-8; it is also rather more than 10 percent thirstier in the standard EEC tests. Since both SL500 and SL600 are limited to the same maximum speed and the smaller version is more economical and faster off the mark, why have an SL600? Simply because it represents the pinnacle of Mercedes technology; they may not make the fastest cars in the world but there is nothing finer than the ultimate in Mercedes engineering.

Mercedes' governors limit the 600SEL to the same top speed as the SL but the big 4-door is little slower in acceleration taking 15.8 seconds from 0-100 mph.

The big V-12 adds a lot of weight to the SL but offers the ultimate refinement.

SPECIFICATION	MERCEDES-BENZ 600SL
ENGINE	Aluminium V-12, 5987 cc
HORSEPOWER	394 bhp @ 5200 rpm
TRANSMISSION	Auto 5-speed
CHASSIS	Unitary steel
BRAKES	Discs all round with ABS
TOP SPEED	168 mph
ACCELERATION	**0-60 mph** 6.0 seconds **0-100 mph** 14.4 seconds

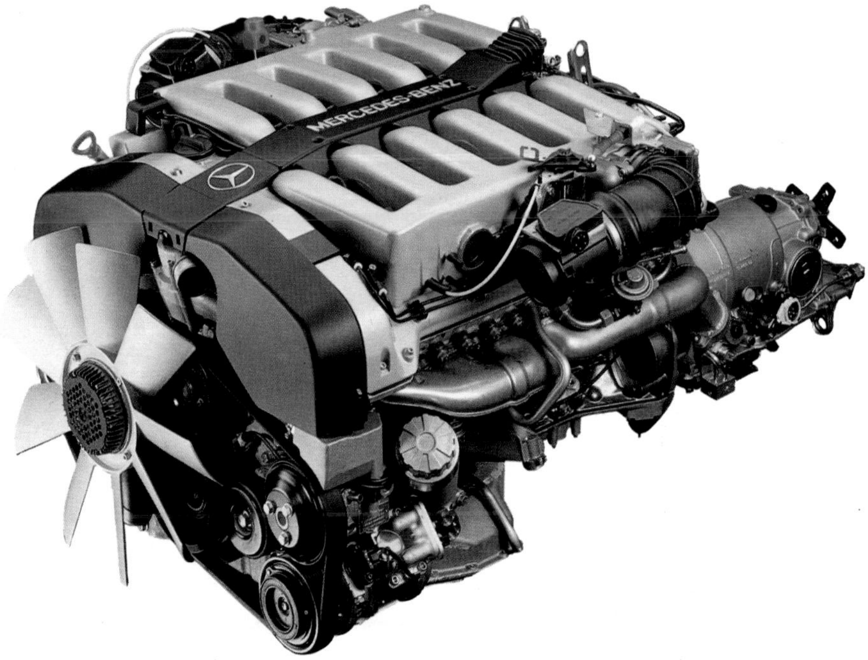

MERCEDES-BENZ CLK-GTR

1997
200+ mph
321+ km/h

'The CLK-GTR weighs 1200 kg, and is expected to be capable of reaching 60 mph in a mere 3.5 seconds and have a top speed in excess of the magic 200 mph.'

Mercedes-Benz, with a racing pedigree that reaches back to the dawn of motoring, has produced a sensational 200 mph roadgoing version of the sports racer it intends to campaign in GT events during the 1997 season.

This is a series that attracts the likes of the Porsche GT1 and the McLaren F1 GTR and the new road car is intended to help Mercedes-Benz shed its refined but rather staid image.

It is hoped that the CLK-GTR will do wonders for the company's appeal among the younger generation of potential purchasers. That is certainly the hope of Jurgen Schrempp, chairman of the firm's Daimler-Benz parent, who is intent on endowing Mercedes-Benz with an enhanced, performance-honed profile.

The silver-hued coupé, for which the company has revived the traditional but unofficial Silver Arrow designation, has been developed in conjunction with its Stuttgart-based AMG tuning partner.

The distinctive gull-wing doors are in the spirit of Mercedes-Benz' legendary 300SL coupé of the 1950s. That model featured them because of an innovative spaceframe chassis although this latter-day version has a carbon-fibre hull. Its lines are loosely based on those of the company's new CLK coupé, introduced in the summer of 1997, and aimed foursquare at a market dominated by BMW's Series 3 coupé.

The four distinctive, slightly reclining oval headlights were first seen on a concept coupé that, to the surprise of many, Mercedes-Benz unveiled at the 1993 Geneva Motor Show.

This was the first outward manifestation of the company adopting a more distinctive appearance to its magnificently engineered products. The new nose, complete with the traditional Mercedes-Benz radiator daringly inclined, made its production debut on the new E-class cars of 1995.

The company has made great play of the fact that the contours of its nose closely resemble those of its famous 1950s sports racing SLR roadster, so underlining its competition pedigree.

These features were subsequently adopted in essence, if not detail, for the smaller CLK coupé but despite their use on the sensational racer

If appearance is anything to go by, this Mercedes-Benz should be a formidable performer on both road and track. This is the roadgoing version based on the new CLK coupé although only the radiator and lights are related. It is thought that about 50 will be produced over the next two years.

tamed for road use, this car was otherwise mechanically unrelated to it.

For while the CLK is powered by a choice of front-mounted, four-cylinder unit or the new V-6 engine, on the GTR power comes from a mid-located, longitudinally-mounted V-12 which, in essence, first appeared in the company's commodious S-Class range introduced in 1991.

This 90 degree V unit, with twin overhead-camshafts per cylinder bank and four valves per cylinder, in 6-litre form developed 389 bhp. But for this stunning two-seater, complete with obligatory rear wing, the engine is enlarged to 6.9-litre and develops no less than 560 bhp.

This has been created with input from the British Ilmor Engineering of Brixworth, Northants, a firm that designs and builds racing engines, in which Mercedes-Benz has a financial interest. It is responsible for the V-10 unit that powers the current Formula 1 McLaren-Mercedes racer.

In the GTR it is attached directly to the composite hull and thus has a supporting role. Drive is taken via a six-speed sequential gearbox and the rose-jointed coil and wishbones suspension is bolted directly to it. Dampers are adjustable and the wheels substantial 18-inch diameter units.

These mechanicals are cloaked with an impressive Kevlar coupé body which retains the familiar Mercedes-Benz oblong radiator grille and even features the marque's famous tristar mascot.

The cockpit comes complete with an integrated roll cage and is surrounded by energy-absorbing, so called, crash boxes. Both driver's and co-driver's airbags are also fitted, so underlining the car's safety qualities.

The CLK-GTR weighs 1200 kg, and is expected to be capable of reaching 60 mph in a mere 3.5 seconds and have a top speed in excess of the magic 200 mph.

While Mercedes-Benz is only required under the GT racing rules to produce one example of the CLK-GTR road car, it seems likely that a limited number will be built. Produced over a two-year period for a handful of lucky owners, a figure of 50 is believed to be the most likely estimate. The cost is thought to be well below the $1 million price ceiling laid down by the FIA.

The racing version was tested by Bernd Schneider, the 1995 German Touring Car Champion and, as a result, the car made its competition debut at the first round of the GT championship at Hockenheim in April. But despite being on pole position, reliability problems resulted in it finishing in only 27th place. Nevertheless, these are early days and Le Mans beckons . . .

The CLK-GTR has been developed by the factory in conjunction with its Stuttgart-based AMG tuning partner, hence the initials on the tail. The car's longitudinally-mounted V-12 engine is bolted directly to the carbon-fibre hull. A number of passive safety features are built into the design.

SPECIFICATION	MERCEDES-BENZ CLK-GTR
ENGINE	Aluminium V-12, 6.9 litres
HORSEPOWER	560 bhp @ 7000 rpm
TRANSMISSION	Sequential 6-speed
CHASSIS	Carbon-fibre
BRAKES	Discs all round
TOP SPEED	Over 200 mph (321 km/h)
ACCELERATION	**0-60 mph** 3.5 seconds **0-100 mph** Not available

PORSCHE 959

1985
197 mph
(317 km/h)

'Tests show a maximum around 200 mph, but a 0-60 mph time of under 4 seconds.'

Loosely based on the faithful 911, the 959 is Porsche's fastest road car yet and, like so many of the Zuffenhausen projects, it was conceived with competition in mind; since Porsche regard competition as a valuable proving ground for road car technology, this was also to prove a mobile test-bed. The 959's four-wheel-drive transmission system has already been carried through to the 911 Carrera 4 and the latest Turbo 4.

Four wheel drive had existed in the Porsche design archives for many years; before and after the war, 4WD derivatives of the Beetle had been built for military use and the post-war Cisitalia GP car had four driven wheels. In the mid-'sixties, Porsche had acquired a Jensen FF to study the pros and cons of four-wheel-drive for road cars. Then their close association with Audi brought them into contact with the Quattro system prior to its 1980 launch. Porsche's first public show of 4WD interest was to present a 911 Cabriolet with 4WD as a design study in 1981. Two years later the 959 was presented as a Group B study.

Group B was the competition category for low volume production GT cars or highly modified saloons and 200 had to be made. In the early 'eighties, it was the Formula for International rallying where Audi and the Lancia Stratos were making the running; Porsche thought they would join in. They were winning most of the sports-car races (Group C) with the 956, privateers were winning Group B classes with 911 variants, and the company didn't want to go into *Grand Prix* racing, so rallying was the next challenge. The 911 had been a familiar and successful sight in 'sixties rallying, but specialism had marched on since then and four wheel drive had become essential for the loose surfaces used.

With most front-wheel drive cars the gearbox is either under a longitudinal engine or at the end of a transverse one – driving the other axle requires considerable redesign. The Audi was alone in putting the engine ahead of the front wheels, so that a normal gearbox behind it could still drive the front wheels; the Porsche 911 layout was a reversal of the same – the engine was outside

The 911 for Group B rallying retained its factory 959 number and had some success in long-distance raids.

the wheelbase. For both it was relatively easy to provide drive to the other axle and both needed it, as their basic design is fundamentally wrong for safe, easy handling; the success of both has always been a triumph of development over design. Where the 959's system stood apart from all other 4WD systems was in how it allocated the driving effort between front and rear axles; all have . some control system, but the 959 used a multitude of sensors to feed a computer which took the decision, or it could be over-ridden by the driver.

The 959's chassis was basically that of a 911 but the bodywork was mostly in Kevlar composites to keep the weight down. Considerable wind tunnel study had created a shape that was fundamentally 911 but which produced aerodynamic downforce. The engine was still a flat-6 but owed more to the Group C racing programme, which also provided the massive disc brakes. The engine was a 2.85-litre unit with twin turbo-chargers operating sequentially to cut down the turbo lag – the time required for the turbos to spin up to the right speed; this produced 450 bhp with plenty of low-down pulling power. The resultant performance figures are dramatic; various tests show a maximum around 200 mph, but a 0-60 mph time of under 4 seconds.

In fact the 959 wasn't able to take the rally world by storm as the regulations had changed again by the time that the 200 had been completed in 1988. However, a 959 prototype – 4WD without turbos – won the very tough Paris-Dakar rally in 1984, and a full 959 won it in 1986; so the systems were vindicated. The 156 mph Carrera 4 adopted the 4WD, while the new Turbo has the 4WD and twin turbos on its 408 bhp 3.6-litre engine; ten years on and the 959's supercar performance for 200 lucky owners is now more readily available as just another production model.

SPECIFICATION	PORSCHE 959
ENGINE	Aluminium flat-6 twin turbo 2850 cc
POWER	450 bhp @ 6500 rpm
TRANSMISSION	Manual 6-speed 4-wheel-drive
CHASSIS	Steel monocoque, Kevlar bodywork
BRAKES	Discs all round with ABS
TOP SPEED	197 mph (317 km/h)
ACCELERATION	**0-60 mph** 3.7 seconds **0-100 mph** 8.5 seconds

PORSCHE 928 GTS

1992
168 mph
(270 km/h)

Perhaps it is because all Porsches set out with a long model life ahead of them that the first models are not always impressive performers; they need something in hand to allow a steady increase of power during the years to come alongside the inevitable increase in technical sophistication and to offset the extra weight that comes with it. Over 15 years, the 2+2 928 has gradually changed from a 260 bhp 140 mph fast tourer to a 350 bhp 168 mph sports coupé with supercar performance; instead of being part of the high performance herd, it is now a class leader with no loss of usability on the way. It is still a very practical car that can be guaranteed to keep going for many thousands of trouble-free miles like any other Porsche – a standard setter for cars like the Aston Martin DB7.

'Rounded and almost aggressively graceful it was also good aerodynamically.'

The 928 story goes back as far as 1971. Amazingly, with hindsight, it was conceived as a replacement for the 911 which was never expected to have a model life of over 30 years. Where the 911 was really a sports car with a fairly narrow cabin and nominal space for two children in the rear, the 928 would be a spacious grand tourer in a different market sector within which driving skills could not be taken for granted; hence it would be front-engined but with handling that would still satisfy the sporting driver. The engine would be an entirely new V-8, a configuration with which the American market would feel comfortable; with 260 bhp from a single overhead camshaft design of 4.5-litres, it was not particularly stressed.

But it was to be 1977 before the car was launched, as other factors intervened. First, the 1973 oil crisis made many manufacturers think twice about big-engined cars. Secondly, VW-Audi decided not to go ahead with the little sports car which Porsche had been developing for them around many VW parts; Porsche took over the project themselves and launched the resultant 924 in 1975. By the time this was under way, the world had again become receptive to the larger cars, so work on the 928 was resumed. Styled by American Tony Lapine, it followed the family line set for the new front-engined cars; rounded and almost aggressively graceful it was also good aerodynamically but the flat-fish headlights – seen previously on the Lamborghini Miura – have never been an artistic success.

The 4.5-litre cars were capable of 137-143 mph, depending on whether the rear-mounted gearbox was a manual 5-speeder or an automatic. Road-testers liked the car – it was also chosen as a Car of the Year in 1978 – but the chassis was so good that they wanted more power. This came with the 928S version in 1979; increasing the

SPECIFICATION	PORSCHE 928 GTS
ENGINE	Aluminium V-8 5397 cc
POWER	360 bhp @ 5700 rpm
TRANSMISSION	Manual 5-speed transaxle
CHASSIS	Unitary steel
BRAKES	Discs all round with ABS
TOP SPEED	168 mph (270 km/h)
ACCELERATION	**0-60 mph** 5.4 seconds **0-100 mph** 14.3 seconds

cylinder size brought the capacity to 4.7-litres, the power to 300 bhp and the maximum speed up to 155 mph; there were a few visual changes like the front air-dam and a rear spoiler while lower profile tyres went on wider wheels. Porsche owners still wanted sporting cars.

And the steady increase in power and sophistication has continued ever since. The 1984 S2 had a little more power from the same 4.7-litre to reach 157 mph. Then 1987 saw the 5-litre version with four valves per cylinder giving 320 bhp and 160 mph. By now Porsche had replaced the 2-litre 924 with the 2.5-litre 944, which used, in effect, half the 928's V-8; the 944S was the four-valve version which arrived at the same time as the 928S4 which now had exactly the same bore and stroke as the 944. While the little 924s and 944s had turbo derivatives, the 928 has always used the less stressed alternative.

In 1990, the S4 became the 928GT with 330 bhp, and the final version so far is the GTS, now increased to 5.4-litres and a healthy 350 bhp. On a straight road, it would be a genuine 170 mph car. The 928 was developed at a time when it required faith to invest in big engines, but the continued demand for the car has fully justified that faith and the 928 has become just as much a classic in its own time as the 911.

The 928 was conceived as a full four-seater family GT to replace the 911, but the rear-engined warrior refused to die. The 928 interior is certainly spacious.

Twenty years on and the 1995 928 is some 30 mph faster than the original. Overall lines have changed little.

PORSCHE 911 TURBO

1995
181 mph
(291 km/h)

'Twenty years on the cult is as strong as ever.'

Any Porsche 911 is a fast car but the Turbo range have been spectacularly fast since the launch of the first one in 1975. While BMW were the first manufacturer to attach a turbocharger to the exhaust system of a production car with the 1973 2002, Porsche arguably gave credence to the cult-following that was to keep growing long after BMW had dropped the idea. Twenty years on the cult is as strong as ever.

Motor racing has always had considerable influence over Porsche's management thinking. The company had enjoyed considerable success with the 917 during the 1969-72 Sports Car Championship until the ruling body killed the formula in favour of thinly disguised 2-seater *Grand Prix* cars. Porsche competition interest then switched to the Stateside Can-Am races where rules were less restrictive; initially open versions of the 917 were used with the 4.5 or 5-litre flat-12 engines of the earlier cars. Seeking even more power, the engineers decided to turbocharge the existing engines rather than develop anything physically bigger; the ultimate version was the 917-30 with the engine increased to 5.4-litres and turbocharged to produce a phenomenal 1100 bhp – it won the championship in 1973.

Meanwhile the sports car racing rules were set to change again for 1975 to cater for cars that at least looked like road cars (Group 5) and others that were road cars (Group 4). Armed with their recent turbo experience, Porsche began to develop a turbo-charged 911 and were running it during 1974 alongside the open two-seater cars. This was to be the basis of the 935, which carried all before it when the championship finally started in 1976. However, a new car was also needed for the Group 4 category, a customary Porsche preserve; hence a road-going version of the 934 was launched in March 1975 – the Porsche Turbo.

While the racing versions were able to develop over 500 bhp, and last the distance in endurance racing, the production car had a relatively leisurely 260 bhp from its 3-litre engine – enough for a comfortable 155 mph. It still looked like a 911 from the side, but wide tyres with massive wheel arch flares and a big rear wing set the Turbo apart; the wing certainly helped to improve the stability at high speed as it always felt a little nervous when being driven fast. But despite all that power it was very tractable, with so much torque that Porsche only gave it four speeds.

When the 911 SC engine was increased to 3.2-litres in 1977, the Turbo went one better to 3.3-litres

Latest Turbo follows 959 technology with four wheel drive and twin turbochargers to produce massive 408 bhp from 3.6-litres of flat-6.

With over three times the power that the original 911 afforded in 1965, this 1995 4WD turbo can reach a top speed of 181 mph.

Below: First of the Turbos came in 1975 as the road-going version of the 911 that Porsche wanted to race alongside the 935 and 936. The 911 Turbo might have been the 930, but marketing sense prevailed.

and 300 bhp in European trim, quite a big increase, helped by an intercooler to drop the temperature of the incoming air, and enough to take the maximum speed to 162 mph. While some 1983 revisions gave the engine more torque, the next major change was to wait until 1990, following a temporary cessation of Turbo production while the Carreras 2 and 4 came along. The new version still used a 3.3-litre engine but, with further modifications, the power was raised to 320 bhp; installed in the cleaner Carrera 2 shape, this raised the maximum speed to 167 mph, and a five-speed gearbox helped to lower the 0-60 mph time to a dramatic 4.7 seconds.

Late 1992 saw the arrival of the 3.6-litre version, outwardly unchanged apart from taller wheels, but now with 360 bhp and a 174 mph maximum speed. Vital tenths are difficult to shave from 0-60 mph times whatever the power increase, but particularly with a rear engine adding to the grip; this one recorded 4.6 seconds, but nearly a second off the 0-100 mph time showed that the new-found power was for real.

But at Porsche development never stops. When everyone thought the 911 had reached its peak they launched the Carrera Turbo, a Carrera 4 with twin turbos and 408 bhp, but everyone else just calls it Turbo. In reality it is a refined 959 with even more modern technology and with 4WD and a 6-speed box, it is almost as fast off the mark as the 959. Thirty years on and the same basic design now handles over three times the power with as much appeal to today's enthusiasts as the original 911 afforded back in 1965.

SPECIFICATION	PORSCHE 911 TURBO (1993)	PORSCHE 911 TURBO (1995)
ENGINE	Turbocharged flat-6 3600 cc	Turbocharged flat-6 3600 cc
HORSEPOWER	360 bhp @ 5500 rpm	408 bhp @ 5750 rpm
TRANSMISSION	Manual 5-speed	Manual 6-speed 4WD
CHASSIS	Unitary steel	Unitary steel
BRAKES	Discs all round with ABS	Discs all round with ABS
TOP SPEED	174 mph (280 km/h)	181 mph (291 km/h)
ACCELERATION	**0-60 mph** 4.6 seconds **0-100 mph** 10.6 seconds	3,7 seconds 9.2 seconds

PORSCHE 911 GT1

1997
190 mph
305 km/h

The roadgoing GT1 closely resembles the sports racer on which it is based. Being 911-related, it is powered by a flat six-cylinder turbocharged engine although mid- rather than rear-located. It produces a formidable 550bhp which is only some 40bhp less than the competition car.

A top speed of over 190 mph and a price tag approaching £600,000 are the mouth watering specifications of the GT1 that Porsche unveiled in April 1997. This exclusive supercar, of which just 30 will be built, is the most potent roadgoing Porsche ever, its mid-located six-cylinder engine developing 544 bhp.

The GT1 project represented an attempt by Porsche to re-establish its dominance of sports racing and, in 1996, came the welcome return of a works entry at Le Mans.

Work on the DM 10 million (£4.2 million) project began at the firm's Weissach technology centre in August 1995 and was completed a record eight months later. The first road test took place there on March 14th 1996, just 14 weeks before the 24-hour race.

Eligible for the Global GT Championship, this series required that the sports racer needed to resemble a road car but, at that stage, the regulations did not specify whether it came before or after the racing version. It is for this reason that the GT1 was superficially akin to a 911 and that the road car appeared some 10 months after its Le Mans debut.

The GT1 is, in essence, the front end and floorpan of a 911, attached to the rear of Porsche's formidable 962 sports racer. This has been dictated by aerodynamic considerations to a great extent because, unlike the 911 that has a rear-mounted, flat-six engine, the 962's is mid-located, thus permitting more slippery body contours.

The bodywork was made from light, but costly, carbon-fibre and Kevlar and the outcome is a shape that is lower and squatter than the 911's although still recognisably related to it.

The car's rear was dominated by a spoiler intended to help keep the 600 bhp generated by the 3.2-litre twin turbocharged, water-cooled, flat-six on the track. Power was conveyed courtesy of a six-speed gearbox.

Two GT1s appeared at Le Mans where they immediately showed their worth and were strongly tipped to win, but placed second and third. There

Left: Close-up of the GT1 road car featured on the Porsche stand at the 1996 British Motor Show. The bodywork is so designed to permit hot air to escape from the front wheels, particularly after the brakes have been applied.

was some compensation for the German make because the race was won by the Porsche-engined TWR Porsche.

Although a single GT1 went on to trounce the McLaren F1 GTRs to win at the four-hour Brands Hatch GT race later in the season, it ceded the championship to the cars from Woking, Surrey. But the factory clearly means business and the menacing GT1s were back in 1997 for their second racing season.

When Porsche announced that it would be producing a roadgoing version of the sports racer, it declared that its output would be detuned by half, to a still respectable but non turbocharged 300 bhp. However, Porsche's project director, Norbert Singer, has said that although 20 to 30 individuals indicated their interest, this was conditional on more power being available.

The factory's response was to take it or leave it, so the potential customers left it . . . Porsche therefore reinstated turbocharging, output shot up to 544bhp and the roadgoing version was back on stream.

A further bonus for using the 911's existing steel hull was that it would not be necessary to crash test a roadgoing version for homologation. With each racing GT1 reputed to have cost around £1 million apiece this is an important consideration.

No motoring magazine has tested a GT1 road car at the time of writing but the factory claims a top speed of over 190 mph, with 62 mph arriving in the blink of an eye, in just 3.7 seconds.

Such astounding acceleration must be allied with impressive braking and the GT1 uses anti lock racing brakes with eight piston calipers at the front and four at the rear. They are backed up by an advanced Bosch anti lock system.

Further refinements include twin catalytic converters, although power steering was a feature of the competition GT1. The two leather-upholstered bucket seats contrast with the single accommodation of the racer.

The car will only be available in left-hand drive form although air conditioning is an optional extra. The interior comes in just one colour: black. However, the customer can specify the body colour of this quicksilver coupé.

'The factory claims a top speed of over 190 mph, with 62 mph arriving in the blink of an eye, in just 3.7 seconds.'

SPECIFICATION	PORSCHE 911 GT1
ENGINE	Turbocharged flat-6, 3200 cc
HORSEPOWER	544 bhp @ 7000 rpm
TRANSMISSION	Manual 6-speed
CHASSIS	Unitary steel
BRAKES	Ventilated disc all round with ABS
TOP SPEED	Over 190 mph (305 km/h)
ACCELERATION	**0-60 mph** 3.7 seconds **0-100 mph** – no figures available

Bare essentials! As befits a model developed from a racer, interior fittings are relatively basic although positively luxurious when compared with the original.

RENAULT ALPINE A610 TURBO

1992
161 mph
(259 km/h)

'It had become a very quick car with a remarkable level of comfort and well developed handling.'

The French challenge to the Porsche 911, the Alpine was for many years the only sporting machine to be produced in a country more concerned with utilitarian transport than exhilarating motoring. Times change and the French market has long had its own share of native sporting hatches, but the Alpine continued to offer fast and comfortable GT 2+2 motoring at a reasonable price; it actually deserved a wider appreciation than it achieved – sadly it ceased production at the end of 1994.

The Alpine has more similarity to the Porsche than just a share of the same market. The layout, with the engine mounted behind the rear axle, is the same and for similar reasons; both trace their origins back to developments of rear engined saloons. Where Porsche eventually made their own engine for the 911, but retained the layout, Alpine have always used Renault engine/gearbox units; the original 1955 A106 used parts from the Renault 750-4CV, and the subsequent A110 shared its drive-train with the R8. When Renault switched to front-wheel-drive, the Renault 16 was the donor for the 1969 Alpine 1600S – a very successful rally machine; a longitudinal engine/gearbox can just as easily be mounted at the back as the front. By now Renault were 30% shareholders and Alpine was Renault's competition department.

Seeking to move up-market Alpine added the A310 in 1971 as a 2+2 using the same running gear under a new distinctive shape. As with its predecessors, the body was a glass-fibre shell mounted on a tubular back-bone frame, but the rear suspension now featured double wishbones rather than the original swing-axles from the earlier Renaults. And it was developed and trimmed to proper GT levels. By the mid-'seventies Renault owned 87% of Alpine whose production now encompassed A110s, A310s and R5 Alpines – the 1975 total was 4500 vehicles; the A110 ceased in 1977.

SPECIFICATION	RENAULT ALPINE A610 TURBO
ENGINE	Turbocharged V-6 2975 cc
POWER	250 bhp @ 5750 rpm
TRANSMISSION	Manual 5-speed transaxle
CHASSIS	Steel backbone, g/fibre bodywork
BRAKES	Discs all round with ABS
TOP SPEED	161 mph (259 km/h)
ACCELERATION	**0-60 mph** 5.8 seconds **0-100 mph** 15.8 seconds

In 1980, the A310 gained a power unit more appropriate to its GT status with the 2.7-litre Peugeot-Renault-Volvo unit to give a 140 mph top speed. As this was also from a front-wheel-drive Renault – the 30 – the engine was still behind the rear axle. Five years on, the sleeker GTA replaced the A310, with the 160 bhp 2.85-litre V-6 or a 200 bhp 2.5-litre Turbo version, giving just over 150 mph; the chassis design remained the same but the car was longer, lower, wider and heavier as refinement and luxury were added. It had become a very quick car with a remarkable level of comfort and well developed handling.

The final version is the substantially similar A610 Turbo introduced in 1991. The body, still glassfibre, has been widened to accomodate a larger track and the front smoothed with pop-up headlamps. But the biggest change was the use of the 3-litre PRV engine, turbo-charged to produce 250 bhp which propels this low-drag coupé to 161 mph. Alpine has a strong track record, the A610 is a well developed car and was considerably cheaper than a Porsche 911; it should have sold better.

The interior had all the luxury trimming expected in a GT; at speed it was a remarkably quiet car.

The French answer to the Porsche 911, the A610 was a fast and effective 2+2 with a glass-fibre body on a steel chassis using turbo-charged Renault power. Despite competition breeding, it was not as popular as it deserved to be.

TVR CERBERA

1996
168 mph
270 km/h

The Griffith is an exhilarating mixture of retro style with modern performance, with an agility that few mid-engined cars can match.

More TVRs emerge from Blackpool in a year than the combined production of Newport Pagnell Aston Martins and Malvern Morgans, but the marque has been far less known outside enthusiast circles than either of those two establishment names. Gradually that is changing; the open TVRs are instantly eye-catching even before the raucous sound of a powerful V-8 turns the heads. And the latest Cerbera 2+2 coupé is just as striking but with TVR's own, more refined, AJP 4.2-litre V-8.

American legislation and litigation deter many small manufacturers and TVR can sell all they want to make elsewhere. So TVRs no longer go to the USA, which is a shame when you look at the origins of the Griffith, the first of the new generation TVRs. Jack Griffith was the American garage-owner who first tried to squeeze a Ford V-8 into the 1600 Mk IIA TVRs that were competing in the 1962 Sebring 12-hour race. From this early attempt came the Griffith 200, a Mark III TVR using a strengthened chassis with the 4.7-litre Ford V-8 installed in either 195 or 271 bhp forms. The Griffith 400 followed in early 1964, the first of the Manx-tailed TVRs. Unfortunately these were not properly developed and affected the TVR reputation; a prolonged US dock-strike hit both companies and bankrupted TVR. Although few Griffiths were sold outside America, the replacement Tuscan V-8, the first of the new Lilley management, was a success and gave over 150 mph in 1967. Tuscan V-6s, Vixens, M-series and Taimars (including the first convertible) took the company through the 'seventies without recapturing that performance level.

The new wedge-shaped Tasmin was the

design for the 'eighties, initially with Ford V-6 power which also temporarily returned the cars to the US market, by which time current owner Peter Wheeler had taken charge from 1981.The Tasmin name was dropped when the Rover unit arrived in 1983 for the 350i convertible. By the mid-'eighties every sports car had to have real performance, so the Rover engine grew to extend the range, providing the 145 mph 390SE and later the 150 mph 420SEAC (Special Edition with Aramid Composite bodywork).

Rover power was used for a special one-make TVR-sponsored Tuscan Challenge for 1989; by the time the 36 race cars were built, TVR had uprated the engines to a dry-sumped re-cranked 4.4-litre developing 350 bhp with four down-draught Weber carburetters, and reworked the chassis to cope with the extra power. The resultant racing was, and still is, a great success, but we had to wait until 1992 for the Griffith, the road-going version of the Tuscan racers.

When the Griffith finally arrived, it had a 4.3-litre Rover unit with 280 bhp installed in a chassis that had learnt the lessons of Tuscan racing, all clad in a curvaceous body that was old and new at the same time, together with an extremely effective quick-action soft-top. The Chimaera followed a year later, a little longer for more luggage space and a little softer for more comfort, with similar lines carrying different detailing. As this was given the option of 4.0 and 4.3-litre units, the Griffith had to move up a league with a 5-litre version developing a massive 340 bhp; gearing limits the top speed of Rover-powered versions to around 161 mph, but the acceleration of the Griffith 500 is brutally quick with 0-100 mph in just over 10 seconds – and it is less than half the price of a Ferrari 355.

Above and left: A permanent hard-top plus an extra 11 inches in the wheelbase make the Cerbera into a reasonable family coupé.

'The Cerbera uses TVR's new overhead camshaft engine which will rev more freely.'

However the Cerbera uses TVR's new overhead camshaft engine which will rev more freely. A little more power and better aerodynamics will lift the maximum speed towards 170 mph, although the initial acceleration will be less dramatic due to the extra weight of a 2+2 coupé. With an extra 11 inches in the wheelbase the new family TVR should considerably broaden the marque's appeal.

SPECIFICATION	TVR CERBERA
ENGINE	Aluminium V-8, 4185 cc
HORSEPOWER	360 bhp @ 6500 rpm
TRANSMISSION	Manual 5-speed
CHASSIS	Tubular frame, grp body
BRAKES	Discs all round
TOP SPEED	168 mph (270 km/h)
ACCELERATION	**0-60 mph** 4.5 seconds **0-100 mph** 9.9 seconds

VAUXHALL LOTUS CARLTON

1990
173 mph
278 km/h

The Lotus Carlton is such an unlikely car. Derived from Vauxhall's top of the range saloon, normally a fast and comfortable 5-seater with few sporting pretensions, it is a product of General Motors' 1986-94 ownership of the Norfolk sports car specialist. GM had bought Lotus for Lotus Engineering rather than the low-volume production side and the Lotus Carlton was as much a flag-ship for engineering ability as for the Vauxhall range. Despite its GM parentage, Lotus Engineering was a facility that also worked for other manufacturers once they were convinced that GM did not have access to the confidential files; the Lotus Carlton was a demonstration of what could be done – it was also sold as the Opel Lotus Omega.

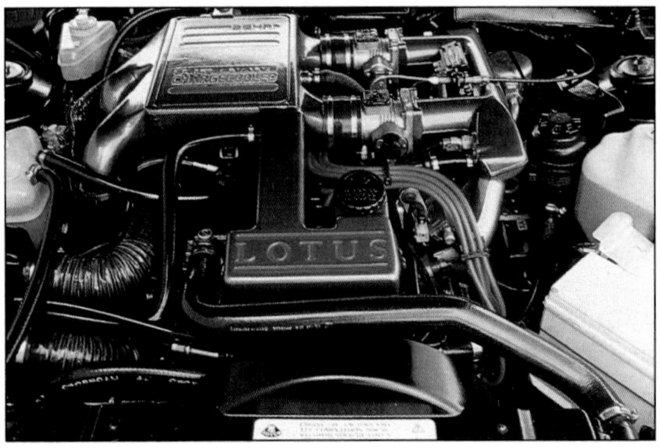

Twin turbochargers and an extra 670 cc capacity help to increase 24-valve Carlton power from 204 to 377 bhp.

At the time of its June 1990 production start, the 173 mph Lotus Carlton cost £48,000 while the 146 mph 3.0 GSi 24-valve Carlton from which it came was a mere £25,635.

It was a Vauxhall which went straight into top BMW and Mercedes territory and out-performed them all – the subsequent BMW M5 6-speed was its nearest equivalent – but for all its performance it was still a Vauxhall or an Opel and never had the cachet required for that end of the market. It ran for just over two years.

The basic Carlton 3.0 GSi 24-valve engine develops a useful 204 bhp at 6000 rpm using twin overhead camshafts and Bosch fuel injection. Lotus squeezed the maximum out of the 6-cylinder block by a small overbore but made a new crankshaft to increase the capacity from 2969 to 3638 cc; to this were added a pair of Garrett T25 turbochargers to give 10 psi pressure – two small turbos give less turbo-lag than a single larger one – with Rochester (from GM US) fuel injection. The result was 377 bhp at 5200 rpm with torque (mid-range pulling power) more than doubled. All this required a new, stronger gearbox which came from ZF as a 6-speeder with a very high top gear ratio to give 70 mph at just 1650 rpm.

Such a performance increase obviously demanded chassis improvements to be safe; the brakes use ventilated discs with four-pot calipers at the front and the new alloy wheels are taller with low profile tyres and wider, increasing the track at both ends.

Big alloy wheels, revised front end and rear wing give a distinctive appearance to the Lotus version.

The standard system of independent suspension is retained, but stiffened and strengthened, while the rear suspension features variable rate coils and self-levelling suspension to ensure that the car remains at the right height for the aerodynamics to work effectively however much weight is being carried – the front spoiler and the rear wing combine to create zero lift, while the drag factor is an impressive 0.307.

While the basic bodyshell comes from the standard Carlton, it looks quite different with the spoiler, side skirts and rear wing; it has the distinction of being the world's fastest ever production 5-seater. Although the model was not a success, lessons have certainly been absorbed within GM. In fact, some of its design stemmed from the work that Lotus did for GM in the development of the Corvette ZR-1 which was the first to use that ZF 6-speed gearbox coupled to a Lotus-designed 32-valve V-8 engine; the standard Corvette uses the same 6-speed gearbox mated to a normal GM 16-valve 5.7-litre V-8, a combination that is now used in the faster of GM's other sporting cars, the Chevrolet Camaro Z-28 and the Pontiac Firebird Trans-Am. With 277 bhp, the latter clocks 158 mph and can reach 100 mph in 16 seconds – it goes as well as it looks. The Lotus Carlton is the ultimate wolf in sheep's clothing.

'The Lotus Carlton is the ultimate wolf in sheep's clothing.'

SPECIFICATION	VAUXHALL LOTUS CARLTON
ENGINE	Turbo straight-6, 3638 cc
HORSEPOWER	377 bhp @ 5200 rpm
TRANSMISSION	Manual 6-speed
CHASSIS	Unitary steel
BRAKES	Discs all round with ABS
TOP SPEED	173 mph
ACCELERATION	**0-60 mph** 5.3 seconds **0-100 mph** 10.9 seconds

Is this the fastest five-seater? At 173 mph this is a shade faster than BMW's latest M5.

VENTURI 400GT

1995
175 mph
281 km/h

When such revered names as Delage, Delahaye, Bugatti, Talbot died in the wake of post-war luxury taxes, France cut off its performance heritage. Since then, the Ligier road cars have come and gone, Renault with Alpine persevered until the A610, too, has ceased, and it is now left to the little firm of Venturi to resuscitate a tradition of French sporting machinery that stretches back to the beginning of motor racing.

Founded in 1984 by two racing enthusiasts, Claude Poiraud and Gerard Godfroy, Venturi showed its first prototype later that year; the Paris Show in 1986 saw the official launch of the first of the high quality mid-engined sports cars that are now assembled in Nantes. Turbo-charged V-6 engines and transmissions came from Renault, but, unlike the Alpine, these were mounted amidships rather than behind the rear axle, and the power outputs were higher with more turbo boost pressure. For the chassis they used a full length pressed steel frame well boxed for stiffness; wishbone suspension is used at the front while the rear has upper and lower radius arms with transverse links, single at the top and a parallel pair below, following racing practice.

'It is impressively fast – stable too – and will reach 180 mph.'

This is all covered by composite bodywork of a striking, yet simple, shape with built-in downforce and a low drag factor of 0.31. Inside it is trimmed with all the care that goes into an Aston Martin with taut leather and polished wood veneers, and there is air-conditioning too. The first one, now the 210, used the 2.5-litre V-6 with a single Garrett T3 turbocharger working to 0.85 bar pressure for 210 bhp to give a maximum speed around 152 mph; the comparable Renault 25 installation produced 182 bhp. The 260 with the 2.85-litre V-6 received similar treatment and 1 bar of boost pressure to give 260 bhp and a maximum of 165 mph; the 260 comes in normal 1255 Kg form and as the lightened Atlantique at 1110 Kg dispensing with such heavyweight luxuries as air conditioning, electric seat adjustment and radio/cassette system in the quest for faster acceleration.

Both 210 and 260 are offered in coupé and 'Transcoupé' form. The latter is an ingenious convertible; you can have *coupe de ville* motoring by removing one or both of the two roof panels, or go one stage further for full open motoring by pressing a button to hinge the rear window/roll-bar assembly forward so that it lies flush with the

With PRV V-6 engines mounted amidships the Venturis are neat and effective machines, ranging from the 2.5-litre 210 to the twin-turbo 3-litre 400GT; shown is the intermediate 300.

rear deck – a true convertible. When up, it is a notchback coupé without the little rear wing that sits across the tail on the coupés.

As part of the promotion of the new Venturis, a one-make race series was organised from 1992 as a support race to major International events; called the Gentleman Drivers Trophy, it was for enthusiastic but skilled amateurs who would pay to race factory-prepared identical cars. For this Venturi produced the 400, using twin turbos on the 3-litre V-6 to generate 408 bhp and special dog-clutch close ratios within the standard casing; the chassis was widened and lengthened to accept the bigger power pack, increase high speed stability and provide higher cornering power. The body grew an integrated Ferrari F40-style rear wing and was 11 inches wider to accommodate a wider track and wider tyres and provide side scoops for engine air and brake cooling; the nose was shorter and blunter with the previous pop-up headlights now partially exposed. They were successful racers for the two seasons, so a road version was produced as the 400GT reverting to the road-going synchromesh gearbox; with 408 bhp in 1150 Kg it is impressively fast – stable too – and will reach nearly 180 mph.

The 400GT is the road-going development of the cars used for the Gentleman Racer series; with 408 bhp in 1150 Kg it is very fast.

SPECIFICATION	VENTURI 400GT
ENGINE	Aluminium V-6 twin-turbo 2975 cc
HORSEPOWER	408 bhp @ 6000 rpm
TRANSMISSION	Manual 5-speed
CHASSIS	Steel chassis, composite body
BRAKES	Discs all round
TOP SPEED	175 mph
ACCELERATION	**0-60 mph** 4.7 seconds **0-100 mph** 10.4 seconds

Some of the 400's features have now been carried across to the tamer Atlantique 300, which uses the 3-litre engine and a single turbo to generate 270 bhp; this has the longer wheelbase but narrower rear tyres than the 400, so that it is only 5.5 inches wider than the 210/260; the extra width slows it down so the maximum is similar to that of the 260.

Few testers have sampled the Venturis, so the figures above are conservatively approximate based on calculations and the few reports that have appeared. They won't be far out and show that the Venturi 400GT is a serious supercar, compact and effective.

Venturi in its simplest body style is shown with this 260 with no extra rear intakes, no wheel-arch flares.

THEY HAVE ALSO RUN . . .

We close with a handful of cars for which full independent performance figures have not been taken. They have all been, or are still, in limited volume production – they are all fast and deserve a place in any book on fast cars.

Isdera Imperator 108i
top speed 176 mph

Eberhard Schulz, an engineer with Porsche's external research and development facility, established Isdera (an acronym for *Ingenuieuboro fur Styling, Design and Racing*) in Stuttgart in 1981. As an advertisement for his abilities, he built the mid-engined Spyder (open) 033i with spaceframe chassis. A 2.3-litre, four-cylinder engine by Mercedes-Benz was employed, a make that then powered all subsequent Isderas.

When the inevitable requests came for replicas, Schulz obliged and also produced the supplementary 036i 3-litre six.

This was followed in 1984 by the Imperator 108i gull-wing coupé on similar lines but using the 5.8-litre V-8. Based on a 1978 Mercedes-Benz design with which Schulz had been involved, the 176 mph car was able to reach 60 mph in 5 seconds and 100 mph in 10.8 seconds.

Later, in 1993, came the 112i Commendatore, a coupé named in tribute to Enzo Ferrari that cost the equivalent of £350,000. The well appointed car was powered by the 6-litre V-12 engine used in the top line S-Class Mercedes saloons. There was an alternative 6.9-litre unit with a claimed top speed of 230 mph and a 0-62 mph time of 4.1 seconds.

Spectre R42
estimated top speed 176 mph

An all-new mid-engined luxury supercar, the Spectre R42 was the product of Poole-based GT Developments, who produced over 330 GT40 replicas in the last ten years. The R42 embodied all that experience into newer technology; it uses an aluminium honeycomb chassis with steel sub-frames, the rear one carrying a 350 bhp version of the 4.6-litre 4-cam 32-valve Ford V-8, mated to their own 5-speed transaxle. Carbon-glass-fibre composites are used for the body which is styled very much as a road-going sports racer. Low drag

The Stuttgart-built exclusive mid-engined Isdera Imperator 108i coupé of 1987, based on Mercedes-Benz design study CW311. The two cars are outwardly very similar, even down to roof-mounted rear view mirror!

Left: A 1996 Spectre R42. The firm's new owners, headed by Swedish entrepreneur Olaf Hildebrand, are planning to market an improved version. The intention is that output will reach 200 units by 1998.

and light weight ensure that it is very quick. And it is comfortable, too, with well padded leather interior, good sound deadening and enough suspension compliance to keep road noise down and ride comfort up.

In the final phase of prototype development, GTD was taken over by Spectre Motor Car Inc., a US company quoted on the NASDQ bulletin board. The R42 is substantially the same as the GTD version but power steering has been added. It is now in production and over 20 have been completed. Racing versions – GTRs – will be available for the International GT events and the company plans to race its own car in 1997.

Vector W8

estimated top speed 200 mph

Founded in 1978, Vector produced a handful of exotic hi-tech performance cars before the W8 arrived in 1990 – at least 22 were built. These have a carbon-fibre monocoque, gull-wing doors in a composite body with a transverse mid-mounted twin-turbo 634 bhp Corvette 6-litre V-8 mated to a GM 3-speed automatic transmission. The earlier, similar W2 used an aluminium honeycomb chassis, as does the more modern-looking WX3, shown at Geneva in 1993. The company was taken over by MegaTech in 1994 and should benefit from some Lamborghini input but was in trouble again at the end of 1996.

Left: The Los Angeles-built Vector W2, introduced in 1980, powered by a 5.8-litre twin turbocharged Chevrolet V-8 engine with a special alloy block and drive taken through a reversed Oldsmobile Toronado transmission.

Monteverdi Hai 650F1

estimated top speed 190 mph

Peter Monteverdi began making high performance GTs in Switzerland in 1967 using a big Chrysler 7-litre in a steel frame de Dion-axled chassis with elegant Fissore bodywork. The 375S and 400SS were joined by the 375L 2+2 using a similar body style. In 1971, he introduced the mid-engined Hai 450SS using the powerful Chrysler 7-litre Hemi in a Fiore-styled Fissore body; only a few were made. Other models included the hemi-powered Berlinetta and the Palm Beach convertible. To celebrate 40 years since the first Monteverdi, 1992 saw the Hai 650 F1 of which four have been built; carbon fibre is used for chassis and bodywork with 650 bhp supplied by a Cosworth DFR 3.5-litre F1 power unit – a road-going *Grand Prix* car.

Ascari FGT

estimated top speed 175 mph

The race bred mid-engined Ascari GT of 1995. As this is the road going version, a BMW V-8 engine was employed. Otherwise the theme is conventional with the good looking glass-reinforced-plastic coupé body.

A racing version of the new Ascari FGT appeared in the April 1995 Le Mans pre-qualifying event, but a gearbox problem intervened. However honour was satisfied in the late season Le Mans 4-hours when the car finished third and another won the final National GT race at Silverstone. The design is that of Lee Noble who has produced racing GT cars for the UK Prosport 3000 series, and the Ultima, two of which were used as mechanical mules for McLaren F1 development. Noble's partner in Ascari Cars Ltd is Klaas Zwart, a businessman racing driver.

The construction is traditional, with a tubular space-frame boxed by aluminium panels bonded and rivetted into place under a well finished and attractive grp body. While the racing versions have used the big 5.7-litre pushrod Ford V-8, road cars will now use the BMW 4-litre V-8 with around 325 bhp instead of the planned Ford quad-cam; this will be mated to a Porsche 6-speed gearbox. The plan is to produce 50 cars a year, some of which will be track cars.

CLASSIC
Cars
FROM AROUND THE WORLD

MICHAEL BOWLER

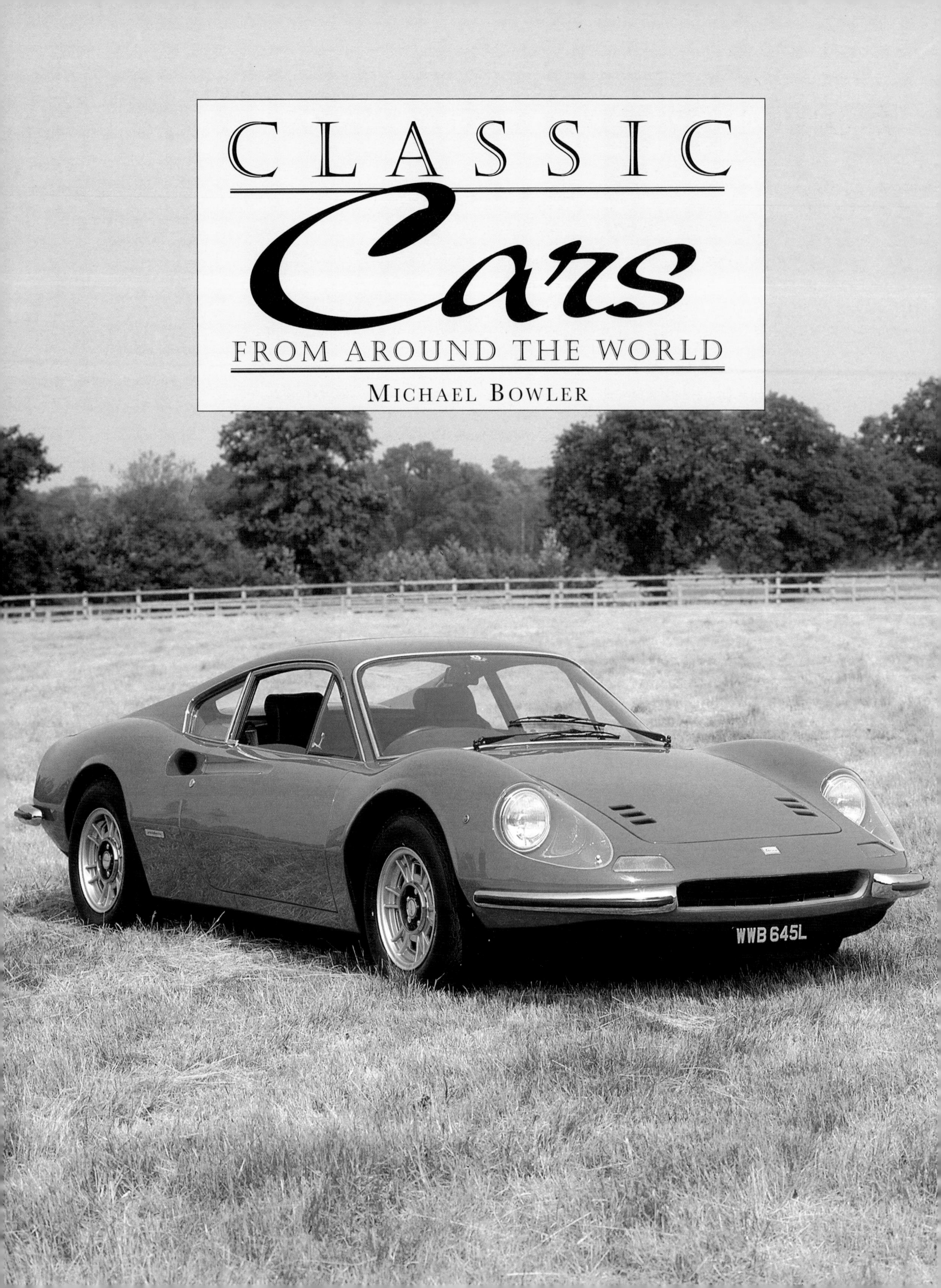

Contents – Classic Cars

Left: The classically stylish Ferrari 275 GTB: this is a 1965 'short-nose'.

Opposite page: The beautiful Dino 246GT was not strictly a Ferrari, but was intended to establish a new sub-Ferrari marque; its successor was eventually promoted to full Maranello status.

Introduction

Classic is one of those terms that every like-minded enthusiast understands but few can define to the satisfaction of all. In broad terms it seems to apply to any obsolete car for which there are sufficient enthusiasts to form a car club, but the ability of a handful of cars to survive the ravages of time and rust should not automatically make them classics; if they were regarded as unimpressive in their day, they don't get better. So today's classic car should have been at least a little out of the ordinary in its day, even if it's only the top of an otherwise mundane range – the Cortina GT might qualify but everyman's Cortina 1200 shouldn't.

Outside the USA, Classic has become the catch-all term for anything that seems to be old and well looked after, and it also embraces periods for which there are established definitions. Within the USA there is a nation-wide Classic Car Club which caters for carefully selected grander cars from the 1925-42 period plus a few younger ones of particular merit. Around most of the rest of the world the definitions have stemmed from the great British obsession with the older car – the International body FIVA has endorsed their years of change if not necessarily their names.

The oldest have been called Veterans since the 1930 foundation of the Veteran Car Club which was set up for cars made before 1905 – the cars which take part in the annual London-Brighton run. From 1943, they also included the 1905-1919 cars that the English call Edwardians. The Vintage Sports-Car Club was formed in 1936 for Vintage (pre-1931) cars because they believed that the advent of mass production marked the end of proper motor cars; they later retracted to some extent by accepting certain cars of the 'thirties as Post-Vintage Thoroughbreds and even later extended their interests to post-war front-engined *Grand Prix* cars, termed Historic Racing Cars. Post-war divisions and names have rather run out of imagination; it is only the racing fraternity that needs tight year definitions to recapture previous eras, leaving the rest to make do with marques and models, decades or the overall age of the car. So a convenient, all-embracing term like Classic was very necessary to provide an umbrella for all the post-war cars that generate a following.

While Classic *is* used to apply to pre-war cars, most people consider that the classic era covers

With little change from the pre-war design, the MG TC was the first sports-car on the post-war market.

post-war cars, which can now be up to 50 years old. The classics in this book are all post-war cars, although some of their stories may start before the war. Within the 44 double-page spreads 132 classics are featured in some detail, ranging from the cheapest with which you can join some form of classic car club through to the most expensive classics of tomorrow. There are a number of American models, too, which are just as likely to have supporting clubs in any country as will the British and Continental equivalents.

It is the classic car clubs that are the backbone of the classic movement. Pre-war cars are covered by marque and general interest clubs, but most post-war cars will be covered by the marque or even model club. Almost any obsolete car will have a car club somewhere, and this should be your first port of call if you are thinking of buying a classic; there may even be one for sale from a club member in the newsletter – it is best to buy a known quantity. If not, there will be a club official who will be happy to guide you to the right model and tell you what to look for. Where to find the club?

There are a number of classic magazines whose pages or enquiry desk will give you club secretary addresses. The magazines will also tell you when the major classic events are taking place; the big classic car shows and concours couldn't function without the help of the clubs, many of whom will have stands or gathering points at these events. If you haven't been a part of the classic scene before, don't rush into a purchase; talk to as many other owners as possible beforehand. Unless you want to do a lot of restoration work yourself at zero cost per hour, you are always best to buy a restored example; the high cost of a professional restoration plus the cost of the purchase will always leave you on the downside if you need to sell quickly. If you want to join in the fun, but don't know what to buy choose a car with good spares availability; many car clubs make their own spares and there are also many specialists in the various models. If you buy an ex-British Leyland model, there is the whole backing of British Motor Heritage with archives and spares to draw upon.

What else do the clubs offer? All have newsletters of varying standards and all arrange gatherings whether these are competitive or not. They may be concours or driving tests, swap-meets or sprints. Whatever it is, you will soon find that a car club will add another dimension to your social life. You may think that insurance will be an expensive deterrent but it isn't. Most clubs have access to a specialist insurance broker who knows the classic car scene well and will offer low premiums for low annual mileages – 3-5,000 miles a year is a typical level – and they know that the classic owner is going to drive in a way that will preserve his investment.

So take a look through these pages and hopefully you will gain some inspiration either to join the classic movement or to change marques within it. Happy dreaming and then, happy classic motoring.

Once the Chevrolet Corvette took on V-8 power, it became America's own sporting car; this 1959 model is from the second generation.

'The classics in this book are all post-war cars, although some of their stories may start before the war.'

AC ACE, ACECA, COBRA 289

'Ace-Bristol was to prove very effective on the race tracks at the end of the 'fifties.'

From their home in Thames Ditton, Surrey, AC were never a large manufacturer. Starting in 1903 with the Autocarrier, they always produced cars which were well engineered to the standards of the times, but not very exciting. After the last war they continued to produce the elegant tourers and sports cars which had served them well during the 'thirties, but these were inevitably becoming old-fashioned. They needed a new range.

Meanwhile an enthusiastic Cambridge engineer, John Tojeiro, had been building a few specials for club racing. British sports cars had fairly basic chassis designs in 1950, so Tojeiro decided to produce something more sophisticated. The frame was modelled on the successful pre-war BMW 328 with twin large diameter tubes to which was attached an independent front suspension system using a transverse leaf spring with lower wishbones; he used the same system at the rear. The aluminium body was wrapped around small diameter tubes and looked very similar to the Ferrari that had won the first post-war Le Mans 24-hour race in 1949. One car was built for Cliff Davis with the Bristol 2-litre engine which had been developed from the BMW 328, while a second had a Lea Francis unit; Davis was particularly successful in the Tojeiro-Bristol.

It was an ideal car for AC to develop as their own road car, initially alongside their saloons which were still using the 2-litre 6-cylinder engine that had originally been designed in 1925 – it was this engine that was installed in the new AC Ace when it was launched in 1953. Old it may have been, but it was still good for 85 bhp when equipped with three SU carburetters; in a car weighing only 15cwt (760 Kg) this gave 100 mph performance and 0-60 mph in 12 seconds.

A year later, AC introduced the Aceca, another pre-war model name. This was the fixed head Grand Tourer version with very elegant lines and used the same 2-litre engine to give comfortable high speed cruising. While the AC-engined cars had reasonable success on the track, the chassis could take more power. So 1956 saw the introduction of the Ace-Bristol with 105 bhp for the Aceca and 120 bhp for the Ace which became a very quick car, capable of 115 mph.

By now AC were beginning to export cars to America, and the Ace-Bristol was to prove very effective on the race tracks at the end of the 'fifties; they had the roadholding but could take even more power. This encouraged Carroll Shelby to install a Ford 260 4.2-litre V-8 into one of the cars in 1961; it worked very well and AC adopted the idea, strengthened the chassis and transmission, widened the bodywork by two inches for bigger tyres, and the AC Cobra was born – now a 150 mph car which could reach 100 mph in 13 seconds. It suited AC well as the Bristol unit was going out of production; lesser Aces would continue to be available with the Ford 2.6-litre six-cylinder engine.

Soon the 4.2-litre was replaced by the 271 bhp 4.7-litre 289, and in 1964, Shelby went several stages on and inserted the 425 bhp 7-litre 427 into a chassis that had been redesigned by Ford using bigger chassis tubes and wishbone/coil spring suspension with ever wider wheels and tyres. While these now very fast cars had some success on American race-tracks, it was the 289 in open and closed forms that gave the

The post-war Ace was launched in 1953, with the Bristol engine option coming in 1956. This is a 1959 Ace-Bristol.

SPECIFICATION	AC ACECA (1954)	ACE-BRISTOL (1958)	AC 289 (1967)
ENGINE	6-cyl 1991 cc	6-cyl 1971 cc	V-8 4727 cc
HORSEPOWER	90 bhp @ 4500 rpm	125 bhp @ 6000 rpm	271 bhp @ 6000 rpm
TRANSMISSION	4-speed manual	4-speed manual	4-speed manual
CHASSIS	Twin tube frame with independent suspension all round (*all models*)		
BRAKES	Drum brakes	Disc option/drum	Disc brakes
TOP SPEED	105 mph	115 mph	144 mph
0-60 MPH	13.5 sec	9.0 sec	5.2 sec

Cobras the International GT championship in 1965. The big Cobras were not sold in Europe, but AC used the revised (Mk.III) chassis as the AC 289, 4 inches wider than the original leaf-sprung 289 and arguably the nicest of all the V-8 powered ACs in looks and road manners.

While production of the Mk.III ceased in 1969, AC restoration specialists Autokraft got permission in 1983 to bring out a Mk.IV, a Cobra in all but engine specification – still a Ford V-8, but a modern 5-litre unit. You could still buy a new one over 40 years after the original Ace arrived in 1953 – that's classic for you!

Left: The fixed head AC Aceca came in 1954, the first one being this prototype.

Nicest of all the post-war two-seater ACs was the Mk.III 289, using the new Ford-designed chassis – a 1966 example here.

ALFA ROMEO GIULIETTA SPRINT, SPIDER, DUETTO

'The Sprint engine used twin Weber carburetters and developed a remarkable 80 bhp.'

A competition heritage stretching back to its 1910 origins has ensured that an Alfa Romeo is always just that much more sporting than its equivalents from other manufacturers. Through the 'twenties and 'thirties, the cars were the ones to beat in single and two-seaters, culminating in the Tipo 158/159 which swept all before it in the post-war years until 1951, when the company withdrew from racing to concentrate on producing road cars in larger volumes than ever before.

Work started on the new small Alfa, the Giulietta, in 1952. It had a pressed steel chassis, independent front suspension and a well-located live rear axle; like its larger predecessors, the 1900s, the new car had a twin overhead camshaft engine, a 4-cylinder 1290 cc unit developing 53 bhp for the saloon car; few other volume production cars had single overhead camshaft engines and no others had two. Unusually, though, the saloon wasn't the first version to be launched.

Alfa Romeo had been state-controlled through IRI (Institute for Industrial Reconstruction) from 1933, and were to remain so until Fiat took them over in 1986. In 1953, IRI sought to raise money for Alfa by a bond issue and offered new Giuliettas as prizes; at this stage the new saloon's platform was developed but the superstructure was still under way. Alfa's way out was to find a specialist coachbuilder to produce a limited run of sporting versions and take some as prizes. Bertone was entrusted with the task of creating and producing the two-door Sprint coupé; demand far exceeded expectation and Bertone had to set up a production facility for it – over 25,000 were produced from 1954-61. The Sprint engine used twin Weber carburetters and developed a remarkable 80 bhp which was enough to give the sleek little car a maximum of 100 mph.

The saloon duly followed in spring 1955 and the Spider came shortly after, a two-seater built by Pininfarina on a shorter wheelbase. Veloce versions of the Sprint and Spider appeared in 1956 with 90 bhp engines and some aluminium panels to reduce the weight for competitions. Two more 'external' variants arrived in 1960 using the Spider

SPECIFICATIONS	GIULIETTA SPRINT (1954)	GIULIA SPIDER (1962)	DUETTO 1600 (1966)
ENGINE	4-cyl dohc 1290 cc	4-cyl dohc 1570 cc	4-cyl dohc 1570
POWER	80 bhp @ 6300 rpm	92 bhp @ 6200 rpm	109 bhp @ 6000 rpm
TRANSMISSION	Manual 4-speed	Manual 5-speed	Manual 5-speed
CHASSIS	Unitary steel body/chassis (*all models*)		
BRAKES	Drums	Discs all round	Discs all round
TOP SPEED	100 mph	108 mph	111 mph
0-60 MPH	13.2 sec	12.9 sec	11.2 sec

The Giulietta Spider arrived in 1955 on a shorter wheelbase and was built by Pininfarina. This too had a 1600 cc engine until it was replaced by the Duetto.

Opposite: Launched in 1966, the 1600 Spider was later called the Duetto, until it became the 1750 in 1968; the 2000 (1976 here) replaced the 1750 in 1971.

platform, the Giulietta SZ (Sprint by Zagato) and the Giulietta SS (Sprint Speciale by Bertone) both with 100 bhp and 5-speed gearboxes; produced in low numbers these two were particularly attractive and the SZ was very successful in Italian racing.

Come 1962 and the Giulietta was replaced by the Giulia with a 92 bhp 1570 cc engine on a slightly longer platform. The Sprint, Spider and SS continued as Giulia 1600s – Zagato's 1963 derivative being the competition Giulia TZ (Tubolare Zagato). In that year the Giulia Sprint was replaced by the new Sprint GT, a Bertone design but the first to be built in the new Alfa factory at Arese; Bertone's own Sprint didn't die, but returned as an economy version with the 1300 engine again for 1964. The Giulia, too, had an economy 1300 added to the range; for a bewildering period, old and new models were being produced at the same time with interchangeable engines. More powerful 112 bhp engines were used for the 1963 Giulia Super and the 1964 Spider Veloce. The Sprint GT spawned the cabriolet GTC in 1965, by which time the original 1955 Spider shape was looking a little dated.

The answer lay in an elegant prototype that Pininfarina had been developing; with a low nose and a tapering tail, it was lower and wider than the old Spider. However on its introduction in 1966 it too was called the 1600 Spider; Alfa Romeo launched a competition to decide a name and avoid confusion – Duetto was chosen. But by 1968, the Alfa saloon capacity had increased to 1779 cc and the car became the 1750 Spider Veloce, earning a chopped tail in late 1969. After the change to 2000 cc in 1971, the car was to continue in production until 1993 with only minor revisions, a classic feat second to none.

Originally designed as a stop-gap, Bertone's Giulietta Sprint was a remarkable success, and went on to use the 1600 cc engine for 1962/3.

ALFA ROMEO 2600 SPRINT, MONTREAL, GTV6-2.5

'The silken six transformed the image and the appeal.'

Since the Giulietta went into volume production in 1954, Alfa Romeo's four-cylinder cars have overshadowed their bigger brothers that were produced in much smaller quantities. But they were fine cars nevertheless and much rarer. Our chosen three were all styled by Bertone and represent some of his finest work of the 'sixties and 'seventies; the 2600 Sprint dates from 1960, the Montreal from 1967, and the GTV6 from 1974.

After the war, Alfa had continued to produce big six-cylinder cars based on pre-war designs, cars with separate chassis which could be supplied to coachbuilders. They were still thinking big in 1950 when they introduced the 1900, the first unitary-bodied Alfa Romeo; work wasn't to start on the high volume Giulietta until two years later. The 1900 used a twin-cam four-cylinder 1884 cc unit developing 90 bhp. Over the next eight years, the range would include the 4-door saloon and the 2-door Sprint as a coupé or cabriolet with the capacity enlarged to 1975 cc in 1953; fastest was the 1900 Super Sprint with 115 bhp. Some 19,000 were produced of which only 1800 were Sprints. These were the chassis on which the famous Disco Volantes and BAT cars were mounted.

In 1958, the new 2000 range used a new chassis and body styles with the same big four-cylinder engine in its 1975 cc form. Over the next three years the factory produced just 2892 saloons, 3443 Touring Spiders and 700 Bertone Sprints, the latter from 1960. The cars looked good but lacked the expected performance and refinement until the six-cylinder 2600 was inserted in 1962; this engine was modelled on the Giulia unit, still featuring twin camshafts, and produced 130 bhp for the saloon and 145 bhp for the Spider and Sprint. The silken six transformed the image and the appeal; the Sprint became a very attractive 125 mph car. When the Sprint GT 1.6 arrived, it was easy to see where the lines had come from.

The 2600 range continued through to the late 'sixties by which time the Giulia had grown into the 1750 and then the 2000, offering similar performance and accommodation in a more modern chassis; the big cars had become superfluous but the company lacked a flagship. This was to come in the shape of the Montreal, Bertone's contribution to the Canadian Expo 67; with its lines inspired by the mid-engined Lamborghini Miura, the show car was adopted by Alfa to take a de-tuned version of the light-alloy V-8 which had powered the Tipo 33, the company's 1967 return to sports car racing. The Montreal took quite a time to reach production, but was finally ready for 1971 using a 2.6-litre version of the 4-cam, dry sump, fuel-injected engine with 200

Named after the Expo 67 show for which Bertone produced a concept car, the Montreal went into production in 1971 as Alfa's flagship, using a detuned version of the racing V-8.

bhp, mated to a ZF gearbox. Its chassis followed familiar Alfa practice with a well-located live rear axle. It was a superb looking 135 mph car, but a short-lived casualty of the fuel crisis.

The next big-engined coupé started its life in 1974 as the Alfetta GT. The Alfetta 1.8 saloon had arrived in 1972 slotting in between the 1600 Giulias and the 2000, which it was eventually to replace. Its particular novelty was a de Dion transaxle system for the rear end. The coupé version followed on a shorter wheelbase. Its clean lines were also to be seen on the Alfasud Sprint from 1976. A year later the Alfetta coupé became the GTV2000 finally replacing the original Giulia-based GT. While the Alfetta continued until 1984, when it was replaced by the 90, a new big-car range was launched in 1979, the Alfa 6. This had an all-new 2.5-litre V-6 with belt-driven single overhead camshafts, a superbly smooth engine that lives on in today's 164. When this was inserted in the coupé in 1980 to create the GTV 6, Alfa once again had a flagship sporting machine. Although its 160 bhp wasn't as powerful as the Montreal's V-8, the neater, lighter GTV 6 was almost as fast – an under-rated car that typifies the Alfa sporting spirit – fine looks and a magnificent engine.

SPECIFICATIONS	2600 SPRINT (1962)	MONTREAL (1971)	GTV 6 2.5 (1980)
ENGINE	6-cyl dohc 2584 cc	V-8 dohc 2593 cc	V-6 sohc 2492 cc
POWER	145 bhp @ 5900 rpm	200 bhp @ 6500 rpm	160 bhp @ 5600 rpm
TRANSMISSION	Manual 5-speed	Manual 5-speed	Manual 5-speed
CHASSIS	Unitary steel construction (*all models*)		
BRAKES	Disc /drum	Discs all round	Discs all round
TOP SPEED	125 mph	135 mph	132 mph
0-60 MPH 0-100 MPH	10.4 sec 25.6 sec	8.1 sec 21.7 sec	8.4 sec 22.4 sec

Above: When the 2-litre 4-cylinder engines were replaced by the new 2.6-litre 'six' in 1962, the big Alfas had the performance to match the image.

Below: Under-rated style; the GTV 6 used the smooth 2.5-litre V-6 in what had started life as the Alfetta Coupé with a 1.8-litre four-cylinder.

ASTON MARTIN DB4, DB4GT ZAGATO, DB6

'A lot of publicity was gained by the claim that this was the first production car to achieve 0-100-0 mph in under 30 seconds.'

When the 3.7-litre DB4 was announced at the 1958 Motor Show, it was just what the British motoring scene needed, a car to match the Italian Ferraris and the German Mercedes 300SL and hold its place in the top flight of *Gran Turismo* machines. Good though the DB2 had been in its day, it didn't have the outright performance to match even the Jaguar sports cars. But the DB4 had the 140 mph pace and it looked the part; it was styled by the Italian coachbuilder Touring in Milan, and featured Touring's Superleggera principle of using a multiplicity of small tubes to carry the aluminium bodywork. It was also a proper four-seater.

The DB4's chassis was a steel platform made from a number of small pressings welded together in a large jig; given the expected numbers it wasn't viable to make a large single pressing tool. Its suspension system was conventional for the day with a double wishbone system at the front and a well located live rear axle, and disc brakes were used all round. Tadek Marek designed a new engine, an aluminium straight-six with twin overhead camshafts; in its first form it developed a genuine 220 bhp which was enough to give the car a remarkable 0-100 mph time of 20 seconds, ten seconds faster than the 3-litre DB2/4 had managed. A lot of publicity was gained by the claim that this was the first production car to achieve 0-100-0 mph in under 30 seconds.

Using Italian Touring bodywork, the DB4 was Britain's answer to Ferrari when it arrived in 1958. Convertible versions joined the range in 1961, this being a 1963 model.

Much of Aston Martin's credibility had been based on racing success and the 'fifties DB3 , DB3S and DBR-1 sports-racing cars had used developments of the DB2 engine. Long distance racing in the early 'sixties was moving towards GT cars, so Aston Martin introduced the DB4GT in 1959 – a DB4 with 5 inches removed from the wheelbase and the engine tuned with triple Weber carburetters to produce a genuine 272 bhp, enough to take the maximum speed up to 152 mph; since it reached 100 mph in 14 seconds, the DB4GT's claim for 0-100-0 mph was under 20 seconds.

Racing thoughts went one stage further in 1960 with the introduction of a new version of the DB4GT using lightweight bodywork from Zagato, also from Milan and thus neighbours of Touring. While the road versions were only a little lighter than the DB4GT, the racing versions could be a useful 150 lbs lighter; the performance was in fact very similar, but the DB4GT Zagato was to prove one of the greatest shapes of all time and with only 19 built, it was also one of the rarest production cars. In 1962/3 Aston Martin also built four very special racing GT cars; Project 212 and 215 were prototypes, but the two Project 214 cars used nominal DB4GT chassis, so the Zagato-bodied cars were really only raced by privateers.

The Project cars were the last Aston Martins to be raced directly by the factory. The DB5 that followed in 1963 was built solely to provide comfortable high speed touring; with its engine size increased to 4-litres, it was faster than the DB4 but couldn't match the lightweight versions. In style it was a DB4 with the cowled head-lights of the DB4GT, but it became the best known Aston shape of all thanks to the James Bond film *Goldfinger*.

Two years on came the DB6 with an extra 4 inches in the wheelbase to make the back seats a little more comfortable; the main recognition point though was the flat vertical tail panel with a slight kick-up on the boot-lid, introduced to improve high-speed stability. Overall the style remained

SPECIFICATION	DB4 (1958)	DB4GT (1959)	DB6 (1965)
ENGINE	6-cyl 3670 cc	6-cyl 3670 cc	6-cyl 3995 cc
HORSEPOWER	220 bhp @ 5500 rpm	272 bhp @ 6000 rpm	270 bhp @ 6000 rpm
TRANSMISSION	Manual 4-speed	Manual 5-speed	Manual 5-speed
CHASSIS	Steel platform chassis with aluminium body panels (*all models*)		
BRAKES	Disc brakes all round (*all models*)		
TOP SPEED	140 mph	152 mph	152 mph
0-60 MPH 0-100 MPH	8.9 sec 20.9 sec	6.4 sec 14.2 sec	6.0 sec 14.9 sec

Zagato, Milan built just 19 special DB4GTs in the 1962-4 period, although they built a further four replicas in 1989.

Below: Although the DB4 had two rear seats, an extra 4 inches in the DB6 wheelbase made it somewhat more comfortable for adults.

very similar to that of the original DB4, but the Superleggera construction system had been replaced by conventional and heavier steel pressings. The most powerful DB6 had a genuine 270 bhp which gave it a maximum speed of 150 mph and acceleration to match the DB4GT.

By the time the DB6 Mk.II came out in 1969 with wider wheels and optional fuel injection, the new generation DBS had already been in production for two years and the V-8 engine had arrived. Convertible versions of all three models were produced, but the name Volante was only introduced for the DB6 – a DB6 Mk.II Volante is still owned by HRH Prince Charles.

'This began to look more like an American muscle car than the best of British.'

ASTON MARTIN DBS, VOLANTE, VANTAGE ZAGATO

From its concept in the late 'thirties, the *Gran Turismo* had grown from a two-seater with luggage space to the 2+2, for the sporting driver with small children. Many sports car manufacturers have stopped there, unwilling to stretch their cars further into the realms of the saloon. But Aston Martin moved on to ensure that the keen owner didn't have to sell the car when his children got too big, and he could reasonably consider using it as company transport. The DB4 and DB5 could just carry four adults, the DB6 made the back seat comfortable for longer journeys, but the DBS was conceived to carry four adults and luggage for as far as they wanted, in as much comfort as could be expected back in 1967.

SPECIFICATION	DBS (1967)	V8 VOLANTE (1988)	VANTAGE ZAGATO (1987)
ENGINE	Straight 6, 3995 cc	Aluminium V-8, 5340 cc with injection or Webers	
HORSEPOWER	270 bhp @ 6000 rpm	305 bhp @ 5500 rpm	432 bhp @ 6200 rpm
TRANSMISSION	Manual 5-speed ZF with 3-speed automatic optional on non-Vantage		
CHASSIS	Steel platform with aluminium body panels (*all models*)		
BRAKES	Disc brakes all round (*all models*)		
TOP SPEED	141 mph	145 mph (auto)	186 mph
0-60 MPH 0-100 MPH	7.1 sec 18.0 sec	7.7 sec 17.3 sec	4.8 sec 11.3 sec

The first DBS models used the old six-cylinder engine before the V-8 came in 1969; this is one of the prototypes which came in between.

Although three of the major Italian design houses – Bertone, Touring and Zagato – had been associated with various DB4 models, the DBS was the work of Aston's own young designer William Towns. It followed the classic fast-back shape, but brought in elements of the British razor-edge where top joined side; in its early days with the edges still sharp it had a graceful elegance that it was to lose as humps and protrusions were added during the 20 years that it was to stay in production.

The problem with adding refinement and space is that weight and size increase, so you need a bigger engine to run at the same speed, let alone keep ahead of the field. The new V-8 engine, designed for the DBS, still wasn't ready when the rest of the car was poised to start production, so the top DB6 engine was inserted, the 4-litre straight-6 developing 280 bhp; while this propelled the DB6 at 150 mph, the heavier wider DBS would only manage 140 mph and was left behind in the dash from the lights. But that really didn't matter too much; it was a far more refined car. When the 5.3-litre V-8 arrived two years later it used Bosch fuel injection to deliver 315 bhp and a lot more torque; straight away it was a 160 mph motorcar – refinement now with performance.

Over the years, emission laws have made it harder to produce the power, so the standard V-8 was producing just 305 bhp twenty years later, once more with fuel injection, but very much cleaner. Meanwhile a Vantage high performance version had arrived in 1977 with 375 bhp; with wider wheel arch flares, a kick-up tail spoiler and a front air-dam, this began to look more like an American muscle car than the best of British – ten years of panel beating had worn the sharp edges of the formers too, so the lines were no longer so well defined.

The convertible Volante followed a year later in response to American demand and remained a very popular model until it was replaced in 1989; it is still very much in classic demand, as many prefer its lines to those of the current Virage. For most of its life it was powered by the standard V-8, but towards the end there were Vantage Volantes with the extra power and the muscular bulges if you wanted them – the Prince of Wales didn't on his latest Volante.

Fast though the Vantage was with a maximum speed around 170 mph, people expected even more from the mid-'eighties supercars although most of those were mid-engined two-seaters. Aston Martin once more tied up with Zagato to produce a limited edition lighter, more aerodynamic body for the Vantage for which Aston would produce a special 430 bhp version of the faithful 5.3-litre V-8; launched as a concept in 1986, the Vantage Zagato started production in 1987. With the full 430 bhp and gearing to match, the car tested recorded 299 km/h (186 mph) – just short of the target 300 km/h; most, though, were made with a smaller quieter exhaust system and gearing more suited to traffic. Just 51 were produced before a more exclusive convertible version arrived, the Volante Zagato; only 36 of these were built and used the 305 bhp fuel injection engine, so their bonnets lacked the Vantage hump.

The DBS was a very elegant car in its own right, but it spawned some fascinating derivatives too.

The elegant Volante remained one of the most popular V-8 models from its 1978 inception through to 1989; a 1980 model is shown.

To put the name up amongst the 300 km/h supercars, Aston Martin returned to Zagato to clothe a 430 bhp version of the Vantage. This 1987 car was the 22nd out of a 51-car run.

AUSTIN-HEALEY 100/4, SPRITE, 3000

'It was certainly a genuine 100 mph car which was an instant success.'

Following the war, British motor industry policy was to export as much as possible in the quest for harder currencies, America being the obvious target. But the product had to be right too. Lord Nuffield's MG had already established its name. Leonard Lord's 1948 Austin Atlantic – styled specifically for the American market – failed and had gone by 1952. Lord needed a proper British sports car, so he approached two established members of the sports car set in early 1952, Jensen and Frazer Nash to propose a new design using Austin components. He knew that Donald Healey was working on a similar car as he had already agreed to provide A90 engines and gearboxes. All three were planning to exhibit their 'Austins' at the 1952 Motor Show.

Frazer Nash simply inserted an A90 engine, gearbox and back axle into an existing model which could never have been volume produced. Jensen produced a nice looking coupé but didn't make the show. The Healey 100 arrived late but made an instant impact on visitors including Leonard Lord and Lord Nuffield – Austin having merged with Morris earlier that year to make BMC. That night, Healey and Lord agreed terms and the next day the car was rebadged as an Austin-Healey.

The new 100 used a simple platform chassis which was mated to the Gerry Coaker designed body by Jensen, who gained the contract to assemble body-chassis units for all the big Austin-Healeys, bar a handful, for Austin to assemble at Longbridge, before this was transferred to Abingdon in late 1957. The A90 engine was a simple low-revving four-cylinder which developed 90 bhp in Healey tune; the initial series used the A90 gearbox without first gear, but coupled the upper two ratios to a Laycock overdrive to give a choice of five gears. Maximum speeds obtained by the magazines varied from 101 to 108 mph depending mostly on whether the ingenious screen was folded flat or not, but it was certainly a genuine 100 mph car which was an instant success. A second series in 1955 brought in a 4-speed gearbox from the 6-cylinder A90, still with an overdrive which was to remain a big Healey feature.

Based on Austin A90 components, the Healey 100 was a simple but very effective design which marked the transition from cycle-winged MGs to modern style, here a 1955 example.

Although the 100M engine modifications could take the output to 110 bhp, and the competition S would produce 132 bhp, a new 102 bhp 2639 cc Austin 6-cylinder unit was inserted in 1956 to make the 100/6 a smoother and slightly faster car. For 1959 this was enlarged to 2912 cc and the legendary Healey 3000 was born. Over the next nine years the power was gradually increased from the initial 124 bhp to 150 bhp for the 3000 Mk.III, by which time the car had wind-up windows and a wooden dash to make it a very civilised road sports car, still with the good looks of the original 100, albeit in a chassis that had been lengthened to take the six.

Throughout its life the big Healey was an effective competition car, particularly in rallying, even when long-distance road events changed to forestry stages where the Healey's limited ground clearance could be a problem – they used side exhausts. It finally ceased production in 1968 when American safety laws became too stringent; despite the fact that over 80 per cent of the 73,000 big Healeys went to America, it was judged too costly to modify the design.

SPECIFICATIONS	100/4 (1952)	3000 Mk.III (1964)	Sprite (1958)
ENGINE	4-cyl , 2660 cc	6-cyl 2912 cc	4-cyl 948 cc
POWER	90 bhp @ 4000 rpm	150 bhp @ 5250 rpm	43 bhp @ 5200 rpm
TRANSMISSION	Manual 3-speed & o/d	Manual 4-speed & o/d	Manual 4-speed
CHASSIS	Unitary steel chassis (*all models*)		
BRAKES	Drums	Disc/drum	Drums
TOP SPEED	103 mph	122 mph	83 mph
0-60 MPH	11.7 sec	9.8 sec	20.5 sec
0-100 MPH	—	23.7 sec	—

Above: The frog-eye Sprite arrived in 1958 using the BMC A-series engine in a new unitary chassis, to give cheap 80 mph performance for the young enthusiast.

Left: The big Healey gained a 2.6-litre six-cylinder engine in 1956; this became the 3000 in 1959. This Mk.II version has the nominal extra rear seats.

At the time that the big Healey was about to become a six-cylinder, Donald Healey was working on a little sister using the A-series power train, thus giving BMC a complete sports car range; the MGA used the B-series and the big Healey the C-series. The new Austin-Healey Sprite, the original frog-eye, came out in 1958 with a little 948 cc engine producing 43 bhp; while this was less than even an MG TC, its light weight and full-width bodywork allowed it a maximum speed of over 80 mph and reasonable acceleration – it wasn't fast but it was a very good, cheap sports car. Unfortunately it lost its cheeky looks when the Mk.II came out with a parallel MG Midget in 1961. Over the ensuing years, the engine was gradually uprated to 1275 cc and the last Sprite and the last Austin-Healey were built in 1971.

BENTLEY CONTINENTAL

Only a handful of British cars have won the great 24-hour race at Le Mans, and Bentley won it five times in the period 1924-30. Then came the Depression and Bentley was taken over by Rolls-Royce in 1931, but the Le Mans reputation has been preserved; the Bentley has always been considered as the sporting Rolls even though the basic engines have been shared. Through the 'thirties, the Bentley was 'The Silent Sports Car', the cars very different in outward appearance and their engines more powerful. In the post-war period, most Rolls models have had a matching Bentley with just a radiator change, but there have been a number of more sporting Bentleys with no Rolls equivalent; some have simply had more sporting bodywork, others have had more power. Over the period from 1952, the Continentals have mostly offered both; more performance and their own distinctive lines.

First of these were the 1952 R-type Continentals, based on the Bentley R-type and Rolls Silver Dawn. Both were available as chassis only for the coachbuilders and a handful were bodied by other specialists, but the true Continental was only bodied by H.J. Mulliner. Quite unlike any previous standard model, it featured a streamlined body with a long sloping tail, flanked by rear wings finishing in razor-edged fins; powered by an improved version of the standard 4566 cc six-cylinder, the prototype lapped the banked Montlhery circuit at 118 mph at a time when the standard saloon could only just achieve 100 mph; the Continental had a higher back axle ratio as well as closer ratios in the manual gearbox – it would do nearly 80 mph in second gear!

That such a normally conservative company could produce a car designed unashamedly for high speed was largely due to the Paris distributor, Walter Sleator, and Bentley's chief engineer, Ivan

The R-type Continental was one of the most desirable cars of all in the early 'fifties, combining genuine high performance with Bentley comforts.

When the S-type arrived, the Continental chassis was used by other coachbuilders for elegant two-door styles including convertibles.

Evernden. They were responsible for the creation of La Streamline, a 1938 4.25-litre with a striking fastback body by Van Vooren, commissioned for Andre Embiricos. The factory, too, had van Vooren create the Corniche in 1939; it too featured a non-Bentley radiator, but its fastback was interrupted by a small boot bulge. The next stage in the saga moves to the 1948 Paris Motor Show for which Sleator commissioned Pinin Farina (still a separated name then) to produce a new 2-door fastback saloon. Its profile followed that of the epochal Cisitalia GT, while the frontal aspect featured a Bentley grille of altered proportions; the grille was changed for 1950. Bentley's John Blatchley then made subtle alterations to what had been termed Corniche II, insetting the headlights from the wings, installing a proper full Bentley radiator and breaking up the flanks with a pronounced rear wing line. The resultant Continental was launched in 1952 as the world's fastest four-seater.

When Bentley introduced the S-type with a 4.9-litre engine, the Mulliner Continental continued alongside Park Ward's saloon and convertible versions. The fastback shape ceased in 1959 after a total of 411 had been built, due to the introduction of the S2 with the new V-8 engine which brought the saloon performance up to Continental levels. The Continental name was subsequently used to separate equivalent Rolls and Bentley models, but 1985 saw the first stage of bringing back a separate Continental model. At the Geneva Show, the company displayed a prototype two-door fast-back, the work of John Heffernan and Ken Greenley; called the Bentley 90, it was the forerunner of the new Continental R launched in 1991 using the 6.75-litre Turbo R model as a base.

Rolls had introduced the Mulsanne name (after the Le Mans straight) in 1980 to separate the Bentley from the identical Rolls Silver Spirit, but the introduction of the 320 bhp Mulsanne Turbo in 1982 was a positive move to establish separate marque identities (Rolls have never published power figures). This became the Turbo R in 1985. The big turbo engine received a 40 bhp increase in 1993, and in 1994 a limited S version was introduced with over 400 bhp. These engines are used in the Continental R and S to create the first Bentleys to exceed 150 mph, although the S was discontinued at the beginning of 1995. However the Bentley Continental is back with a classic vengeance.

With the 1991 Continental R, Bentley once more had an unique style not shared with Rolls-Royce. This 1994 example has the later lower profile tyres.

'It would do nearly 80 mph in second gear!'

SPECIFICATIONS	R-TYPE (1952)	S-TYPE (1956)	R (1991)
ENGINE	6-cyl 4566 cc	6-cyl 4887 cc	Turbo V-8 6750 cc
POWER	Not quoted	Not quoted	c.360 bhp @ 4200 rpm
TRANSMISSION	Manual 4-speed	Manual 4-speed	Auto 4-speed
CHASSIS	Separate steel chassis with steel body		Unitary steel
BRAKES	Drums	Drums	Discs with ABS
TOP SPEED	117 mph	120 mph	152 mph
0-60 MPH	13.5 sec	12.9 sec	6.2 sec

BMW 507, 3.0CSL, 635CSi

'Only just over 1000 CSLs were built and it has remained a desirable classic.'

Bayerische Motoren Werke has its roots in the building of World War I aero engines; the blue and white roundel comes from the image of a spinning propeller. The production of engines for planes, trucks and cars, was to continue through the 'twenties, with the company starting its famed motor cycle range in 1923 with the flat-twin shaft drive R32; the configuration has remained unchanged. But it wasn't until they took over the Eisenach Dixi company in 1928 that the company finally became motor manufacturers.

SPECIFICATION	507 (1956)	3.0CSL (1971)	635CSi (1978)
ENGINE	Aluminium V-8, 3168 cc	Straight-6, 3003 cc	Straight-6, 3453 cc
POWER	155 bhp @ 5000 rpm	200 bhp @ 5500 rpm	218 bhp @ 5200 rpm
TRANSMISSION	Manual 4-speed	Manual 5-speed	Manual 5-speed
CHASSIS	Steel frame	Unitary steel/ali panels	Unitary steel
BRAKES	Drums	Discs all round	Discs all round
TOP SPEED	125 mph	134 mph	140 mph
0-60 MPH 0-100 MPH	8.8 sec 22.6 sec	7.8 sec 20.2 sec	8.4 sec 19.8 sec

While there had been Dixis large and small, it was the production of the Austin 7 under licence that formed the basis of the BMW cars that were to follow. Early BMWs were small cars recognisably based on the Austin 7, but 1932 saw the arrival of the 3/20 as the first true BMW. A year later the 303 was launched with a little 1173 cc six-cylinder overhead valve engine in a twin-tube chassis with independent front suspension, first of the line that was to yield such sporting legends as the 2-litre 328 and the coupé 327/80 which formed the basis of the first post-war Bristol.

After the war, BMW production could only start slowly with revised, and bigger versions, of the pre-war cars, the 501 appearing in 1951. The 502 followed with an all-aluminium 2.6-litre V-8; this engine, enlarged to 3.2-litres, was used in the first post-war coupé and its convertible equivalent the 1956 503, as well as the short-wheelbase 507 two-seater sports car; with 150 bhp this was a 125 mph sporting machine of very elegant style. But all the 50 series cars were produced in small numbers, 6000 502s over seven years and only 253 of the 507 in four years; BMW's volume manufacture was concentrated on the Isetta, using a motor-cycle engine in what was initially just a town car before it grew to the 700 range.

A major shake-up brought an all-new range out in 1961, the four-door 1500 with a style and an

BMW production started slowly after the war with large saloons. The first sports car came in 1956, the 507, which went as well as it looked with a 155 bhp 3.2-litre V-8.

The 3.0CSL was very similar to the CSi but formed the basis of the racing version; with all its extras, it could look like this 'Batmobile'.

engine design that has continued recognisably through to the present day. When the four-cylinder grew to six with the 1968 2500 range, BMW moved back into the luxury class and brought out a coupé version once more, the 2800CS; that style was to stay through to 1975 by which time it had become the 3.0CSi. This was the basis for BMW's touring car racing entry, the CSL which used aluminium panels for its bonnet, boot and doors; a small bore increase in 1972 gave it just over 3-litres to change its racing class and a longer stroke in 1973 gave it 3.2-litres and 206 bhp. Only just over 1000 CSLs were built and it has remained a desirable classic, separated visually from its more numerous cousins by discreet coach-lines.

Meanwhile BMW had started to denote the different model ranges with the numerical series which remain to this day; first had been the 1972 5-series. Thus the new coupé replacement became the 6-series in early 1976, starting with the 630 and 633 CSi; while these were quite quick, they were no faster than the old 3.0CS or the four-door 7-series which followed in 1977. It wasn't until the arrival of the 218 bhp 635CSi (6-series, 3.5-litre engine, fuel injection) that the coupé had the performance to match its style, which had been enhanced by the usual sporting appendages – a front air-dam, a boot lid spoiler and coach-lines.

By the time BMW's motorsport division had produced the M635CSi in 1983 with a new 4-valve twin-overhead camshaft engine with 286 bhp, it had become a very fast car capable of over 150 mph; brakes and suspension had been suitably uprated. While most BMW coupés had been saloons with mildly altered two-door bodywork, 6-series was a separate model in its own right – a prelude to its 8-series replacement.

With the 6-series, BMW coupés returned to their own individual styles. With the Motorsport divisions' M-series came further body changes and 286 bhp for the M6.

CHEVROLET BEL AIR, CORVAIR, CAMARO

'Its long bonnet, low roof, short tail ponycar hallmarks would match many European GTs.'

Chevrolet wasn't the first to join General Motors; William Durant created that around Buick in 1908, and was in trouble by 1911. He left to form Chevrolet; five years later he exercised a reverse take-over and once more headed the giant. Chevrolet eventually became the model for the multitude. While the corporation developed economies of scale in the supplies of parts, each division retained a remarkable degree of autonomy for many years in style and power units.

After the second world war Chevrolet continued to produce their 1942 range, the first all-new model coming in 1949, the Styleline. The Bel Air joined the range as the the two-door hardtop for 1950 during which year Chevrolet offered their first automatic transmission, the Powerglide. Until 1955, the power unit had been a pre-war six-cylinder unit of varying capacities between 3.54 and 3.85-litres; however that year saw the introduction of Ed Cole's small-block V-8, initially a 4.34-litre, which gave a lift to the Corvette as well as the Bel Air's top line models.

This was the era of heavy chrome, tail fins and Chevrolet's new wrap-round screen with its vertical pillars. The 1957 range had everything in abundance and there were 19 models in the range of which the convertible was top; it had 110 mph performance too with the latest V-8, in fuel-injected 4.6-litre form, producing 283 bhp. The '57 Bel Air convertible was one of the great cars of that fabulous finny era.

Meanwhile Chevrolet had been developing a compact to take on the growing number of smaller imports like the VW Beetle. While Ford produced the conventional Falcon, Chevrolet took the unorthodox route and created the Corvair for 1960 as a grown-up VW with American styling; uncertain of the reaction to a rear-engined car, they styled it deliberately to look a front-engined car, albeit without a radiator grille. The VW design features that influenced the Corvair were the swing-axle rear suspension and an air-cooled engine, a flat-6 2.3-litre with 80 or 95 bhp. It was also Chevrolet's first unitary construction chassis.

The Corvair was really quite a good car; its styling was refreshingly clean after the finny era and the 2-door Monza Coupé was attractive to any eyes. The engine was good, too, but the handling was even-more tail-happy than a Beetle's and safety campaigner, Ralph Nader, effectively killed the car. Even a change in rear suspension to a double wishbone principle failed to convince the

Heavy chrome bumpers, exaggerated tail fins and a powerful V-8 made the 1957 Bel-Air one of the classic American cars of the late 'fifties.

The Corvair had a refreshingly uncluttered style that should have appealed to America as the home-grown answer to the VW Beetle, but safety campaigner Nader killed it.

American market that the Corvair was a nice car quite capable of taking the 180 bhp of the top 2.7-litre turbocharged version. Production ran through to 1969 but the numbers never justified the bold step of selling a radical design to America.

In the wake of the Compact market for down-sized leviathans came a demand for affordable sports compacts, cars that would satisfy the desire of American youth to drag-race away from the lights, but equally be a stylish second car. The Ford Mustang was first in the frame in 1964. GM had hoped the revised Corvair would find its place in this new Ponycar market, but Nader ensured it didn't. However, Chevrolet had a possible alternative on the back-burner, but Ford had two years of unrivalled sales before the new Camaro arrived. This was an all-new car, not just a rebodied version of the Compact Chevy II. While it was essentially a unitary construction car, it had a separate rubber-mounted front sub-frame for a more comfortable shock-free ride; as with Ford there was a low-cost base model with a 140 bhp 'six' but a host of performance options up to a 325 bhp 6.5-litre V-8; Regular Performance Options – RPOs in Chevrolet language – would include such as RS (Rally Sport handling pack) and SS (Super Sport performance pack) complete with body decals.

The Camaro certainly had style; its long bonnet, low roof, short tail ponycar hallmarks would match many European GTs; like many of those, there was also a version that could be converted for racing, Trans-Am saloon racing with the Z-28 package. To match the regulations, the Z-28 was a 5-litre unit developed from the small-block 327 cu.in with a forged short-stroke crankshaft with a factory rating of 290 bhp, although a blue-printed 400 bhp was possible; period observers reckon the Z-28 had nearer 350 bhp. It proved to be a race-winner and Z-28 Camaros won their Trans-Am category in 1968 and 1969, after which Z-28 became a model rather than just an RPO.

The Camaro name has lived on through many changes but always a high-style pony car and still with a live rear axle, but even the top 1995 car cannot match the Z-28 for sheer power performance.

Chevrolet's Camaro pony-car arrived two years after the Mustang, but came with all possible options. This 1967 car has the Z-28 engine with the Rally Sport handling package.

SPECIFICATION	BEL AIR (1957)	CORVAIR MONZA (1966)	CAMARO Z-28 (1968)
ENGINE	V-8 4637 cc	Flat-6 2683 cc	V-8 4949 cc
POWER	283 bhp @ 6200 rpm	140 bhp @ 5200 rpm	290 bhp @ 5800 rpm
TRANSMISSION	Manual 4-speed	Manual 4-speed	Manual 4-speed
CHASSIS	Separate steel chassis	Unitary steel	Unitary steel
BRAKES	Drums	Drums	Disc/drum
TOP SPEED	112 mph	106 mph	133 mph
0-60 MPH	8.6 sec	11.4 sec	7.4 sec

CHEVROLET CORVETTE, STING RAY, STINGRAY

'The Corvette began to develop a muscle-car image that had been lacking.'

Returning from Europe at the end of the second war, the motor-minded GI brought back an MG; it was the nearest thing for wind-in-the-hair sports car motoring to the Jeep that so many had enjoyed driving on active service. European sports cars were lapped up by post-war America, particularly the offerings from MG and Jaguar.

General Motors were the only ones to pick up the gauntlet with any real determination, starting work on the Corvette in 1951. Styled by the legendary Harley Earl with a chassis drawn up by European suspension expert Maurice Olley it was well received when it was launched in 1953, but its reliance on existing saloon car hardware nearly spelled disaster; a two-speed automatic transmission, and a 3.8-litre six – even when tuned to 150 bhp – did not spell sporting performance when measured against the Jaguar XK120. Sales were slow until 1955 when a manual 3-speed gearbox became available and the first V-8 was installed with 195 bhp; sales improved but it wasn't until the 1956 restyle that the Corvette began to develop a muscle-car image that had been lacking .

Available horsepower increased by leaps and bounds during the six-year production run. The original 265 cu.in (4.3-litre) had 225 bhp in 1956 which gave nearly 120 mph; the capacity grew to 283 cu.in and 283 bhp for the top option in 1957 together with a 4-speed manual transmission. For 1962, the 283 had been enlarged to 327 cu.in (5.3-litres) with up to 360 bhp on tap with fuel injection; the rounded rear end had been given a duck-tail the year before and the Corvette grille 'teeth' replaced by a mesh. Much of the credit for taking the Corvette forward into the high-performance league is due to Zora Arkus-Duntov who had joined GM in 1953, and he continued to be known as the father of the real Corvette.

The first big step in the Corvette's design story came in 1963 with the Sting Ray – a European-type fast-back coupé and an equally attractive convertible. Under the new skin was a redesigned chassis featuring independent rear suspension for the first time, and disc brakes were soon to be an option. The same engines were carried over and the fastest version could almost reach 150 mph, but it was the acceleration figures

Low nose, coke-bottle sills and a T-bar roof made the 1968 restyle even more European, but emission laws gradually stifled performance during its 15-year model life.

that were impressive in European terms with 0-60 mph in 6.2 sec and 0-100 mph in 15.6 sec.

From the introduction of the V-8 onwards, Corvettes had been very much a part of the American racing scene, but by 1965 they were being consistently beaten by the 7-litre Shelby Cobras. Even more power was needed. Just as Shelby had taken out Ford's small-block 289 cu.in from the AC and dropped in the big-block 427 cu.in, so Duntov put a Chevrolet big-block engine into the top Corvette; this was a 425 bhp 396 cu.in (6.5-litre) for 1965, enlarged the following year to 427 cu.in. There was always a variety of axle ratios available but Americans preferred the lower ones for acceleration; with such a ratio, the Corvette 427 could reach 100 mph in 11.2 sec, but it was limited to 140 mph – longer ratios would give nearer 160 mph. Classic Corvette enthusiasts go for the last two years of the Sting Ray's production; the emission-conscious 'seventies were to see emasculated outputs severely restricting performance.

The next style in 1968 produced an even more European shape, longer, lower and less aggressive with coke-bottle sills and a neat removable T-bar roof; after its first year it became the Stingray (one word). Initially the same range of engines gave similar performance to that of its predecessors, but from 1972 onwards this declined. Even the big block engine was down to 270 bhp before it was dropped in 1974; by 1978 the 350 cu.in engine (5.7-litres) was only giving 185 bhp. More performance had to come from less weight which was progressively reduced over 1980-82.

The final version of the big Corvettes was the 1982 Collector Edition. The shape had received a soft front end in 1974, losing its chrome bumpers, and a fast-back rear window in 1978; for this edition the large rear window became a hatch-back. It was a desirable final fling before the new car arrived in 1983.

SPECIFICATION	CORVETTE (1953)	STING RAY (1967)	STINGRAY (1978)
ENGINE	6-cyl 3860 cc	V-8 5360 cc	V-8 5735 cc
POWER	150 bhp @ 4200 rpm	360 bhp @ 6000 rpm	185 @ 4000 rpm
TRANSMISSION	Auto 2-speed	Manual 4-speed	Auto 3-speed
CHASSIS	Steel with glassfibre body panels (*all models*)		
BRAKES	Drums all round	Disc brake option	Discs all round
TOP SPEED	105 mph	147 mph	125 mph
0-60 MPH 0-100 MPH	11.0 sec —	6.2 sec 15.6 sec	8.7 sec 25.0 sec

This 1954 Corvette is one of the original series with the sluggish six-cylinder engine; the arrival of the V-8 in 1955 set the true Corvette on its muscular way.

European fast-back styles influenced the 1963 Sting Ray which came in coupé and convertible forms.

CHRYSLER 300B, DODGE CHARGER, PLYMOUTH GTX

'These fantastic looking cars would lap some of the ovals at over 200 mph.'

This Chrysler trio were all about performance, whether on the street, the drag-strips or the high-speed Ovals. American auto enthusiasm in the 'fifties and 'sixties was very straight-line orientated; roadholding and braking were lesser considerations. Europeans preferred road-racing where sheer power was only part of the equation in making a car quick around a track with corners. Thus, to Europeans, these American classics are rarities; they are each pretty rare in America too. However Jensen, Bristol and Facel-Vega, appreciating the engineering, adopted complete Chrysler engine/transmission units, so the name was associated with high performance in Europe.

Chrysler was a late starter in automobile manufacture. Walter Chrysler had risen through the Buick ranks to become its president in 1920; after a couple of years with Willys he joined Maxwell and the Chrysler marque was created from that in 1924. Four years later he launched the low-cost Plymouth range and took over Dodge (founded in 1914). Chrysler was on his way to make the big two (Ford and General Motors) into the big three; by the time he died in 1940 they had toppled Ford from the second slot.

As with the rest of the American auto-makers, Chrysler's post-war production was pre-war based, a new range only emerging for 1949; this was over-conservative and a sales slip behind Ford demanded a hefty restyle. This was entrusted to Virgil Exner; having headed Pontiac style pre-war, followed by Studebaker with Raymond Loewy, he joined Chrysler in 1949 but spent his first four years designing idea/dream cars in association with the Italian Ghia company who put them into the metal; Exner's take-over as design chief in 1953 was to draw heavily on the advanced themes established during the Italian association.

A striking addition to the 1955 range was a revised and regrilled 2-door New Yorker called the 300, Chrysler's answer to the Ford Thunderbird; what set it apart was the adoption of Chrysler's V-8, the first Hemi (short for the hemispherical combustion chamber with inclined valves), which had been brought into the range in 1951. With 331 cu.in (5.4-litres) and 300 bhp it was the most powerful engine on the American roads. With this, Chrysler won two stock-car (showroom stock – near standard) championships in 1955, but they only built 1725 of this version. It was the start of the 'win on Sunday, sell on Monday' philosophy in Detroit.

For 1956, the 300B was restyled at the rear with fins reminiscent of the Ghia FliteSweep and

The Dodge Charger was Chrysler's other racer to match the Plymouth Belvedere. This 1970 Special Edition has the 440 cu.in wedge-head engine.

the engine uprated still further to 5.8-litres and 355 bhp; 1957's 300C went still further with a 390 bhp 6.4-litre. American manufacturers agreed to stop racing at the end of 1957, and hemi-engines were expensive to build, so 1959 saw a change to wedge-head, still with engines over 6-litres; the 300s were to continue but lacked the charisma of the 300B and 300C.

Racing gradually returned on the manufacturer's agenda and Chrysler built a new race-only 426 hemi (6.98-litres) for the 1964 NASCAR season; after Chrysler products had swept the board, NASCAR rules demanded 500 identical cars. After a year off, Chrysler responded with the Dodge Charger using a 426 street-hemi developing up to 425 bhp; the Plymouth Belvedere followed suit and soon the hemi was available in the Dodge Challenger and Plymouth Barracuda pony-cars. NASCAR racing still occupied the Chrysler mind each year, and 1969 saw the Dodge Daytona Charger complete with droop-snoot nose, retracting headlights and a massive rear wing on tall side-plates. Plymouth's Belvedere had steadily developed through the GTX into the Superbird Road Runner of 1970 to match the Daytona Charger. Chrysler cleaned up in 1970 and these fantastic looking cars would lap some of the ovals at over 200 mph and reach 60 mph in under 5 seconds; although around 1500 were built, NASCAR forced wing-cars to have smaller engines for 1971.

Meanwhile the hemi-option had been somewhat expensive for the non-racer who still wanted to burn up the street tarmac, so the 1966 range also included a conventionally-headed 440 cu.in V-8 (7.2-litre). A high performance Magnum version (Super Commando for Plymouth) was introduced for 1967 with 375 bhp. A revised Dodge Charger shape came along in 1968, longer and cleaner, and a new 6-pack carburetter was added to the option list in 1969 to give 390 bhp. Chrysler continued their high-power options through 1971, when a new Charger shape came out, but that was the last year of the classic muscle cars.

The 1955 300 was the first of the American muscle cars with a 300 bhp hemi V-8; this 1956 300B had 355 bhp.

Shown below is the 1967 Plymouth Belvedere GTX440.

SPECIFICATION	CHRYSLER 300C (1957)	DODGE CHARGER (1967)	PLYMOUTH GTX (1968)
ENGINE	V-8 Hemi, 6426 cc	V-8, 7210 cc	V-8 Hemi, 6974 cc
POWER	390 bhp @ 5200 rpm	375 bhp @ 4600 rpm	425 bhp @ 5000 rpm
TRANSMISSION	Auto 3-speed	Auto 3-speed	Auto 3-speed
CHASSIS	Separate steel	Unitary steel	Unitary steel
BRAKES	Drum brakes	Drum brakes	Disc/drum
TOP SPEED	125 mph	128 mph	144 mph
0-60 MPH	8.4 sec	6.8 sec	6.3 sec

CITROEN LIGHT 15, DS19, SM

'This was one of motoring's great moments in history, a car so advanced that everything else was hidden in its technical shade.'

Citroen have long been known for producing slightly quirky cars, cars that are out of the ordinary run and frequently herald the way ahead for the motor industry. The company was founded by Andre Citroen in 1913 as gear manufacturers, hence the famous herring-bone motif. Cars came in 1919, with the popular 5CV soon to contribute to a production rate of 250 cars per day by 1924 – a pressed steel saloon version arrived in 1925; Citroen factories were set up in Britain (1926), Germany and Italy.

The famous Traction-Avant arrived in 1934. This set Citroen on the front-wheel-drive path; the compact power train system had obvious advantages which would be proved with time, but the distinguishing feature then was the attractively low lines that could be achieved without a prop-shaft – the gear lever came through the dashboard. With independent torsion bar suspension at the front and a light beam axle at the rear, it was also advanced in comfort. Its construction, too, was *avant-garde* with a pressed steel unitary frame while the engine was an overhead valve unit with pressed in wet liners – both features well in advance of others. Initially the engine range covered 1303 cc – the French 7 was the English Super Modern 12 – and 1529 cc 7S; for 1935 both were given a longer stroke, so the 7 grew to 1628 cc which was still called a 12HP as the English system calculated tax horsepower on the engine bore regardless of stroke, the French using a different system. The 7S with 1911 cc became the *Onze Legere*, the English Light 15, and the longer *Onze Normale* became the Big 15.

For 1939, a six-cylinder 2.9-litre (same bore and stroke as the 1911cc four) was added – 15CV for the French and 22.6HP for the English who just called it the Six.

The Light 15 and Six continued in production after the war until 1955, although a French *Onze Legere* was still available until 1957. It was a remarkable production span for a car that was still very modern in design. For 1954, the Six had been given oleo-pneumatic independent rear suspension as a prelude to the launch of the DS19 the following year.

This was one of motoring's great moments in history, a car so advanced that everything else was hidden in its technical shade, even the 'Mark I' Jaguar of the same year. To start with, it was aerodynamically styled by the same Bertoni who had designed the Light 15 shape; it had no obvious grille as the radiator intake was under the bumper line. Its construction extended the unitary principles by having a complete welded-up pressed steel frame with detachable wings and glassfibre

The Traction Avant was launched in 1934 but it was still a remarkable car in 1953 when this Light 15 was made.

roof. And the Six's hydraulic suspension system had expanded to control front and rear suspensions, brakes, clutch and provide steering assistance. Even though the chosen engine was based on the old 1911 cc 'four', this had been developed with a new cylinder head with hemi-inclined valves and a twin-choke compound Weber carburetter, so the unit developed the same 75 bhp as the previous Six. Where the Six could reach 83 mph, the new DS19 was 5 mph faster. While it took a little time to learn to drive such an unorthodox car, the rewards came with a very comfortable ride, easy high-speed cruising and spacious, airy seating for five adults.

Over the next 20 years there would be a few changes but nothing fundamental. A cheaper ID19 version had a single-choke carburetter and a normal gearchange; new short-stroke 1985 cc engines came in 1966 with a DS21 having a 2175 cc version. In 1968 the headlights were hidden behind glass as part of an even cleaner front end style, and a DS23 – 2347 cc and 115 bhp – came in 1972; when electronic fuel injection was specified, 130 bhp made the DS23 into a 120 mph car.

Meanwhile Citroen had effectively taken over Maserati in 1969. The Italian company designed a four-cam 2.7-litre V-6 for a new sporting DS, a little shorter, but with recognisable family styling. Given 170 bhp, the SM could achieve 135 mph. While the suspension was firmer and the steering more direct, the basic Citroen hydraulic system was retained; it was a remarkably comfortable high speed tourer which, like the DS, was rewarding once you were accustomed to its intricacies.

Over that 40-year period, Citroen became renowned for advanced technology. Sadly the founder had seen none of its success. He had to sell out to Michelin in 1935 and died from cancer the same year.

SPECIFICATION	LIGHT 15 (1948)	DS19 (1957)	SM (1970)
ENGINE	Four-cyl, 1911 cc	Four-cyl, 1911 cc	Dohc V-6, 2670 cc
POWER	56 bhp @ 4250 rpm	75 bhp @ 4500 rpm	170 bhp @ 5500 rpm
TRANSMISSION	Manual 3-speed	Semi-auto 4-speed	Manual 5-speed
CHASSIS	Unitary steel	Unitary steel	Unitary steel
BRAKES	Drums	Disc/drum	Discs all round
TOP SPEED	76 mph	87 mph	135 mph
0-60 MPH	20.6 sec	23.3 sec	9.9 sec

Above: Although the 4-cylinder engine was similar to that of the Light 15, the rest of the DS19 was all-new from its remarkable style to its complex, but effective, hydraulic systems.

A product of Citroen's short-lived ownership of Maserati, the SM had a delightful four-cam V-6 power unit that would be shared with the Maserati Merak.

FIAT DINO 2.4, DINO 246GT, FERRARI 308GTS

'The Dino 246GT had taken Ferrari into the Porsche market.'

Although it is always referred to as the Ferrari Dino, the first mid-engined road car to emerge from Maranello was officially just a Dino, bearing the diminutive name of Alfredino, Ferrari's son who died tragically young in 1956. Putting the maker's name first also serves to differentiate this one from the front-engined Fiat Dino which shared the V-6 engine.

Alfredino had been working with Vittorio Jano on a 65-degree V-6 for the 1957 Formula Two racing; that was for 1500 cc engines but Ferrari saw to it that the engine could be increased in capacity to function as a *Grand Prix* engine. The four-cam V-6 had limited F2 success but went on to power Mike Hawthorn to his world championship in 1958. That formula ran out at the end of 1960 when *Grand Prix* rules dictated a change to 1.5-litres; while the original Dino engine was used early on, the team moved on to wide-angle V-6, V-8 and then flat-12.

It was when the 1600 cc formula 2 was planned for 1967 that the Dino engine came back to life. The only problem was that this required a production cylinder block of which 500 had been made. Ferrari persuaded Fiat to produce a sports car using a 2-litre version of that light-alloy engine. Within 20 months Fiat had dived into the parts bin to create a steel frame and partially 'productionised' the V-6 at 1978 cc, while Pininfarina had produced a delightfully aggressive, curvaceous Spider for launch at Turin in late 1966; at the same time, Fiat launched the 124 Spider, also designed by Pininfarina – they had been busy. March 1967 saw longer versions of each as coupés, a Bertone Fiat Dino and Fiat's own style for the 124S Coupé.

Ferrari's Dino came a little later. Its concept was first shown as a Pininfarina styling exercise on a mid-engined 2-litre racing chassis in 1965; Ferrari wanted an entry level model that would take the company into the higher volume 911 market but needed to gauge reaction first. While the concept car had a longitudinal engine and gearbox, the road car used the Fiat engine – with a nominal power increase from 160 bhp to 180 bhp – set transversely with the gearbox contained in the rear of the sump. Shown as a prototype at Turin in late 1967, it finally went into production in late 1968 as the Dino 206, the year in which

With Pininfarina's Spider and Bertone's 2+2 coupé bodywork, the Fiat Dino 2.4 was one of the best sports cars that Fiat ever made.

Ferrari's F2 car won a couple of races. Fiat had produced 1163 Spiders and 3670 coupés, and Ferrari had made perhaps 150 Dino 206s when Fiat radically altered their cars into the form they would have liked, without the rush to build 500 units. For 1970, the engine became a quieter 2.4-litre using a cast-iron block, the Fiat box was replaced with one from ZF and independent rear suspension was adopted. Although these were significantly better cars, fewer were produced over the 1970-73 period – 420 Spiders and 2400 coupés.

Ferrari also adopted the 2418 cc engine – 195 bhp against Fiat's 180 bhp – for the Dino 246GT, which became a superb little jewel of a car with near 150 mph performance, remarkable ride and roadholding and wonderful style. Meanwhile the (Ferrari) Dino engine/gearbox package was used to power the highly successful Lancia Stratos rally car – another homologation special of which 500 should have been built during 1973-4; it won the World Rally Championship in 1974-6. That original *Grand Prix* winning V-6 sired quite a family.

The Dino 246GT had taken Ferrari into the Porsche market, but it needed another two seats to match the 911. For the extra weight, a bigger engine was needed. Ferrari chose an aluminium 3-litre V-8, dimensionally two-thirds of a 365 V-12, but with its twin overhead cams driven by toothed belts; this was installed in the first Bertone-designed production Ferrari, the Dino 308 GT4 with 8 inches extra in the wheelbase; although never as highly rated as the two-seaters, the GT4 stayed in production from 1973 until 1980. But to keep up with Porsche's increasing engine sizes, the two-seater 246GT, which had been joined by the Targa-top GTS in 1972, also needed uprating; the 308GTB arrived in 1975 using the same 255 bhp V-8. Early models used glass-fibre bodywork but switched back to steel in 1977, by which time the cars had been officially called Ferraris. Pininfarina's 308GTB has long been rated as one of his best ever styles; it was joined by the removable top 308GTS in 1977. Increasing emission control demands brought a change to fuel injection in 1980, which lost some power, but this was largely recovered by the 1982 adoption of 4-valve heads. It was to be 1985 before the 308 engine was increased to 3.2-litres for the 328 range.

Never labelled as a Ferrari, the Dino 246GT was the first mid-engined road car to be built at Maranello.

SPECIFICATION	DINO 246GT (1971)	FIAT DINO 2.4 (1970)	FERRARI 308GTS (1975)
ENGINE	Dohc V-6, 2418 cc	Dohc V-6, 2418 cc	Dohc V-8, 2927 cc
POWER	195 bhp @ 7600 rpm	180 bhp @ 6600 rpm	255 bhp @ 7700 rpm
TRANSMISSION	Manual 5-speed	Manual 5-speed	Manual 5-speed
CHASSIS	Steel frame and body	Unitary steel	Steel chassis, grp body
BRAKES	Discs all round	Discs all round	Discs all round
TOP SPEED	148 mph	130 mph	154 mph
0-60 MPH 0-100 MPH	7.1 sec 17.6 sec	8.7 sec 19.9 sec	6.8 sec 16.5 sec

First of the 308s was the 1973 GT4, followed by the GTB in 1975 and this Spider GTS in 1977.

FERRARI 250GT SWB, 250GT LUSSO, 250GTO

'The new shape was carefully sculpted at Ferrari to aim for 175 mph.'

One of Pininfarina's best Ferrari shapes, the 250GT Short Wheel Base was a very successful racer in Grand Touring events as well as an effective road car, for which steel bodies were used instead of aluminium.

Ferrari is still a great name for stirring the blood of every car enthusiast despite the fact that others have built faster cars or won more races in one or other International category. The 250GT series was the start of serious road-going Ferrari production, and the start of the long-standing relationship with the Pininfarina styling house which has always ensured that Ferraris look as striking as their performance reveals.

Enzo Ferrari loved motor-racing. A successful driver in his own right during the 'twenties, he had then formed Scuderia Ferrari to race Alfa Romeos, before running the factory Alfa Corse team before the war. After that, he decided to build his own cars and the first Ferrari 125 appeared in 1947, using a 1.5-litre V-12 designed by Colombo. Over the next six years, Ferrari produced a wide variety of racing machinery and road cars in very small numbers using different versions of the Colombo engine as well as a bigger V-12 designed by Lampredi. While the variety was to continue throughout the 'fifties, it was in 1954 that the 250GT series began with the Europa, fit for road or track; Pininfarina bodied some 30 of them around Ferrari's simple but effective ladder-frame chassis with the Colombo V-12 now at 3-litres – Ferrari type numbers revealed the size of a single cylinder.

From this point, Ferrari began to build both road cars and raceable cars. To win races at International level you needed a purpose-built car; while a GT car could always be driven on the road, cars designed for the road had become too laden with comforts to be effective track cars. As demand for Ferraris for road use had gradually increased on the back of their racing reputation, Ferrari's 250GT production diverged into the road-going 250GT Coupé bodied to Pininfarina design by Boano and the 250GT Berlinetta dubbed the *Tour de France* after successes in that event.

The racing Berlinettas were given more power from the 3-litre engine – up to 280 bhp – while their bodies were made in aluminium by Scaglietti to Pininfarina's design. Some were more beautiful than others, but all were extremely effective on the track; until the 1959 version, the front end tended to look narrow, while the rear wings ended in light-carrying fins. Come the second 1959 model, the front end had evolved into the aggressive forward leaning stance while the rear wings blended smoothly into the rear panel; this was the stepping point for the 250GT SWB line – arguably one of Pininfarina's top designs for its combination of compact aggression and simple elegance.

All the *Tour de France* models had been built on a 2.6 m wheelbase. The new car, introduced in late 1959, was shorter and lighter on a 2.4 m wheelbase. The simple ladder chassis still carried wishbone independent front suspension and the live axle was supported by leaf springs but well located with four radius arms. The engine remained the magnificent V-12 whose glorious sound had thrilled so many race spectators. This model was soon a success in the GT categories.

However, increasing competition from the likes of Jaguar and Aston Martin forced Ferrari to go a stage further and produce a limited series with lower, lighter and more aerodynamic bodywork; the GT racing rules allowed this, so the 250GTO was introduced in 1962 – O for Omologato showed that the motor sport authorities had 'homologated' it, agreeing that it was a production model.

While the 250GT had been capable of speeds around 155 mph, the new shape was carefully sculpted at Ferrari to aim for 175 mph, thanks to a sharper front profile and a better understanding of air flow at the rear, complete with a lip to reduce aerodynamic lift which had made the previous model unstable at high speed. The chassis too was improved with a Watt linkage to hold the rear axle transversely while the engine was further tuned to give 300 bhp, still from the 3-litre V-12. That Ferrari won the International GT category in 1962-4 is adequate testimony to the efficiency of the 250 GT SWB and the 250GTO.

Meanwhile on the road-going scene, the 250GT Coupé with Boano bodywork had been supplemented by a Cabriolet and the California Spyder, the latter really an open version of the competition *Tour de France* cars. The coupé was then replaced by a new model designed and, now, built by Pininfarina from 1958, and still called 250GT; in contrast to the muscular lines of the competition car its slab sides and angular front were elegant but unexciting – people wanted road-versions of the competition car and Ferrari wanted to build them to reach the necessary numbers for GT racing. So this 250GT 2-seater gave way to road-going steel-bodied versions of the competition car in 1960, when it was juggled internally to become the 250GT 2+ 2.

Come the changeover from competition GT to GTO, Ferrari needed another 2-seater road coupé, so Pininfarina created the beautiful 250GT Lusso, *Lusso* meaning Luxury. The same engine was now de-tuned a little to give just 250 bhp.

The main body was in steel, but doors, boot and bonnet were in aluminium. It was the final version of the 250GT series; Ferrari was now an established producer of road cars and the Ferrari-Pininfarina relationship was set to continue to the present day.

SPECIFICATION	**250GT SWB** (1959)	**250GTO** (1962)	**250GT LUSSO** (1964)
ENGINE	V-12 2953 cc	V-12 2953 cc	V-12 2953 cc
HORSEPOWER	260 bhp @ 7000 rpm	300 bhp @ 7200 rpm	250 bhp @ 7000 rpm
TRANSMISSION	4-speed manual	5-speed manual	4-speed manual
CHASSIS	Tubular ladder frame with steel or aluminium body panels (*all models*)		
BRAKES	Disc brakes all round (*all models*)		
TOP SPEED	155 mph	165 mph	150 mph
0-60 MPH 0-100 MPH	6.6 sec 15.2 sec	6.0 sec 14.0 sec	6.8 sec 16.6 sec

When the 250GT SWB ceased production, Ferrari introduced a new more luxurious two-seater GT, the Lusso meaning luxury; with elements of 250GT and GTO it was extremely elegant.

Below: Shaped by the wind tunnel, the 250GTO has become one of the most sought-after Ferraris, and proved a very effective competition car, giving Ferrari success in the GT championship from 1962-3.

FERRARI 275GTB, 330GTC, 365GTB4 DAYTONA

'It had elegance without the poised sprinter look.'

While the Ferrari 250GT series started as race-cars adapted for the road, the 275 series were the first Ferraris to be designed as road cars; sure the 275 could be raced, but track cars were becoming ever more removed from road cars by this time, and winning GTs had mid-engines.

The 275 was the last of the small-block engines that had originally been seen in the first Ferraris after the war; its V-12 3.3-litre engine was mounted in the front but the gearbox, now with five speeds, was moved to the rear to keep the weight distribution more even. The chassis followed the familiar tubular space-frame principles but independent rear suspension was a welcome change.

The new model was announced at the 1964 Paris Show in two Pininfarina-styled forms, the open 275GTS, which was to be built at Pininfarina's factory, and the coupé 275GTB which was built by Scaglietti, near the Maranello factory. In the GTS, the engine developed 260 bhp at 7000 rpm but the GTB had a choice of two outputs, 250 bhp with three downdraught Weber carburetters, or 280 bhp at 7500 rpm with six Webers. After a year, the body was altered with a longer nose to reduce front end lift at high speed. The final version came in 1966, the 275GTB/4 with four overhead camshafts, two per bank of six cylinders, and dry sump lubrication; while this was rated at 300 bhp at 8000 rpm, increased torque made it more tractable for road use. During the three year span of the 275GT series, only a little over 1000 were built.

But while the 4-cam version extended the life of the 275, a new 330 range had been presented earlier that year. A new longer block with the traditional V-12 single-cam allowed a capacity increase to 4-litres to give a lazier 300 bhp at 7000 rpm. The chassis design was similar to that of the 275, but a torque tube joined the engine to the rear gear box for smoother, quieter running. Like the 275, it was offered in two body styles, 330GTC and 330GTS; the new shape lost the fastback style and had a lower waistline with more glass area – it had elegance without the poised sprinter look.

The single-cam long-block engine had already been used in Ferrari's sports-racing 330P in 1964; this had been enlarged to a 4.4-litre 365 for the non-factory cars while the works continued to develop the 330 to the point where the 1967 P4

Fastback styling of the 250GT series was carried through to the 275GTB, but the chassis was all-new with a transaxle and independent rear suspension. This is a 1965 'short-nose' 275GTB.

had four cams, three valves, twin plugs, fuel injection and 450 bhp. That 4.4-litre was first used as a production engine in 1967 for the 365GT 2+2, an extremely graceful Pininfarina lengthening of the 330GTC with 25 cm more in the wheelbase but with an overall length increased by 58 cm to provide more luggage space as well as the extra seats; the rear suspension had a self-levelling system to maintain the ride height whatever the loads. It was the following year before the 330GTC and GTS were uprated to 365-series; this was to have a new flagship in the 365GTB4, more commonly called the Daytona as a tribute to the success of the P4 at the 24-hour race and consequent appeal to the American market.

Ferrari needed a classic fast car to replace the 275GTB and it needed to be a four-cam unit to match those of Lamborghini, Aston Martin or Maserati. While the road-engine didn't carry through the P4's 3-valve design, it had new four-cam heads with six downdraught Webers and dry sump lubrication; with 352 bhp at 7500 rpm it was usefully more powerful than the 320 bhp at 6600 rpm achieved by the two-cam cars with lower compression ratios and triple Webers. While the chassis was basically that of the 365GTC/S, the Pininfarina body was quite different, a dramatic reversion to the powerful haunch style of a fastback with a distinctive sharp front end; early cars had the headlights visible behind a perspex band running across the nose, but later ones had this replaced by body-colour metal and the headlamps became swivelling pods. Other variants included a convertible – 100 only – and the 365GTC4, a 2+2 Daytona slightly lengthened with less horsepower and a revised front end which was available in 1971/2 following the phasing out of the previous 2+2. But the Daytona stayed in production until 1974; over 1300 were built in its six-year life against 350 of the 275GTB4 in just two years.

With less aggressive styling the 330/365 GTC single-cam cars were softer, more practical and easier to drive than the Daytona; here, a 1967 330GTC.

SPECIFICATION	275GTB4 (1966)	330GTC (1968)	365GTB4 (1971)
ENGINE	Ali V-12, 3285 cc	Ali V-12, 3967 cc	Ali V-12, 4390 cc
POWER	300 bhp @ 8000 rpm	300 bhp @ 7000 rpm	352 bhp @ 7500 rpm
TRANSMISSION	Manual 5-speed transaxle carrying final drive (*all models*)		
CHASSIS	Steel tube frame with steel or aluminium (competition) bodies (*all models*)		
BRAKES	Disc brakes all round (*all models*)		
TOP SPEED	159 mph	147 mph	174 mph
0-60 MPH 0-100 MPH	6.2 sec 15.2sec	6.8 sec 15.8 sec	5.4 sec 12.6 sec

Below: 1973 Ferrari 365GTB4 Daytona.

FERRARI TESTAROSSA, 288GTO, F40

'The shape was really dramatic this time.'

The big mid-engined Testarossa is a beautiful and very striking car which did all that it set out to do, but during its 1984-1992 lifespan Ferrari brought out two other remarkable but considerably less practical machines – the 288GTO and the F40. As a result, the best of the Boxers never quite had the appreciation it deserved.

The model originally started in production in 1973 as the 365GT4BB, BB denoting Berlinetta Boxer – the flat-12 boxer engine configuration. At the time of its design Ferrari were using a 3-litre flat-12 in GP and Sports Car racing; it gave a usefully low centre of gravity and was very effective. It was a good layout for road cars too, as the width of the engine was not a problem and it allowed a low rear deck for better rearward visibility than many mid-engined cars offered. Making use of existing machinery, Ferrari opted to open out the 60-degree V-12 to 180 degrees which allowed considerable development and component carry-over, although the four camshafts adopted belt drive; at 344 bhp it was a little less powerful than the Daytona due to lower compression ratio and more cramped exhaust system. But instead of putting the gearbox in the conventional racing position behind the final drive, they kept the gearbox mass inside the wheelbase and mounted it within the rear of the sump, causing the engine to sit higher than it might have done.

As ever, the body was styled by Pininfarina but was somewhat understated. Underneath, it used a steel space frame with steel body panels, although the front and rear 'bumper' assemblies were in glass-fibre. Its performance was similar to the Daytona's but the difficulty of rapid take-off with a mid-engined car meant the front-engined one was quicker in the 0-60 mph tests.

While the engine was uprated to 5-litres (BB512) and given a dry sump in 1976, and fuel injection (BB512i) was added in 1981, the first big change came in 1984 with the arrival of the Testarossa, still with 5-litres but now with 4-valve heads and 390 bhp to bring the performance back. The shape was really dramatic this time; the previous front radiator was split into two rear ones fed by giant straked intakes just ahead of the rear wheels, the smaller front intake remaining to cool the brakes. With the side radiators and ever bigger wheels the Testarossa was 6 ins wider than the BB512 and five inches longer. It was a big car compared with the GTO and the F40.

Like its predecessor of 20 years earlier, the GTO was conceived in response to racing rules; Group B required 200 to be built in a year to enable them to take part in GT racing and rallies. Ferrari wanted a weapon to match the Porsche 959 which was the ultimate development of the 911, so they used the 308GTB as a basis and fitted

Conceived as Ferrari's response to the Group B race/rally Porsche 959, the 288GTO used the 308 as its basis, but used a twin-turbo V-8 set fore-and-aft with a longer, wider composite body.

twin turbochargers to a 2.85-litre version of the quad-cam V-8 to develop 400 bhp in road form; to allow a conventional gearbox with changeable ratios, the engine was mounted fore-and-aft with the box behind the axle, so the 308 chassis had to be stretched by four inches. While the body was recognisably 308, it was also some 7 inches wider to accommodate bigger wheels and tyres, and made from a mixture of composite materials to keep the weight down. Launched in 1984, it immediately attracted premium prices; unfortunately suitable Group B competitions failed to materialise, but any Limited Edition Ferrari is a classic even without a track record.

Less limited but even faster was the F40 developed to celebrate Ferrari's 40 years of manufacture in 1988. While the chassis used a similar space frame it had carbon fibre bonded to it as lightweight stiffening. The engine, too, was similar but used more turbocharger pressure to develop 478 bhp from a 2936 cc version of the V-8. Even wider wheels and a latter-day approach to aerodynamics and ground effects saw the latest Pininfarina creation look far more track orientated than did the GTO; the body and interior made liberal use of composites for appearance and weight reduction. While the Testarossa could reach 182 mph and the GTO nearly 190 mph, the F40 all but joined the 200 mph club; they were a fascinating trio from the height of the supercar boom.

While the preceding BB models were somewhat understated overgrown Dinos, the Testarossa made a bold statement when it arrived in 1984.

Under an all-new race-style skin, the F40 chassis was very similar to that of the GTO, but used composite panels to reinforce the steel frame.

SPECIFICATION	TESTAROSSA (1985)	288GT0 (1986)	F40 (1990)
ENGINE	Flat-12, 4942 cc	Turbo V-8, 2885 cc	Turbo V-8, 2936 cc
POWER	390 bhp @ 6300 rpm	400 bhp @ 7000 rpm	478 bhp @ 7000 rpm
TRANSMISSION	Manual 5-speed	Manual 5-speed	Manual 5-speed
CHASSIS	Steel frame and body	Steel frame with composite body work	
BRAKES	Disc brakes all round (*all models*)		
TOP SPEED	182 mph	189 mph	198 mph
0-60 MPH 0-100 MPH	5.7 sec 11.9 sec	5.0 sec 11.0 sec	4.1 sec 7.6 sec

FORD LOTUS CORTINA, CORTINA 1600E, CAPRI 3000GT

When Ford launched the Consul Cortina in September 1962 it was the start of a new design era – a proper four-seater designed down to a weight by current stress techniques. It was a full 100 Kg lighter than the next one up, the Consul Classic introduced in May 1961. Consul was the broad range between the Anglia and the Zephyr/Zodiac and covered three very different models.

This was the period of Ford's Total Performance strategy to capture the youth market. Within a year the Cortina had been joined by a 1500 cc model, the 1500GT and the 'Consul Cortina Sports Special' – the Lotus-Cortina to everyone but the Ford marketing department. In a bid to win saloon car races outright where the Anglias had won classes, Ford commissioned Lotus to make a road-going racer out of the family saloon. Lotus had already developed a twin-cam head for Ford's new five-bearing 1500 cc engine as the power unit for the Lotus Elan launched at the 1962 Motor Show. In fact, Ford wanted 1588 cc to make the car better suited to the 1600 cc race category and Lotus subsequently used the same engine for the Elan. Aluminium door skins, boot and bonnet replaced Cortina steel units and wings were slightly flared to take 5.5J rims but the major change was to the rear suspension; the leaf springs were replaced by radius arms while brackets welded to the old forward spring mount dropped down to carry an A-bracket picking up on the axle casing, and coil spring/damper units operated on the radius arms. The springing was much firmer and the car sat two inches lower. Most of the cars were converted from white Cortina 1200 to white/green Lotus Cortinas at the Lotus factory in Cheshunt, but Ford took over once the move to Hethel was imminent.

When the Lotus-Cortina was announced in January 1963 it was an immediate sensation; with 105 bhp it would reach 108 mph and the Elan close-ratio gearbox ensured that it would reach 60 mph in second gear 10.1 seconds after take-off. On the track the car did all that was asked of it,

Although some race teams used other colours, all production Lotus Cortinas were white with green stripes and carried discreet Lotus badges in the revised grille and on rear wings, flared to take wider tyres.

The Capri followed the American Ford Mustang in offering a two-door coupé with as many options as possible. This 1600GT was mid-way through a range that ran from 1300 to 3000GT.

winning races and championships in the UK and Europe, but it wasn't a very reliable road car and certainly had no chance in rallies where Ford stuck to the stronger and less powerful Cortina GT; the rear axle location was the major problem – the stresses were too high to keep the oil in and the linkage was too low for forest rallies. Once the car had been accepted for International competition there was a gradual switch back to standard body panels, but it was to be mid-1965 before the axle went back to leaf springs with additional radius rods – the handling wasn't the same but it stayed together.

When Ford brought in the Mk.II Cortina in mid-1967 there was still a Lotus version uprated to 109 bhp to carry the heavier shell, which retained the same design of lowered suspension as the final Mk.I – regular colours and a discreet Lotus badge made the new one less conspicuous. Part of the Mk.II package was the new cross-flow engine, which gave 88 bhp for the 1600GT, 10 bhp more than the old 1500GT. But the best of the new range was a cross between the two; the 1600E was a 1600GT with the lowered suspension, wide wheels and an executive level of trim – thicker sound deadening, wooden facia and door cappings, better seats and paintwork to match. It was almost a 100 mph car with acceleration not far behind the Cortina Lotus, the new official name, and soon generated quite a following.

When the Mk.II Cortina arrived in 1967, the 1600E version was a luxury Cortina GT which used Cortina Lotus suspension and wide wheels; it soon became a classic.

At the time of the original Cortina announcement the Classic was joined by the two-door Capri – an attractive coupé that used the 1340 cc, 1500 and 1500GT engines. Such was Cortina success that the Classic/Capri only lasted until 1964, but the Capri name was to be revived in 1969 for a new fast-back coupé evolved along the lines of the American Ford Mustang – long bonnet short tail style with as many options as you can make available. Its running gear followed the usual Ford suspension systems with a choice of half a dozen engines from 1300 cc to the 3-litre V-6, added in 1970; this was uprated in 1972 with an extra 10 bhp and a higher final drive which gave it a 120 mph maximum and Porsche level acceleration.

The Capri – the car you always promised yourself – was a great success running through two face-lifts and numerous refinements until 1987, a final Limited Edition being the Brooklands model using the German 2.8-litre V-6 which had replaced the Essex 3-litre in 1982. While Ford have never made traditional sports cars, they have made some pretty sporting saloons.

'When the Lotus-Cortina was announced in January 1963 it was an immediate sensation.'

SPECIFICATION	LOTUS-CORTINA (1964)	1600E (1968)	CAPRI 3000GT (1972)
ENGINE	Dohc four, 1588 cc	Ohv four, 1599 cc	Ohv V-6, 2994 cc
POWER	105 bhp @ 5500 rpm	88 bhp @ 5400 rpm	138 bhp @ 5000 rpm
TRANSMISSION	Manual 4-speed (*all models*)		
CHASSIS	Steel with ali panels	Unitary steel body/chassis (*both models*)	
BRAKES	Disc/drum (*all models*)		
TOP SPEED	108 mph	97 mph	120 mph
0-60 MPH	10.1 sec	11.6 sec	8.6 sec
0-100 MPH	33.5 sec	—	26.5 sec

FORD THUNDERBIRD, GT40, MERCURY COUGAR

'The T-bird was still trying to outdrag the Corvette, even if it couldn't out-corner it.'

The post-war influx of European sports cars into America caused heartache in the corridors of Detroit power. Ford and Chevrolet responded, but Chevrolet got there first with the Corvette, launched in 1953 despite a 1951 start; it used many standard GM components but it had its own frame and the glass-fibre body was new technology whose short lead-time and low cost tooling enabled Chevrolet to steal a march on Ford. Ford had been looking at a car in the same European sporting mould, but changed tack when the Corvette came out; Ford would create another market and make a two-seater personal car with all 'mod cons' and no compromise to comfort, a two-seater Lincoln.

When the Thunderbird came out in 1955, it had a remarkable elegance and a V-8 engine, two factors that put its sales ahead of the Corvette straight away. The 'vette had started with a sluggish six and was not exactly beautiful; although GM's V-8 came in 1955, and the restyle in 1956, the T-bird got off to a better start. The V-8 was a 292 cu.in. with 198 bhp, enough for 110 mph and a 0-60 mph in under 10 seconds; by 1956 this was up to 312 cu.in and 225 bhp and the spare wheel was mounted on the tail with its own cover. The T-bird was still trying to outdrag the Corvette, even if it couldn't out-corner it, so 1957 saw the addition of a race-level 312 with 285 bhp against the Corvette's 283 bhp 283 cu.in V-8, but a handful of T-birds were given Paxton superchargers and 340 bhp. In shape, the back end grew some mandatory fins, but that was the last of the classic 2-seater Thunderbirds.

For 1958, Ford added 11 inches to the wheelbase and the car became an open four-seater with a hideous amount of front-end chrome. Despite its looks, it sold well with the increased carrying capacity and engine options that ranged from a 300 bhp 352 cu.in to a big block 430 cu.in with 350 bhp. Fortunately the 1961 restyle restored some elegance, and you could have a two-seater by putting a twin-headrest moulding over the rear seats.

While the Thunderbird has lived on as a luxury sporting machine, Ford needed to get back to the true sports-car image and the Mustang (see page 44) was created for 1964; this had stemmed from Mustang 1, a 1962 show car – a mid-engined two-seater – but became a conventional front-engine rear-drive four-seater. Those that had created the two-seater went on to design the GT40, Ford's racing GT challenge to the Ferraris; while this became a joint design venture with Eric Broadley's similar Lola GT, the concept was evolved in America. Using a built up sheet steel frame with glass-fibre doors, engine cover and front end, it used a variety of race-modified Ford

Chevrolet beat Ford to the sports car market, so Ford went for the luxury personal car and came up with the Thunderbird – fast in a straight line.

From the prototype Mustang 1 came three cars – the Mustang pony-car, the GT40 and the Mercury Cougar. This 1966 GT40 is one of the Mk.I street-racers.

engines – 4.2 to 4.7 to 7-litre – in a range of shapes. It served its purpose and the 7-litre cars won Le Mans in 1966 (Mk.2) and 1967 (Mk.IV); the GT40 had started as a prototype but, by 1966 was eligible for the 50-off sports car category. When regulations changed for 1968 to limit prototypes to 3-litres, Ford was well poised with the GT40 of which over 100 were to be produced – it won at Le Mans in 1968 and 1969. It was an impressive four years and did much to strengthen Ford's world-wide performance image.

While Mustang 1 can be said to the ancestor of the production Mustang and the GT40, it also added another dimension to the Mercury range with the Cougar. Ford had inserted the Mercury brand between Ford and Lincoln in 1939. In the immediately pre-Mustang period, its Comet range was somewhat bigger than nominal Ford equivalents. The Mustang had the pony-car market to itself for its first two years, but autumn 1966 saw Chevrolet launch the Camaro and Firebird, Chrysler the Barracuda and Ford's Lincoln-Mercury division produced the Mercury Cougar, a name that had actually been applied in-house to the final prototype Mustang II. The Cougar was the luxury sports-model Mustang with an extra three inches in the wheelbase, its own styling – headlights concealed behind a waterfall grille, sequential turn indicators within a rear waterfall – and all the Mustang engine options; it was a good-looking alternative to the mass-appeal Mustang and came third in the 1967 pony-car sales behind Mustang and Camaro. To launch its performance image Ford campaigned the Cougar in 1967 Trans-Am, but other Mustangs just took the championship. Cougars continue as luxury Mustangs but the first was one of the best.

Below: The Cougar was a luxury Mustang, with 3 inches added to the wheelbase for more comfort, and its own short tail, long nose styling.

SPECIFICATION	FORD T'BIRD (1956)	FORD GT40 MK.III (1967)	MERCURY COUGAR (1967)
ENGINE	Cast-iron V-8, 5115 cc	Cast-iron V-8, 4727 cc	Cast-iron V-8, 6385 cc
POWER	225 bhp @ 4600 rpm	306 bhp @ 6000 rpm	320 bhp @ 4800 rpm
TRANSMISSION	Auto 3-speed	Manual 5-speed ZF	Auto 3-speed
CHASSIS	Steel frame	Steel frame, g/fibre body	Unitary steel
BRAKES	Drums	Discs all round	Disc/drum
TOP SPEED	116 mph	164 mph	122 mph
0-60 MPH	10.2 sec	5.3 sec	7.7 sec
0-100 MPH	—	11.8 sec	—

FORD MUSTANG, SHELBY GT-350, BOSS 351

'The performance image had to be proved in competition too.'

Lee Iacocca's quest for the ideal car for American youth started in 1960, the search for a sports car that was more practical and affordable than a Corvette. 'Affordable' meant high numbers and 'practical' required market research, as this was a new arena.

The first prototype was an engineer's ideal, a neat mid-engined equivalent of a Fiat X1/9 albeit some years ahead of even the concept version; called Mustang 1, it was shown in 1962 but, with a space-frame and glass-fibre bodywork, it was impossible to produce in volume. Those engineers went off to design the GT40, leaving others to create Mustang II on the basis of a shortened Ford Falcon – research had shown that the volume American sports car should have four seats.

The Mustang was duly launched in April 1964 in open and fixed hard-top forms, the fast-back following a little later. Under $2400 for a base model was remarkable value, but there was nothing special about its simple front-engine rear drive design, it was just the style and the option list that made it unique in that market. Ford were committed to a Total Performance programme and Mustang extras were to reflect this. Initially the engines were from the Falcon range – a 2.8-litre six (170 cu.in.) with 101 bhp and the 4.3-litre (260 cu.in.) with 164 bhp at 4400 rpm; the former could manage just over 90 mph and the latter 105 mph. This lack of sporting potential was speedily rectified in September with the base six now at 200 cu.in and the new V-8 of 289 cu.in (4.7-litre) available in 200, 225 or 271 bhp forms; the last would rev to over 6000 rpm, so the performance was vastly increased to give a maximum of 128 mph and 0-100 mph in 19.7 seconds with the manual 4-speed. Sales exceeded all estimates; 100,000 went in four months and the millionth Mustang came in March 1966, still six months before the first rival appeared in this new pony-car market – the Chevrolet Camaro.

The performance image had to be proved in competition too. Carroll Shelby had played his part with the racing Cobras and was looking for a replacement production racer. When the fastback came out in September 1964, Shelby started work and launched the Shelby-Mustang GT-350 in January 1965 – 350 being an inflated horsepower claim; stiffer springing, wider wheels and tyres, race instruments, bucket seats and some glass-fibre

Out in 1964, the Mustang was given a minor face-lift in 1967 with a bigger front grille as the most obvious pointer – this is a 1968 convertible.

panels helped to make it a better track car, while the 289 engine was upped to 306 bhp with a new carburetter and manifold. The Mustang duly won the SCCA Class B against the Corvettes and then went on to win the new Trans-Am championship for saloons in 1966 and 1967.

For 1967 the Mustang had a minor face-lift which made it more comfortable but heavier, so Shelby added the GT-500 to his production, using the 7-litre 428 engine with a lazy 350 bhp. By the end of that year, Shelby had made 4115 GT-350s and 2050 GT-500s; 936 of the 350s used a black and gold colour scheme and were rented out through Hertz as GT-350H. For 1968, emission laws had stopped Shelby making the Cobra and he handed over Shelby Mustang production to Ford, although he still made some convertible versions. In 1968 Ford made 4450 in a variety of forms – GT-350 now with a 302 cu.in.engine, GT-500 with the high performance 427 cu.in engine and GT-500KR (King of the Road) with the 428 engine with 360 bhp. The final year of Shelby production saw another 3150 cars – GT-350s now with the 351 cu.in engine and GT-500s with the Ram Air 428 cu.in engine cut back on non-premium fuel to 335 bhp.

Meanwhile Ford introduced the face-lifted Mustang in 1969 and added the high-performance Mach 1 – after a 1966 show car – and a Grande luxury version; the Mustang was getting soft. And the fastback, now called sportroof, had a race-minded Boss derivative. The Boss series were designed to give Ford the best chance in competition, the Boss 302 with a special stronger engine for Trans-Am and the very limited Boss 429 with 390 bhp to qualify this near race engine for NASCAR. Although they were quick cars they failed to win the 1969 Trans-Am, but went on to win in 1970 by which time a minimum production of 7000 was called for – there are a lot of Boss 302s around. Last of the Boss range was the 1971 Boss 351 which took the Mach 1's 351 cu.in engine out to 335 bhp with high compression and solid valve lifters. It was the last performance Mustang of the muscle-car era.

The 1971 Boss 351 with 335 bhp is shown here in its sportroof form.

Shelby 350GTs were fastback Mustangs built for racing with appropriate chassis mods, some lighter grp panels and the 289 cu.in V-8 uprated to 306 bhp.

SPECIFICATION	MUSTANG 289 (1964)	GT-350 (1966)	BOSS 351 (1971)
ENGINE	Iron V-8, 4736 cc	Iron V-8, 4736 cc	Iron V-8 5750cc
POWER	271 bhp @ 6000 rpm	306 bhp @ 6000 rpm	335 bhp @ 6000 rpm
TRANSMISSION	Manual 4-speed	Manual 4-speed	Manual 4-speed
CHASSIS	Unitary steel for hardtop, fastback and convertible models		
BRAKES	Disc/drum option	Disc/drum	Disc/drum
TOP SPEED	128 mph	135 mph	135 mph
0-60 MPH	7.6 sec	6.2 sec	6.4 sec

Jaguar XK120, C-Type, XK150

From the moment of its launch at the 1948 Earls Court Motor Show, the Jaguar XK120 was destined to become one of the great cars in history. It had a style and a level of performance that transcended anything else that was to appear in those early post-war years. It was just as much at home on road or track with impressive victories in rallies too; while the chassis design was unremarkable, its famous twin-cam six-cylinder engine would go on to power five Le Mans winners and countless road cars before it was finally phased out in 1987.

Before the war, Jaguar was a model name for SS Cars, the company founded by William Lyons on the back of his previous Swallow Coach-building; Armstrong Siddeley used to make a Jaguar aero engine but surrendered the name to Lyons in 1936. Most famous of these was the SS Jaguar 100 two-seater sports car which generated a strong competition following. The name was changed to Jaguar Cars in 1945 in preparation for the launch of the first real Jaguar.

Much of the ground-work had evolved during the latter part of the war; William Lyons and some of his engineers had been engaged in fire-watching and had used the time to decide what the first true Jaguars would be – a 100 mph saloon and a faster sports car, both to be powered by the same six-cylinder twin overhead camshaft engine which would need to produce around 160 bhp. As it turned out they continued to make revised versions of the pre-war saloons until the 1948 launch of both the Mark V with the old 3.5-litre pushrod engine and the XK120 with the new 3.4-litre engine, both having separate chassis with new torsion bar independent front suspension. The 100 mph saloon would wait until the 1951 Mk.VII. When announced, the XK120s were to be bodied in the traditional low volume way – aluminium on wood – but such was the demand that steel bodies were brought in after the first 240 cars. Over 12,000 would be built in open and fixed head coupé forms with the vast majority going overseas in those export conscious days.

The 120 part of the name signified the speed the car was expected to reach; period road tests all

When sports car still meant cycle wings and slab tanks, the arrival of the XK120 in 1948 was a major step forward in sporting design.

While XK120s did well at the 1950 Le Mans, Jaguar wanted outright victory for 1951; the XK120C won in 1951 and 1953.

The XK140 was little changed from the earlier car, but the XK150 was a much more substantial and more comfortable car – here is an XK150 3.4 drop-head coupé.

confirmed it. This high performance made it particularly suitable for rallying where the XK120 scored its greatest International successes – Ian Appleyard's four Alpine Cups among the most noteworthy. They were raced, too, with Stirling Moss' 1950 TT win a highlight, and they had also been to the Le Mans 24-hours that year – although they didn't win, one had always run in the top seven before retiring in the 23rd hour and two others finished 12th and 15th. It was enough to convince Lyons that a lighter purpose-built car could win with the same engine, so work started on the XK120C (Competition), always known as the C-type; which explains why there were never A-types and B-types.

The C used a space-frame chassis with an all-enveloping quickly detachable body with considerably improved aerodynamics. Front suspension followed the 120 but the live rear axle was well located with radius arms and an A-bracket and sprung by torsion bars. With the engine tuned to give 204 bhp, the C-type gained its first Le Mans victory in 1951. C-types were also produced for private racers and would do over 140 mph with 200 bhp. Although rebodied versions failed early in the 1952 Le Mans, lighter versions of the original shape were prepared for 1953 with more power – 220 bhp with triple Webers – and disc brakes; the works cars finished 1st, 2nd and 4th. With two victories in the world's most famous motor race, the Jaguar reputation was well and truly founded.

Thus when the replacement XK140 came out in 1954 it bore a plaque proclaiming the victories. Similar to the XK120, the new car was given a little more interior space by moving the engine forward. With 190 bhp or 210 bhp in special equipment form, the top speed could rise to nearly 130 mph. The model was replaced by the XK150 in 1957 with more comfortable bodywork for the customary fixed head, drop-head and roadster versions, and disc brakes for all; the engine was finally enlarged to 3.8-litres in 1959 with the XK150S 3.8 receiving the 265 bhp which would power the E-type from its 1961 launch. The 'fifties had been an exciting decade for Jaguar.

'The 120 part of the name signified the speed the car was expected to reach.'

SPECIFICATION	XK120 (1949)	XK120C (1952)	XK150S 3.8 (1960)
ENGINE	Straight-6, 3442 cc	Straight-6, 3442 cc	Straight-6, 3781 cc
POWER	160 bhp @ 5000 rpm	200 bhp @ 5800 rpm	265 bhp @ 5500 rpm
TRANSMISSION	Manual 4-speed (*all models*)		
CHASSIS	Steel frame and body	Tubular frame, ali body	Steel frame and body
BRAKES	Drums	Drums	Discs
TOP SPEED	124 mph	144 mph	136 mph
0-60 MPH	10.0 sec	8.1 sec	7.6 sec
0-100 MPH	27.3 sec	20.1 sec	19.0 sec

JAGUAR XKSS, E-TYPE, XJS

Less well-known than the racing Jaguar D-type, the XKSS was the rare road-going version. Arguably the Jaguar E-type was its direct descendant – a race-bred car – before the XJS took over in 1975.

Having won the renowned Le Mans 24-hour race in 1951 and 1953 with the C-types, Jaguar were keen to continue. Not only did such racing improve the road car breed but success, particularly at Le Mans, brought tremendous publicity benefits. Le Mans was a very fast circuit so a low drag shape was very important; aerodynamicist Malcolm Sayer,who had also styled the C-type, evolved the D-type with an elliptical cross-section which helped to reduce drag to around half that of the XK120. It made a big difference in Le Mans lap times.

The chassis construction was very different from that of the C-type. Although there was a square tube frame underneath, the centre section was made into a stressed skin monocoque with metal panels riveted to it, aircraft fashion; the frame extended forwards to carry engine, front suspension, radiator and bonnet mounts. To the rear a sub-frame carried bodywork but the suspension trailed from the rear of the monocoque – still a live axle but with twin radius arm plates and an A-bracket. The XK engine, giving around 245 bhp with triple Webers, was converted to dry sump lubrication to keep the frontal area down. The D's first year was not quite a success; one finished second while the Belgian C-type finished 4th. Down the straight, the D had clocked 173 mph, the C 147 mph while the winning Ferrari reached 160 mph. The next three years saw victory for further developments of the Jaguars, although 1956 and 1957 were due to the private Ecurie Ecosse team – the works had stopped after 1956. Although they were built specifically to win

When the E-type arrived in 1961, it embodied many of the D-type principles, including its monocoque construction and a 3.8-litre XK engine. This is a 1962 3.8-litre roadster.

By 1957 demand for the amateur racer's D-type had dwindled, so a number were converted to two-seater road-going XKSS – as this one.

Le Mans, the D-types won many other races over the period, but by 1957 private entrant demand had slowed; Jaguar decided to produce a road-going version with a soft-top attached to a full width screen, and a nominal silencer for an engine that was identical to the 1954 cars. While over 60 D-types were produced, there were only 16 of these XKSS.

Emphasising that it was the true successor to the D-type rather than an evolution of the XK150, Jaguar's E-type followed the same monocoque construction principles within a Sayer-developed style that was recognisably a stretched D-type – it was six inches longer in the wheelbase and over a foot longer overall which helped to provide luggage space. A major change though was the independent rear suspension which had been tried on the 2nd prototype E2A, which had run at Le Mans in 1960, and was also to be used on the Mk.X announced later in 1961. The XK engine was the same 3.8-litre six that had been developed for the XK150S. On its announcement at Geneva in March 1961, the E-type made just as much impact on the sporting public as the XK120 had done 13 years earlier; roadster and fixed head styles were both capable of around 144 mph, although the press cars were a little faster with the coupé reaching 150 mph for *Autocar*. It was such a well-mannered fast car with a very comfortable ride, that it became everyone's ideal.

Jaguar's new V-12 was first used in the E-type from 1971. This engine and the rear suspension design was all that was carried over to the replacement XJS in 1975.

Over the next 14 years, the XK would increase to 4.2-litres for the same output but more torque, nine inches would be added for a 2+2 version with a raised roof, and a V-12 would replace the XK engine in 1971 to make up for the power lost in reducing emissions. That V-12 had started life in the mid-engined XJ13 which might have taken Jaguar back to Le Mans in 1966/7; then a 5-litre 4-cam engine, it was considerably refined to become a silky smooth 5.3-litre with just a single cam per bank by the time it was inserted in the Mk.III E-type with 272 bhp.

This engine was the heart of the XJS which followed on, although for this it had fuel injection and 285 bhp. Many decry the XJS as an unworthy replacement for such an icon as the E-type, but demand for overtly sporting cars had diminished considerably after the 1973 fuel crisis, and a more comfortable Grand Tourer was what the market wanted. The central monocoque system had gone and the XJS used the conventional unitary construction retaining the rear suspension subframe; with that effortless V-12 power the XJS was a class leader in quiet 100 mph cruising, a far cry from the wind-swept XK120.

'Many decry the XJS as an unworthy replacement for such an icon as the E-type.'

SPECIFICATION	XKSS (1957)	E-TYPE 3.8 fhc (1961)	XJS V-12 (1975)
ENGINE	Straight-6, 3442 cc	Straight-6, 3781 cc	V-12, 5344 cc
POWER	250 bhp @ 5750 rpm	265 bhp @ 5500 rpm	285 bhp @ 5500 rpm
TRANSMISSION	Manual 4-speed	Manual 4-speed	Manual 4-speed
CHASSIS	Ali body & chassis	Steel chassis	Unitary steel
BRAKES	Discs	Discs	Discs
TOP SPEED	149 mph	150 mph	153 mph
0-60 MPH 0-100 MPH	7.3 sec 13.6 sec	6.9 sec 16.2 sec	6.7 sec 16.2 sec

JAGUAR 2.4, 3.8 MK.II, XJ12C

'Inside was all the luxury that had become a Jaguar hallmark.'

Below: The little Jaguar 2.4 was introduced in 1955; rear wheel spats and narrow grille were distinguishing features up to the time the 3.4 arrived in 1957 with partial spats, as this, to allow wire wheels and wider grille, later used on the 2.4 as well.

Once Jaguar had launched the Mk.VII in 1950, there was an obvious need for a smaller saloon if Jaguar were to move into any form of volume production. Given the Jaguar reputation it had to be a sports saloon which was a relatively untapped market in 1955. And moving with the times, it was to be Jaguar's first unitary construction car – Mk.VII and XK120 still having separate chassis.

While its engine might have been the four-cylinder twin-cam that had been considered for a low cost XK100, the final choice was a short-stroke version of the familiar six; with twin small downdraught Solex carburetters it produced a conservative 112 bhp from 2483 cc. For the front suspension, a separate sub-frame was used to isolate road-shocks, so the double wishbone system adopted coil springs rather than the torsion bars of the previous models. At the rear, the live axle was located by twin upper radius arms, a semi-trailing Panhard rod while cantilevered leaf springs, set into under-body channels, acted as lower radius arms – in principle similar to the C and D-types.

As with all Jaguars during his rule, the major styling input came from the boss, Sir William Lyons. Where the XK120 maintained the pre-war theme of separately delineated flowing wings, and the Mk.VII followed suit, the 2.4's waistline was a single sweep from the front to the fallaway tail; the whole was a nice balance of flowing curves and practicality, although the rear wheel spats were a little affected. At the front, the XK140 family style was evident in the grille flanked by inset headlights and prominent horn grilles. Inside was all the luxury that had become a Jaguar hallmark with the polished wooden facia and comfortable leather-covered seating for four.

With the optional overdrive ratio, the 2.4 would just reach 100 mph which was good enough for European markets but Americans were critical of the lack of the easy acceleration offered by their customary big V-8s and automatic transmission. This was remedied by the March 1957 arrival of

SPECIFICATION	2.4 (1956)	3.8 MK.II (1963)	XJ12C (1975)
ENGINE	Dohc 6, 2483 cc	Dohc 6, 3781 cc	Ali V-12, 5344 cc
POWER	112 bhp @ 5750 rpm	220 bhp @ 5500 rpm	285 bhp @ 5750 rpm
TRANSMISSION	Manual 4-speed + o/d	Manual 4-speed + o/d	Auto 3-speed
CHASSIS	Unitary steel construction used for all models from 2.4 onwards		
BRAKES	Drums	Discs	Discs
TOP SPEED	101 mph	125 mph	147 mph
0-60 MPH	14.4 sec	8.5 sec	8.3 sec
0-100 MPH	—	25.1 sec	19.9 sec

the 3.4-litre version which was easily recognisable by its wider grille, twin exhaust tail pipes and rear wheel spats with a partial cut-out to allow the option of wire wheels. With 210 bhp the 3.4 was a 120 mph car with acceleration to match; the US market was further satisfied by the option of automatic transmission. Disc brakes all round became on option for 2.4 and 3.4 within six months.

Good though the compact Jaguars were, the arrival of the Mk.II in October 1959 brought some welcome changes. The rear track had been uncomfortably narrower than the front so this was increased by 3.25 inches to benefit handling; more glass was added by widening the rear window and giving the side-windows simple chromed frames; the grille had a broad strip in the centre and was flanked by fog-lights rather than horns; and the dashboard was redesigned. It was a much better car; the 2.4 received an increase to 120 bhp, the 3.4 stayed at 210 bhp but the new 3.8 gave 220 bhp and 125 mph. It was the Mk.II 3.8 that gave the compact Jaguar its charisma; not only was it a police favourite in the new motorway era, but it was a very successful saloon car racer.

The shape was to continue for many years including the Daimler variant with the 2.5-litre V-8 which came in 1962. The Mk.IIs blended into a new range of 240 and 340 plus the V-8 250 in 1967 as 'cheaper' Jaguars, following the 1963 introduction of the S-types, 3.4 and 3.8. These were basically modernised Mk.IIs with the Mk.X independent rear suspension which necessitated a stronger rear floor area, and earned a longer luggage boot and more rear headroom in the process. The S-range was extended with the 245 bhp 420 in 1966, its front-end style adjusted to match the 420G which took over from the Mk.X. The somewhat bewildering model range was then all rationalised with the overdue arrival of the XJ6 in 1968.

While the E-type continued to sell, all other Jaguars were XJ6 variants which made for new economies of scale to enable Jaguar to maintain its value for money policy. Launched with 2.8 and 4.2-litre engines, the range was joined by the XJ12 in mid-1972. When the Series 2 cars came in 1973, the range included a new 2-door coupé powered by either the 4.2-litre or the V-12. To classic eyes, these were the nicest of the range although there were always problems with sealing frameless windows which had delayed their production until 1975; they sadly disappeared in 1977 after 6505 XJ6C and only 1873 XJ12C had been produced – the XJS served a similar function with fewer problems.

The picture above shows a 1963 Jaguar 3.8 Mk.II.

Less than 2000 of these XJ12C were produced.

LAMBORGHINI 400GT, ESPADA, URRACO

When Italian tractor magnate, Ferruccio Lamborghini, decided that he would build a GT car that would satisfy his perfectionist tastes, he gathered a core of talented young engineers in 1962 to translate his wishes into design and then production. Giampaolo Dallara, Paolo Stanzani were in at the beginning; New Zealander Bob Wallace joined at the end of 1963 for the development of the first car, by which time the new factory at Sant'Agata Bolognese was nearly complete.

While the trio above all had previous Maserati connections, engine design was entrusted to Giotto Bizzarrini who was to go on to design the Iso Rivoltas and his own Grifo derivative, the Strada 5300. Fresh from Ferrari where he had led the 250GTO project, he followed instructions to produce a more modern engine than Ferrari with more power and came up with a 3.5-litre V-12 with twin overhead camshafts, an extrapolated version of a 1.5-litre racing engine he had designed for Ferrari. While that produced over 350 bhp at 8000 rpm on the test-bed it was then tamed for production durability by Dallara to a still respectable 270 bhp at 6500 rpm. Dallara's chassis was a straightforward tubular frame, but it had independent rear suspension which was then a rarity. Gearbox came from ZF and final drive from Salisbury.

Touring produced the production body which was well received at Geneva in March 1964; despite the short development period, production then started with Touring making the bodywork with the chassis also contracted out – then, as now, the Lamborghini line was a final assembly facility built around a machine shop. After a year of 350GT production, the engine was enlarged to 3.9-litres with 320 bhp for the 400GT, which also used Lamborghini's own gearbox and final drive assembly. Maximum speed went from 148 to 156 mph although the 0-60 mph time was slower than before as the car had put on weight – but 7.0 seconds wasn't slow in those days; it was also a very good GT car.

The Lamborghini 350GT was the first from Sant'Agata in 1964; the 400GT followed a year later with its 4-litre V-12 producing 320 bhp, as this 1966 example.

Below: A 2+2 400GT was offered in 1966, but replaced in 1968 by the Islero 2+2. The 4-seater Espada was launched at the same time and continued for the next 10 years; this is a 1972 Espada.

For 1966, a 2+2 was added to the range. On the same wheelbase, extra space was found with a 2-in higher roof-line and adjustment to the rear suspension mountings. It sold better than the 2-seaters, so its replacement Islero for 1968 was also a 2+2; slightly taller, but shorter, than the 400GT 2+2, its shape was created jointly by the boss and Marazzi, a group of ex-Touring employees following the collapse of the Milan coachbuilder. It was clean and simple, but was somewhat overshadowed by the striking Bertone-styled four-seater Espada which was launched at the same 1968 Geneva Show.

While the Islero had continued with the old tubular chassis, the Espada followed Miura thinking and used a sheet steel platform. Its body was modelled on Bertone's Marzal concept car; it was longer, lower and wider than the Islero and featured a fast-back with a lift-up window and an auxiliary glass panel in the tail to assist visibility, the car being only 3ft.11in tall. The engine, now with the 350 bhp version brought in for the Islero GTS, was well forward and it was a genuine four-seater; it was a top seller straight away and continued in production until 1978, by which time Lamborghini had changed hands – Ferruccio had sold out to Swiss interests during 1972/3. Meanwhile the Islero was only in production for two years, being replaced by the Bertone-designed Jarama which had adopted the Espada chassis with nearly 7 inches out of the wheelbase – that continued until 1976.

From early on, thought had always been given to a small Lamborghini for the higher volume, lower price Porsche market. It wasn't until the Dino 246 arrived in 1969 that this was put into action – the Urraco would be a mid-engined 2+2 with a new V-8 engine. This was all-aluminium but used single overhead camshafts driven by toothed belt which gave 220 bhp in 2.5-litre form for the P250 – the gearbox was mounted on the end; a sheet steel chassis carried MacPherson strut suspension at each corner and the body was a very neat and attractive Bertone design. First shown in late 1970, it was well liked and production began in 1972; for 1975, the engine was uprated for the P300 with a 250 bhp 3-litre version with four chain-driven cams, an altogether nicer power unit which gave the car a 158 mph maximum speed. But problems in the factory and world economy limited its production to a mere 205 cars by 1979 against 586 of its smaller predecessor. The concept lived on, though, into the Jalpa.

'The Lamborghini line was a final assembly facility built around a machine shop.'

The mid-engined Urraco with a 2.5-litre V-8 began production in 1972 but was replaced by the better 3-litre P300 in 1975. Bertone styled the little 2+2.

SPECIFICATION	400GT (1966)	ESPADA (1972)	URRACO P300 (1975)
ENGINE	Ali V-12, 3929 cc	Ali V-12, 3929 cc	Ali V-8, 2996 cc
POWER	320 bhp @ 6500 rpm	350 bhp @ 7800 rpm	250 bhp @ 7500 rpm
TRANSMISSION	Manual 5-speed	Manual 5-speed	Manual 5-speed
CHASSIS	Tubular frame	Sheet steel	Sheet steel
BRAKES	Discs all round	Discs all round	Discs all round
TOP SPEED	156 mph	153 mph	158 mph
0-60 MPH 0-100 MPH	7.0 sec 17.1 sec	7.8 sec 17.8 sec	7.5 sec 17.5 sec

Lamborghini Miura, Countach, Diablo

'They performed with all the promise of that exciting design; top speed around 170 mph with roadholding at race-track levels.'

Once the first Lamborghini was under way in 1964, the thoughts of its enterprising young engineers turned towards creating a car that could be used for GT racing, which demanded a mid-engined layout. Although Ferruccio Lamborghini would never sanction a racing project, he encouraged the development which was to lead to the first supercar, the Miura P400, with stunning 2-seater bodywork by Bertone's young designer, Marcello Gandini. It was first shown in chassis form at the 1965 Turin Show, and initial thoughts of producing perhaps a handful were overwhelmed by the interest shown.

The difficulty of fitting the long V-12 350 bhp 4-litre into a mid-engined layout was ingeniously solved by setting it transversely, and integrating the gearbox behind it with a complex crankcase casting which could only have been done in Italy. Its chassis followed modern racing style and used a sheet steel centre section with fore and aft extensions to carry the wishbone suspensions and cradle the engine.

The first prototype was shown at the 1966 Geneva Show from which point road development could only just begin; so the first cars didn't leave until early 1967. They performed with all the promise of that exciting design; top speed around 170 mph with roadholding at race-track levels. Two years later it received more power, a stiffened chassis and some suspension changes to cope with wider tyres; the P400S had 370 bhp. The final version, the P400SV, came a year later with even wider tyres requiring some bodywork flaring, and another 15 bhp. In all, 765 were built; production stopped prematurely in 1971 to hand over to the Countach, but that took two more years to develop after its first showing at Geneva that year. But the Miura had put the Lamborghini star in the supercar ascendant.

For the Countach, Dallara produced a space-frame chassis but took a front-engine gearbox unit and turned it round to put the gear-box nearest the driver; this gave a very short and direct gear linkage. Drive was taken to the rear wheels through drop-down gears and a shaft through the sump under the, thus, slightly raised engine. Although a 5-litre engine had been planned, Lamborghini business problems were to delay that for 10 years, so the 4-litre V-12 continued with 375 bhp. The body again came from Bertone's Gandini – a slender, near-single volume shape that was every bit as breath-taking as had been the Miura's. It was 5 inches wider and a shade taller, so the top speed didn't change significantly, but

The Countach finally got into production in 1973 as the LP400; wider tyres introduced for this LP400S in 1978 brought glassfibre eyebrows over the wheel arches.

Last of the remarkable mid-engined Miuras was the P400SV – this is a 1971 model – with wider tyres and its engine output increased to 385 bhp. The Miura set Lamborghini on the world map.

when it finally went into production in late 1973 as the LP400, it was well worth the wait. Unfortunately its shape had lost much of its unity in development, as the rear-mounted radiators required scoops instead of slats on the engine cover, as well as NACA ducts on the side.

Further desecration of the original shape came with the LP400S in 1978; the arrival of Pirelli's big, low profile P7 tyre brought glass-fibre eyebrows over the wheel arches, the front ones blending into a new chin-spoiler, and revised suspension. The 5-litre (4.75 actually) came in 1982 as the LP500S, but the power output remained the same but at lower revs – emission laws were biting. However the adoption of four-valves per cylinder with a 5.17-litre capacity for the LP5000S QV in 1985 raised the power to 455 bhp and the maximum speed to around 190 mph, the body remaining unchanged. And that was the final version until the Diablo arrived in 1990.

During the Countach's 16-year life, the company had endured its ups and downs, but Chrysler's take-over in 1987 gave them some stability and a chance to get on with a new car. This had a new Gandini shape, much cleaner than the Countach had become, and made good use of a greater understanding of aerodynamics above and below the car. Under the skin it remained very similar to the Countach but the space-frame was slightly lengthened to allow for the option of a four-wheel-drive version. A 5.7-litre version of the V-12 gave 492 bhp; with its more wind-cheating shape, the Diablo could reach 205 mph; the heavier 4WD VT was 3 mph slower when it arrived a year later. Since then we have had the SE30, a special edition (150-off) model to celebrate 30 years (1963-93) of Lamborghini production; this has 525 bhp and has been usefully lightened using some magnesium castings and carbon-fibre composites. You can recognise it by the slatted panel that fills in the valley behind the rear window. But even in its standard form, the Diablo is a worthy successor to the Miura.

SPECIFICATION	MIURA P400S (1970)	COUNTACH LP400 (1975)	DIABLO (1991)
ENGINE	Ali V-12, 3929 cc	Ali V-12, 3929 cc	Ali V-12, 5707 cc
POWER	370 bhp @ 7500 rpm	375 bhp @ 8000 rpm	492 bhp @ 7000 rpm
TRANSMISSION	Manual 5-speed	Manual 5-speed	Manual 5-speed
CHASSIS	Sheet steel	Space frame	Space frame
BRAKES	Discs all round	Discs all round	Discs all round
TOP SPEED	172 mph	175 mph	205 mph
0-60 MPH 0-100 MPH	6.7 sec 15.1 sec	5.6 sec 13.1 sec	4.2 sec 8.5 sec

After 16 years of the Countach, the Diablo arrived in 1990, with a very similar chassis but an all-new, much cleaner Gandini body style. This is a 1994 model.

LANCIA AURELIA, FULVIA COUPÉ, BETA COUPÉ

Lancia has a long history of producing cars that are never mundane and which have frequently been trend setters. Even after the Fiat take-over, the Lancia badge has adorned cars that have little obvious affinity with others in the Fiat line-up, often because Lancia has been the rallying flag-ship with such as the Stratos or Delta Integrale, following on from the traditions of the Fulvia coupé.

'It was a pretty little car with remarkable roadholding and ride comfort.'

The history goes back to 1906 when Vincenzo Lancia founded his own company in Turin; then, as later, model names used the Greek alphabet – those that didn't had other classical connections. By 1922, he had reached the Lambda, which pioneered unitary body/chassis construction, had independent front suspension and an overhead camshaft narrow V-4. The 1937 Aprilia saloon was another trend-setter, a streamlined body, all-round independent suspension and a 1352 cc V-4 giving 47 bhp and over 80 mph – it was Vicenzo's last as he died that year, but the philosophy of innovation continued.

After the war, 1951 saw the legendary Aurelia designed by Jano (from Alfa-Romeo) and Vicenzo's son Gianni. Both saloon and the shorter B20 coupé used a new V-6 engine, initially of 1754 cc, then 1991 cc and finally of 2451 cc with 110 bhp. They also had all-round independent suspension – the pre-war sliding pillar at the front and a semi-trailing system at the rear before the latter was replaced by a de Dion axle – and a rear-mounted gearbox in unit with the final drive. The B20 was technically very advanced and offered exceptional performance, ride and roadholding for its day; it was also the first practical 2+2 style to follow on from Pininfarina's new fast-back look first shown on the 1948 Cisitalia. Over the seven years that the various versions were in production, only some 3600 coupés were built, but they performed so well on the road and in competition that many sought to emulate their stylish characteristics.

The V-6 Flaminia and front-drive flat-4 Flavia followed on with saloon and coupé variants alongside the little V-4 engined Appia which had been launched in 1953 and was replaced by the Fulvia in 1964. This came as a boxy four-door saloon or the neat and compact two-door 2+2 coupé, with a wheelbase 6.4-inches shorter.

Both used the narrow V-4 – with only 19 degrees between the banks, it used a single twin-cam cylinder head – in sizes ranging from 1100 to

All-independent suspension, rear gearbox and a powerful V-6 engine made the Aurelia an advanced car for 1951; this 1953 B20GT shows the elegant fastback lines.

The Fulvia Coupé with front wheel drive was a fast and economical 2-seater that became a rally winner in 1.6HF form during the late 'sixties.

1600 cc; this was mated to a front-drive gearbox while the wishbone front suspension was mounted on a solid sub-frame which absorbed road shocks particularly well. It was a pretty little car with remarkable roadholding and ride comfort; in its 1.6HF form it became an outright rally winner.

Good though the Lancia designs were, they were never produced in sufficient quantities to match their rivals on price and Fiat took over in 1969. The first product of the rationalisation came in 1972 with the Beta, once more front-wheel-drive but using a transversely mounted Fiat twin-cam 'four' of 1438, 1592 or 1756 cc. This came in four-door fast-back saloon form with a two-door notch-back coupé and Zagato built Spider added in 1973. The range was further extended in 1975 with the attractive and effective HPE (High Performance Estate) by which time the 1.8-litre had been superseded by a 2-litre version; at the same time came the Beta Monte Carlo. This followed the theme of the Fiat X1/9 – a mid-engined sports car using a Fiat 128 engine/transmission package – by using the Beta package still mounted transversely but behind the driver; clothed in an attractive body by Pininfarina it certainly had the looks of a mini-Ferrari but not the performance, which was why it didn't sell as well as intended. Production was suspended after 1978 but it came back again two years later and formed the basis of the Fiat group's rally contender; although that was somewhat different under a similar skin, it kept the Monte Carlo flag flying for a few more years.

Early Betas may have had a deserved reputation for rust, but the basic design was good; the survivors are worth keeping.

Fiat's 1969 takeover led to some rationalisation of which the Fiat-powered Beta was the first product in 1972. A coupé and the Zagato-bodied Spider came in '73, this being a 1977 2-litre coupé.

SPECIFICATION	AURELIA GT2500 (1955)	FULVIA COUPÉ 1.3 (1968)	BETA COUPÉ 1.8 (1976)
ENGINE	V-6 ohv, 2451 cc	V-4 dohc, 1298 cc	4-cyl dohc, 1756 cc
POWER	118 bhp @ 5000 rpm	87 bhp @ 6000 rpm	110 bhp @ 6000 rpm
TRANSMISSION	Manual 4-speed t/axle	Manual 4-speed	Manual 5-speed
CHASSIS	Unitary steel	Unitary steel	Unitary steel
BRAKES	Drums	Discs	Discs
TOP SPEED	112 mph	103 mph	109 mph
0-60 MPH	12.3 sec	11.9 sec	10.7 sec

LOTUS SEVEN, ELITE, ELAN

'Elans were quick cars with still exceptional road-holding and remarkable ride qualities.'

While Lotus was a major name in *Grand Prix* circles for some 35 years, the company has been making sports cars for over 40 years. Founder Colin Chapman came up through the early post-war school of special builders, the impecunious enthusiasts who created their own competition cars around Ford or Austin 7 parts removed from tired saloons. Having built several specials and a few replicas for friends, Chapman set up his own company in 1952; his first 'production' car was the Mk.6. A clubman's competition road car, this had an aluminium body rivetted to a space-frame with a divided Ford front axle and a choice of engines. Such a clientele was quite happy to buy the car in kit form and thus avoid purchase tax.

The 7 was set to follow on, but small sports-racing cars (8, 9, 10 and 11) intervened; however, as the clubman demand was still there, the 7 was brought off the design shelves in 1957.

Using a simpler space-frame, this had wishbone front suspension and a glassfibre nose-cone, and was again a kit-car to take a variety of engines. Lotus took this through four series of progressive improvement without loss of character until the manufacturing rights were transferred to Caterham Cars in 1973; and the car is still in production although modelled now on the Series 3. However, those early Lotus sports cars were essentially small, efficient competition cars that could be used on the road, but by then Chapman wanted to produce a genuine road car.

The Elite (Lotus 14) was launched in 1957 with an innovative glassfibre monocoque shell which carried metal inserts for suspension and power train mountings and a steel roll-hoop. Producing a steel chassis was out of the question for the numbers envisaged due to high tooling costs, while space-frames would take too long to build which would make the unit cost too high. Tooling for grp (glass-reinforced plastic) was relatively cheap but it had only been used previously on unstressed bodywork; however by astute use of the various types of grp with a well-boxed structure, Chapman came up with a two-seater fixed head GT which was stiffer than most such cars. The attractive body-style came from Peter Kirwan-Taylor with aerodynamic adjustment by Frank Costin who had developed the wind-cheating sports-racers. All-round independent suspension used MacPherson strut principles which had been used on the Lotus 12, the first single-seater F2 car, together with disc brakes.

Lightweight glass-fibre body/chassis and lightweight Climax engine made the Elite a remarkably efficient machine, which achieved considerable success on the track.

Elite successor, the Elan was simpler to make and faster with its twin-cam 1558 cc engine. This is a Series 4 Elan.

SPECIFICATION	SUPER SEVEN (1961)	ELITE SE (1962)	ELAN (1964)
ENGINE	Ford 4-cyl, 1340 cc	Ali 4-cyl, 1216 cc	Dohc 4-cyl, 1558 cc
POWER	85 bhp @ 6000 rpm	85 bhp @ 6300 rpm	105 bhp @ 5500 rpm
TRANSMISSION	Manual 4-speed	Manual 4-speed	Manual 4-speed
CHASSIS	Steel, ali body	Grp monocoque	Steel , grp body
BRAKES	Drums	Discs	Discs
TOP SPEED	102 mph	117 mph	112 mph
0-60 MPH	8.3 sec	10.7 sec	9.0 sec
0-100 MPH	—	33.9 sec	24.1 sec

All the Lotus cars had used small engines from Ford, BMC or the lightweight all-aluminium Coventry-Climax unit that had been developed for portable fire-pumps; Climax developed the FWE for Lotus with 1216 cc and 75 bhp. With the low drag body this was sufficient to give a 112 mph maximum rising to 117 mph when fitted with the twin carburetter 85 bhp version. With only 13.5 cwt (690 Kg) to propel, 85 bhp produced a 0-60 mph time of 10.7 seconds; it could also be very economical – 45 mpg at 70 mph – and the road-holding was exceptionally good. But despite the appeal to the keen motorist, the Elite was not a commercial success; it was not easy to make and was expensive for the performance.

For its 1962 replacement, the Elan (Lotus 26) again used glassfibre, but only for the body. The chassis was a folded sheet metal backbone with forks at each end to carry engine and front suspension and the rear suspension. Power came from the Ford-based twin-cam engine that Lotus had developed for the Lotus Cortina, with 1558 cc and 105 bhp; front suspension used normal wishbones but the rear retained the coil strut system with rubber doughnuts in the drive-shafts. The body was neat and attractive but lacked the all-time grace of the Elite. In time, it spawned the fixed head coupé (Lotus 36) and, in 1967, the stretched Elan Plus 2, the Lotus 50, arrived with reasonable rear seat space, while the engine output gradually increased to 130 bhp; although the Elans were quick cars with still exceptional road-holding and remarkable ride qualities, they were still quite expensive as they were very much hand-built – as kit cars, though, without purchase tax, they were a better buy. Over 12,000 Elans and 5200 Plus 2s were built in the 12-year production run – but they served to launch Lotus as a maker of genuine road cars.

Lotus built the 7 as a clubman's competition car, but it has remained a popular road car ever since its 1957 launch, now being produced as a Caterham 7. This is a mid-'sixties Series 2.

LOTUS EUROPA, ELITE, ESPRIT TURBO

'Colin Chapman decided that Lotus should make a mid-engined replacement for the Lotus 7.'

By the mid-'sixties Lotus was split into three operations. Lotus Cars built road cars while Team Lotus built and ran their own racing cars (including Elans and Lotus-Cortinas); Lotus Components built customer racing cars and the Lotus 7, but demand was dwindling for this side of the business. As all serious racing cars were mid-engined, Colin Chapman decided that Lotus should make a mid-engined replacement for the Lotus 7. When the Renault 16 arrived in 1964, its front-drive engine/gearbox layout seemed an ideal package for such a car. Despite their allegiance to Alpine, Renault agreed to provide 500 such units for the new Lotus 46, the Europa, which was launched in 1966.

This used what was effectively an Elan backbone chassis reversed to carry the Renault power train amidships; the engine had been uprated by Renault to give 78 bhp. Triumph front suspension assemblies and a simple rear suspension using a fixed length drive-shaft as the upper link kept costs low; as did fixed side windows and fixed seats with pedal adjustment. It had a neat enough low-drag grp body style which allowed 110 mph, but the sail panels behind the side windows obstructed visibility. By the time Lotus had finished, though, the price was nearer that of an Elan than a 7, and most of the first series went to France. An S2 followed in 1968 with such refinements as wind-up windows, a body that was no longer bonded to the backbone chassis and some luggage space behind the engine; some of these Renault-engined ones were sold in the UK, but the best version came in 1971 when the Elan's twin-cam engine was inserted with a stronger Renault gearbox, the rear panels were chopped and the interior made less stark. The final Europa Special version came in 1972 with the engine uprated to 126 bhp with a five-speed box; good for nearly 125 mph, this at last had the performance to match the chassis. Over 9000 Europas were built in the 8-year period.

Best of the Europas was the Special which used the Lotus twin-cam engine instead of the Renault 16 unit; cut down rear side panels improved visibility.

Europas had also been seen on the race-tracks. Lotus Components had built 55 Lotus 47s, Europas with the twin-cam engine, for Group 4 racing during 1967. Then in 1969 a pair of Lotus 62 Europas race-proved a new engine which was to be the prototype for the new range of Lotus road cars. As the twin-cam engine needed replacement, as much for emission reasons as for the fact that it used an obsolete Ford block, Lotus had drawn up a new 2-litre 16-valve slant-4 as half of a potential future V-8; but the arrival of Vauxhall's similar Victor engine saved a lot of development time and was used with a new head and dry sump lubrication for the test-bed racers. In fact this engine was ready for production before the new Lotus cars; with Lotus' own cylinder block and 140 bhp it was used in the Jensen Healey from 1972.

The new estate-style Elite finally arrived in mid-1974 in the middle of the fuel crisis, which should have helped its sales as it was a fast, efficient four-seater with fair fuel consumption.

Under-rated, the new Elite of 1974 was an efficient 2-litre semi-estate car which should have sold well in the aftermath of the 1973 fuel crisis, but was too expensive for its performance.

The backbone chassis principle was retained as was a refined independent suspension; Lotus' full understanding of suspension theory ensured a comfortable ride/roadholding compromise. While the body still used grp, a new Lotus process (Vacuum Assisted Resign Injection) ensured a high quality finish. For their own car, Lotus chose a 155 bhp version of the 16-valve engine which gave it a 126 mph maximum. Somehow it was never a very popular car as only 2400 had been built by the time it was phased out in 1983; even the arrival of the 2.2-litre version in 1980 hadn't helped. Meanwhile 1975 had seen the arrival of two further variations on the theme, the cheaper fast-back Eclat, and the new mid-engined Esprit.

The latter had been seen at the 1972 Turin Show as a Giugiaro styling exercise on a Europa Twin-Cam chassis. Well received, it was quickly incorporated into the new range using a similar back-bone chassis design with a gearbox from the Citroen SM coupled to a 160 bhp version of the slant-4 engine. This gave it a 135 mph maximum which was enough, then, to put it near the supercar category. It finally arrived there in 1980 when the turbocharged 2.2-litre engine was adopted. In much refined form the Esprit is still in production, capable of around 160 mph.

SPECIFICATION	EUROPA SPECIAL (1972)	ELITE (1975)	ESPRIT TURBO (1981)
ENGINE	4-cyl dohc, 1558 cc	Ali dohc, 1973 cc	Turbo 2174 cc
POWER	126 bhp @ 6500 rpm	155 bhp @ 6500 rpm	210 bhp @ 6000 rpm
TRANSMISSION	Manual 5-speed	Manual 5-speed	Manual 5-speed
CHASSIS	Steel backbone chassis with glassfibre bodywork (*all models*)		
BRAKES	Disc/drum	Disc/drum	Discs
TOP SPEED	122 mph	126 mph	148 mph
0-60 MPH 0-100 MPH	6.6 sec 21.6 sec	7.8 sec 24.5 sec	6.1 sec 17.8 sec

The Esprit came in 1975 but had to wait until 1980 before the Turbo took it into the supercar performance club, even if roadholding was second to very few. Two Bond films were graced with the Esprit.

'It wasn't until the factory withdrew from racing in 1957 that road cars could be taken seriously.'

Maserati Mistral, Khamsin, Merak

To the motor sport historian Maserati is one of the great names but, in truth, its world status really only stemmed from the mid-'fifties when the 250F ruled the *Grand Prix* scene and the sports-racing cars, 300S and 450S, were frequent front-runners although rarely winners. The company was founded in 1926 by the Maserati brothers and most of the pre-war cars were built for competition; while some of the post-war 2-litre cars were equipped with road-going bodywork, it wasn't until the factory withdrew from racing in 1957 that road cars could be taken seriously.

This 1976 Khamsin was a product of the Citroen period of ownership. With the big V-8, the Bertone-styled 2+2 was destined for an 8-year run from 1974-82.

For the next ten years these drew heavily on the racing designs which had mostly used six-cylinder twin-cam engines up to 3-litres, with a 4.5-litre V-8 used for that final season. However the camshafts of the road-going engines were driven by chain rather than gears, and lubrication was by wet sump systems. In fact the six-cylinder road-car engine used different dimensions within new castings, but it followed the 250F/300S design and had also been raced in the 350S. The first road car was the 3.5-litre 3500GT 2+2 which used a tubular frame under its Touring bodywork; in the days of separate chassis, coachbuilders would make single models or complete production runs. Vignale brought in the open Spider version on a shortened chassis in 1959, the same year in which the V-8 made its first road appearance for the limited run of 32 5000GT coupés.

The six-cylinder cars received fuel injection in 1962 – 3500GTI – while 1963 saw Vignale make a coupé version of the Spider which would become the Sebring; in the same year Frua produced the Quattroporte with a 4.2-litre V-8 as well as the two-seater Mistral coupé on a further shortened 3500 chassis. By the next year this had a 3.7-litre option which would be further enlarged to 4.0-litre in 1966 when the Mistral Spider was introduced – Mistral lines are recognisable in the AC 428 which was also being built by Frua at the time. That was the last model to use the original 'six'.

The original Touring 3500 had been dropped at the end of 1964, and 1965 saw the 5000GT replaced by the Vignale-bodied Mexico, a low volume luxury four-seater powered by the V-8 in 4.2 or 4.7-litre forms. A year later came Ghia's memorable Ghibli, a supremely elegant fast-back

SPECIFICATION	MISTRAL (1968)	MERAK (1973)	KHAMSIN (1978)
ENGINE	Dohc 6, 4018 cc	4-cam V-6, 2965 cc	4-cam V-8, 4930 cc
POWER	255 bhp @ 5500 rpm	190 bhp @ 6000 rpm	320 bhp @ 5500 rpm
TRANSMISSION	Manual 5-speed	Manual 5-speed	Manual 5-speed
CHASSIS	Steel frame and body	Steel frame and body	Unitary steel
BRAKES	Discs	Discs	Discs
TOP SPEED	145 mph	140 mph	156 mph
0-60 MPH 0-100 MPH	7.2 sec 18.4 sec	7.5 sec 19.9 sec	6.5 sec 16.8 sec

2-seater with the 4.7-litre V-8 (later 4.9-litre), with a spyder version following in 1968. That year Vignale added to his Mexico production with the Indy as a 4.2 or 4.7-litre four seater version of the Ghibli.

It seemed a bewildering range but Maserati just produced their chassis in different lengths with the V-8 engine in various states of tune and left most of the rest to the coachbuilders. When Citroen took over ownership in 1969, rationalisation was gradually brought in, such that by 1974 the front-engined GTs had all faded out in favour of the Bertone-bodied Khamsin 2+2 with the 4.9-litre V-8 engine. A striking looking machine, it was the first front-engined Maserati to feature independent rear suspension; it also had Citroen-style power brakes and steering assistance. The Khamsin was to stay in production until the new Biturbo range came in 1982.

Meanwhile Maserati had ventured into the mid-engined supercar field with the Bora using the 4.7-litre V-8 in a pressed steel chassis. First shown at Geneva in March 1971, this was styled by ItalDesign and was in production at Maserati by the end of the year. Strictly a two-seater, it was reasonably practical with luggage space in the front boot; and with a 160 mph potential it was very fast, well able to hold its head up alongside the comparable Lamborghini Miura. More practicality came with the Merak the following year; outwardly almost identical to the Bora, this used the power pack that Maserati had created for the front-drive Citroen SM – a 4-cam V-6 with transaxle mounted amidships. However as this was somewhat shorter than the V-8 plus ZF transaxle, there was room for a couple of small rear seats, or interior luggage. With only 190 bhp from the 3-litre engine, against the Bora's 310 bhp, it was considerably slower but 140 mph was fast enough for most in 1972. Three years later, the Merak SS had 220 bhp and an extra 6 mph or so.

That was the year in which Citroen retired and de Tomaso took over the reins.

Maserati joined the mid-engined supercar league with the V-8 Bora in 1971. A year later came the Merak with the Citroen SM power train, outwardly similar but with a 2+2 configuration. The Merak SS, as this 1980 example, had 220 bhp.

MERCEDES 300SL, 190SL, 280SL

'While SL had originally meant Sport Light, it had become just another model name.'

Given Mercedes pre-war racing eminence it was hardly surprising that their post-war return to motor sport would produce something pretty special. But success was by no means guaranteed, as there was little money available in the immediate aftermath of the war to spend on expensive racing projects. When the competition 300SL appeared in 1952 it had used most of the running gear from the 300 saloons, but kept the weight down by installing it in a lightweight chassis. It was much the same philosophy that Jaguar had employed with the C-type, only that was an open car; Mercedes decided they couldn't get the outright power to win short races and that aerodynamically efficient closed cars would be faster in long distance events. Trouble was that conventional doors would cut into their space-frame chassis, so they hinged these from the roof centre and the famous gull-wing doors were born.

These new cars only raced in 1952 as the German company was too busy preparing a return to *Grand Prix* racing in 1954; but, despite their six-cylinder 3-litre engines producing less than 180 bhp, they had remarkable success – 2nd and 4th in the Mille Miglia; 1-2-3 at Bern; 1-2 at Le Mans; 1-2-3 at Nurburgring (as open roadsters) and a final 1-2 at 102 mph in the Carrera Panamericana. Although the racing department continued to develop the cars, they didn't race again. However the American importer, Max Hoffman, insisted the company put the 300SL into production and ordered 1000; the new car was launched in February 1954, similar in overall design to the racing coupés, but incorporating some of the later developments, such as the Bosch fuel injection system which lifted the power to 200 bhp – when equipped with the sports camshaft this rose to 220 bhp.

Capable of around 145 mph, it became the instant supercar of the day and continued to be successful in competition, racing and rallying. By the time the coupé was phased out in favour of the roadster in 1957, nearly 1400 had been built; the open car retained the space-frame but conventional deeper doors were fitted. The new car also adopted the low-pivot swing axle of the later saloons; the normal swing axle used at the rear of the coupé had given it a rather tail-happy reputation.

Meanwhile part of Hoffman's proposal had been for a smaller sports car; the 190SL roadster

Conceived as the little brother to the 300SL, the 190SL looked very similar but its 4-cylinder engine produced only 105 bhp against the bigger car's 200 bhp.

The 1952 racing coupé was turned into this enviable 300SL road car with little change to the design thanks to the persuasion of Mercedes' American importer.

was launched at the same time as the 300SL. Outwardly very similar to the later 300SL roadster, this had a conventional saloon car platform with a 1.9-litre four-cylinder developing 105 bhp which was enough for around 110 mph. While it lacked the charisma of its bigger brother, it was a successful model in its own right.

The two roadsters stayed in production until 1963 when they were replaced by the 230SL, based on a shortened version of the 220SE saloon, but with its own distinctive styling. While SL had originally meant Sport Light, it had become just another model name; although all subsequent SLs were sportier and lighter than the saloons from which they were derived, they were fully engineered Mercedes road cars with no competition intention. The 230SL was a 2-seater roadster but could be fitted with a substantial hard-top which turned it into a properly trimmed coupé for winter use – it needed at least two people to remove this elegant pagoda-style roof. With 150 bhp from the 2.3-litre six-cylinder, the 230SL was a 120 mph car, or 115 mph when fitted with the more popular Mercedes 4-speed automatic transmission. Some 20,000 cars later, 1966 saw the 250SL with the same 150 bhp but more torque; another 5000 models on and a year later came the 280SL, still basically the same car but the 2.8-litre six-cylinder now produced 170 bhp which added another 5 mph. This SL range came to an end in 1971. The replacements were very similar but were mostly based on the new V-8 engines, rising to the flagship 500SL in 1985. The current range came in 1989, and like all the SLs are assured of future classic status.

Since the 300SL, the SL ranges have evolved from shortened saloon cars. This '68 280SL was the final version of the first such series which started with the 230SL.

SPECIFICATION	300SL (1955)	190SL (1956)	280SL (1968)
ENGINE	Six-cyl, 2996 cc	Four-cyl, 1897 cc	Six-cyl, 2778 cc
POWER	220 bhp @ 5800 rpm	105 bhp @ 5700 rpm	170 bhp @ 5500 rpm
TRANSMISSION	Manual 4-speed	Manual 4-speed	Auto 4-speed
CHASSIS	Steel frame, ali body	Unitary steel	Unitary steel
BRAKES	Drums	Drums	Discs
TOP SPEED	145 mph	109 mph	121 mph
0-60 MPH	7.2 sec	13.3 sec	9.3 sec
0-100 MPH	16.2 sec	—	25.8 sec

MG TC, TD, TF

While the MG had catered for a very British clientele before the 1939-45 war, the TC was to launch the marque on the world market, thanks in large part to the war. Many of Britain's allied troops had met the little British sports car at that time and fallen in love with it; Americans particularly, accustomed to larger, less sporting machinery, welcomed a car that made motoring enjoyable. To them it was also a natural successor to the Jeep in which many of them had their first experience of sporting motoring.

The initials MG came from Morris Garages, the retail off-shoot of William Morris' Oxford-based factory which had started producing cars in 1913. Cecil Kimber, the father of MG, was the manager of Morris Garages and, in the early 'twenties, decided to produce sporting versions of the Morris Cowley. Thus was born the marque MG. Then, as now, much of its content came from other mass-production models within the same company.

The MG TC was launched in 1945. In fact it was little changed from the TB which had been announced in 1939, but very few were built before the outbreak of war – just 379. And the TB had been the successor to the TA, launched as the T-

The MG TC (red car) took the British sports car into America. Small, agile and fun, it gave the visiting GIs a taste for the open air. Successor to the TC, the TD (green car) brought the front suspension up to date with independent wishbones within the still square-rigged shape.

type in 1936, with the customary MG soubriquet of Midget which had endorsed many of the previous models. The TA had been powered by a version of the Wolseley engine, a four-cylinder 1292 cc unit developing 52 bhp. For the TB this had been changed for the stronger, and potentially more tuneable, Morris engine; although slightly smaller at 1250 cc it developed 54 bhp with its twin SU carburetters.

Came the end of the war and a return to car production, MG abandoned their multi-model policy and concentrated all efforts on the new TC with just a single two-seater body-style. With little time available for development, design changes were kept to a minimum; the cramped cockpit was made four inches wider and the rear spring design was changed for more simple maintenance. So the TC was put quickly into production at a time when most manufacturers were still struggling to get going again.

So the TC was basically a pre-war design and looked it. The chassis was a simple box-section ladder with its axles carried on semi-elliptic springs. It wasn't fast even by period standards – 75 mph flat out and 15 seconds to reach 50 mph. But what it had was charisma. Wire wheels, long bonnet, big radiator grille and slab petrol tank exposed at the back, it looked like everyone's sporting ideal. It rapidly became MG's biggest volume model ever and 10,000 were made by the time it ceased late in 1949; one third stayed in Britain and 2000 went to America.

Pre-war in looks, the TC was also pre-war in road behaviour. Stiff springing gave an uncomfortable ride and poor, if entertaining, roadholding on poor surfaces. The TD was to change that – if not the performance. In 1947, MG had introduced the Y-type saloon; it had a slightly different chassis from that of the TC, but that carried independent front suspension. The TD made use of a shortened version of the Y-type chassis which brought the added benefit of increased track for better roadholding; this was further enhanced by lower, fatter tyres, now 5.50 x 15 instead of 4.50 x 19. The extra width, length and the introduction of bumpers served to add weight, so the same engine made the TD less accelerative than the TC – but it looked more modern and had the right appeal. Nearly 30,000 were sold during its four-year life and the majority were exported.

Last of the T-series, the TF was a belated attempt to bring a modern look to an old style. The 1500 cc engine finally added some performance in the year after this 1953 car.

By 1953, though, demand was falling; the TD was looking old-fashioned and it was slow compared with the new Austin-Healey 100 introduced in late 1952. That was a product of the same BMC, and MG were not allowed to produce another all-new sports car for the same market. The best they could achieve was the TF, a face-lifted TD, lower with a sloping dummy radiator grille, more comfortable and heavier; while its rakish lines increased the appeal, the performance was even slower than that of the TD. In 1954, the insertion of a 1466 cc version of the same engine, increased the power to 63 bhp and sustained some demand for the final year of T-series production – the more modern MGA was launched in late 1955.

Over its 19-year span, the T-series gave International fame to the name of MG. Many racing drivers cut their track teeth on the cars and they embodied all that was best in traditional British sporting machinery, dated though they had become by 1955. Their classic appeal has never diminished.

'Americans welcomed a car that made motoring enjoyable.'

SPECIFICATION	MG TC (1948)	MG TD Mk.II (1952)	MG TF 1500 (1954)
ENGINE	4-cyl 1250 cc	4-cyl 1250 cc	4-cyl 1466 cc
HORSEPOWER	54 bhp @ 5200 rpm	57 bhp @ 5500 rpm	63 bhp @ 5000 rpm
TRANSMISSION	4-speed manual	4-speed manual	4-speed manual
CHASSIS	Steel box frame with separate body panels (*all models*)		
BRAKES	Hydraulically operated drum brakes all round (*all models*)		
TOP SPEED	75 mph	77 mph	80 mph
0-60 MPH	22.7 sec	23.9 sec	19.5 sec

MGA, MGB, MGC

'It was just what the market wanted with near 100 mph performance, good roadholding and attractive modern styling.'

Despite the fact that MG was Britain's traditional sports car, the BMC management of the day nearly let the marque die in the early 'fifties. The T-series cars were looking very old-fashioned, but no-one would sanction the development of the special-bodied MG TD that had been built for Le Mans in 1951; BMC were going to launch the new Austin-Healey 100 at the 1952 Motor Show and didn't need two new sports cars. The TF face-lift was all that was allowed, but the Triumph TR2, which arrived at the same 1953 Show, was another nail in the T-series coffin.

The Y-type MG saloon had likewise been getting a little long in the tooth. This was partially cured with the 1953 launch of the ZA Magnette. This followed on from the Wolseley 4/44 which had been launched the year before using the MG TD's 1250 cc engine, but the MG received the new BMC B-series 1489 cc unit – the Wolseley would get the same engine in 1956 and become the 15/50. The ZA and its ZB successor went on to be highly regarded sports saloons.

While that 1951 Le Mans MG had sat at Abingdon, the new chief engineer, Syd Enever, had made a new chassis which allowed the occupants to sit lower in the same body than had been possible with the TD chassis. While this had been completed in 1952 using the TF 1500 engine, and had been converted to a possible record car in 1953, it wasn't until mid-1954 that Enever was given the order to turn this into a production reality and to use the new B-series engine with 68 bhp. Three prototypes were entered in the 1955 Le Mans 24-hours and two finished, one averaging 86 mph; still as prototypes, three ran in the TT that year and one finished 4th in class behind the Porsches. Finally the MGA was announced for the 1955 Show with an instant competition history. It was just what the market wanted with near 100 mph performance, good roadholding and attractive modern styling – it rapidly outsold all previous MGs. A year later the roadster was joined by the fixed head coupé and in 1958 both became available with a 1588 cc 108 bhp twin-cam engine. The MGA 1600 came in 1959 with 80 bhp and disc front brakes, while the final version from 1961 was the 93 bhp 1622 cc Mk.II 1600. Just over 100,000 MGAs were produced in the 1955-62 period, more than twice the post-war T-series over 1945-55.

MGB production figures were even more impressive; over half a million were to be produced over the next 18 years before the Abingdon factory closed for ever. Higher volumes were always

Although the MGA was late to join the mid-range sports car market in 1955, it soon became a very popular car. The example shown is the rare Twin Cam, easily distinguished by its Dunlop knock-off wheels.

envisaged for the MGA's replacement, so the separate body/chassis construction of the A gave way to the monocoque construction of the B. The power unit was still the trusty B-series now enlarged to 1798 cc and 95 bhp while the 4-speed gearbox could be supplemented with an overdrive. The new sports car was considerably more comfortable than its predecessor with more space as well as a better ride; and it could comfortably clear 100 mph too. As before, the roadster was joined by a coupé, the MGB GT, in 1966. Over the years there was little apparent change to the basic B, apart from the switch from chrome to rubber bumpers, but a host of detail changes came in response to changing safety and emission legislation; and there were two short-lived additional models.

It was safety legislation that was terminating big Healey production. A six-cylinder MGB should have been a suitable replacement. Unfortunately the 3-litre engine chosen for the MGC in 1967 was a particularly gutless and overweight unit developed for the Austin 3-litre saloon; its size and weight caused a front suspension redesign and the handling became most unsporting – it was somewhat better with the GT version which had stiffer rear springs. It actually needed very little work to make the GT into a worthy Healey replacement – better engine breathing and a shorter axle ratio – but this was never done by MG and the model died after just two years and 9000 cars.

SPECIFICATION	**MGA 1500** (1955)	**MGB** (1962)	**MGC GT** (1967)
ENGINE	4-cyl, 1489 cc	4-cyl, 1798 cc	6-cyl, 2912 cc
POWER	68 bhp @ 5500 rpm	95 bhp @ 5400 rpm	145 bhp @ 5250 rpm
TRANSMISSION	Manual 4-speed	Manual 4-speed	Manual 4-speed + o/d
CHASSIS	Steel chassis/body	Unitary steel	Unitary steel
BRAKES	Drums	Disc/drum	Disc/drum
TOP SPEED	98 mph	108 mph	119 mph
0-60 MPH	16.0 sec	12.1 sec	10.1 sec

The other short-term model was the MGB GT V-8; somewhat belatedly the 3.5-litre Rover V-8 was fitted to the GT to provide a very rapid sports coupé from 1972-6, but it was canned after only 2591 had been built, reputedly because Rover needed all the engines for their other products. Maybe the old B design was dated by the mid-'seventies, but the 125 mph B GT V-8 gave very good performance value.

The MGB was designed for big numbers and half a million were produced over 18 years. The GT came in 1966, and the MGBGT V-8 shown here started its short-lived run in 1972.

Conceived as a replacement for the big Healey, the MGC had a gutless six-cylinder engine and poor handling. However, intelligent tuning could transform them into proper sports cars, like this 1968 rally version.

MORGAN 4/4, PLUS 4, PLUS 8

'The Morgan is essentially a 'thirties classic with performance that keeps pace with the times.'

Founded in 1910, the Morgan Motor Company spent its first twenty-five years making three-wheelers, the stable kind with two front wheels set wide apart. They ranged from runabouts to competition speed models, the engines from twin-cylinder air-cooled to four-cylinder water-cooled. Their success was based on sound engineering. What is particularly remarkable is that the first model had an independent front suspension design which is still in use on present-day Morgans – the sliding pillar system.

The first four-wheeler came in 1936; the 4/4 denoted four wheels and a four-cylinder engine, an 1122 cc side-valve Coventry Climax; its design set the pattern that was to follow. Where most used a channel section chassis, Morgan used a Z-section which made it easier to mount the floorboards; at the front was the familiar sliding pillar suspension, while the rear saw a conventional live axle mounted on underslung leaf springs which were inset from the chassis side members. The four-speed Moss gearbox was distanced from the engine by a short tube to ensure that the gear lever could act directly on the selectors without a long lever or remote control. The steel bodywork was mounted on ash frames with contemporary styling – long louvred bonnet with chrome radiator, front wings sweeping into running boards, and twin spare wheels mounted on the flat tail. It was a sleek modern motor car back in 1936 with a maximum speed of almost 80 mph.

Since then, little has changed in the style. The flat radiator gave way to a cowled one in 1954 when the headlights were fared into the wings, while the body is wider than it used to be. A four-seater version was offered in 1937 and is still available. Over the years it is only changing power units that have denoted the different models; although some of the design features have been strengthened and the chassis length has also varied, the Morgan is essentially a 'thirties classic with performance that keeps pace with the times thanks to period engines.

The 34 bhp Climax engine was supplemented with an overhead valve Standard Flying Ten unit of 1267 cc with 39 bhp in 1939. After the war, Morgan continued with the Standard-powered 4/4 while the 3-wheelers were to remain in production using side-valve Ford units until 1950. When Standard decided to use just a single engine

Initially with the Vanguard 2088 cc 'four', the Plus 4 stuck to Triumph TR power through to 1968. This 1966 4-seater uses the TR4's 2138 cc engine.

When the TR5 adopted a six-cylinder engine, Morgan switched to the Rover V-8 to create the Plus 8 which has been the mainstay from 1968 onwards.

for the new Vanguard, Morgan moved with them and adopted the big 2088 cc 68 bhp four-cylinder in 1951 to create the Plus 4. An improved 1991 cc version of this engine was created for the TR2 in 1953 with 90 bhp, but it wasn't until 1955 that Morgan were allowed to use it, and then only in limited quantities; accordingly Morgan brought back the 4/4 range using the side-valve 1172 cc Ford engine and gearbox as the 4/4 Series 2 – with the same power as the pre-war models it is not surprising that the top speed didn't change from 75 mph but it was a popular car. When the 100 bhp TR3 engine was fitted to the Plus 4 from 1956, Morgan had a genuine 100 mph car; Motor's 1957 road test was headed 'A modern vintage sports car with vivid acceleration' . . . but they liked it!

The Plus 4 would continue with the TR engines until the arrival of the six-cylinder TR5 made them obsolete; fortunately for Morgan enthusiasts the six wouldn't fit, but Rover's 3.5-litre V-8 could be shoe-horned in with small increases in chassis length and width; still mated to a Moss gearbox which had been strengthened over the years, the new Plus 8 arrived in 1968 and has been the backbone of production ever since – with 168 bhp it became an instant 125 mph car and could reach 100 mph in under 20 seconds. Still primitive in the comfort department, it was and has remained great fun.

Meanwhile the 4/4 had become a Series 3 using the Ford 997 cc ohv engine in 1961, changing to a Series 4 a year later with the 1340 cc version and a Series 5 with the 1498 cc Ford in 1963. That year saw Morgan's only attempt to modernise the range with a neat two-seater glassfibre coupé body placed on top of the Plus 4 chassis; it was not a success and only 50 were made.

Throughout Morgan existence the cars have been regularly used in competitions, from trials and rallies to circuit racing. The most famous success was with a competition version of the Plus 4 in the 1962 Le Mans 24-hour race; finishing 13th overall, it won the 2-litre class. Today's Morgans are just as much at home on road and track as their predecessors.

The original 4/4 was Morgan's first four-wheeler. Subsequent 4/4 series cars started again in 1955 with Ford power, from the 1172 cc side-valve to the 1498 cc Cortina unit in 1963. This is a 1972 4/4.

SPECIFICATION	4/4 SERIES 2 (1956)	PLUS 4 (1957)	PLUS 8 (1968)
ENGINE	Ford sv, 1172 cc	Triumph ohv, 1991 cc	Rover V-8, 3528 cc
POWER	36 bhp @ 4400 rpm	100 bhp @ 4800 rpm	168 bhp @ 5200 rpm
TRANSMISSION	Manual 3-speed	Manual 4-speed	Manual 4-speed
CHASSIS	Cross-braced Z-section steel chassis with steel bodywork (*all models*)		
BRAKES	Drums	Drums	Disc/drum
TOP SPEED	75 mph	100 mph	125 mph
0-60 MPH 0-100 MPH	26.9 sec —	9.7 sec —	6.7 sec 19.0 sec

NISSAN 240Z, 280ZX TURBO, 300ZX

'With 150 bhp it was a 125 mph car which could reach 100 mph in 24 seconds.'

Arriving in 1969 as the Datsun 240Z, Nissan's all-independently sprung GT coupé, powered by an overhead-cam 2.4-litre six, was the spiritual successor to the big Healey in the eyes of most enthusiasts. It was what the next Healey should have been and made a mockery of the short-lived MGC; it was designed for the American market as a more affordable alternative to Porsches and the Jaguar E; backed by competition success, it received great acclaim – over 156,000 were built in its four-year life with the majority going to America.

The project had actually started in 1963 when Nissan commissioned Yamaha to create a mini E-type from scratch. This was achieved by the end of 1964 using a body style that had been drawn up by Albrecht Goertz – renowned for the BMW 507 of the previous decade. For whatever reason, Nissan did not take this up, so Yamaha offered it to Toyota who turned it into the 2000GT which was announced at the 1965 Tokyo Motor Show. Nissan then returned to the idea two years later and came up with the 240Z which was launched in 1969.

Sporting fast-back style, independent rear suspension, free-revving ohc 'six' – it was just what Healey fans wanted to replace the aging 3000. Datsun gave it to them with the successful 240Z.

This used a unitary construction coupé body incorporating various components from other Nissan/Datsun models. The six-cylinder engine used moving parts from the 4-cylinder Bluebird, the gearbox came from the 2000 Sports and the MacPherson front suspension from the Laurel saloon; struts were also used for the independent rear. Using carefully chosen high volume components for a low volume niche car was what MG had done for years, but Nissan were able to capitalise on the system just at the moment that MG faltered. With 150 bhp it was a 125 mph car which could reach 100 mph in 24 seconds. Competition successes included two consecutive US SCCA Production championships and victories in the East African Safari rally in 1971 and 1973 – it was tough as well as fast.

However, increasingly stringent American safety and emission legislation were beginning to slow the car down with restricted power and more weight. The 260Z went some way towards restoring the balance in 1974, at which point a 2+2 was introduced with an extra 12-inches in the wheelbase. A year later, another engine stretch brought the 280Z with fuel injection but it was still not as accelerative as the original 240Z, which was 250Kg lighter. There was no way that Nissan could go back to the original sports car concept without an all-new design, so they deserted that section of the market and headed for the luxury personal car sector with the 280ZX in 1978.

Although similar in style, the ZX was largely new, and featured a semi-trailing arm rear suspension; the 2.8-litre injection engine was carried over but 140 bhp pushing 2800 lb was a poor comparison with the 240Z's 150 bhp and 2300 lb; a better shape kept the maximum speed up to 121 mph though. In 1980, the 2-seater and 2+2 were supplemented with the T-bar roof version with a pair of removable smoked glass panels, an option which accounted for over half the US sales in 1980. Finally in 1981 came a Z-car that was faster than the original; a turbocharger took the output up to 180 bhp lifting the maximum speed up to 129 mph; improved steering and suspension with bigger tyres also made it a nicer car with some of the sporting appeal restored. It was the last sports car to use the Datsun name.

Only two years later came the first Nissan 300ZX. The engine this time was a two-cam 3-litre V-6 in normally aspirated 170 bhp and turbocharged 225 bhp forms, the American turbo version having 205 bhp. While this was essentially a revamped 280ZX, the body panels were all new and the shape considerably cleaner – the European cars would reach 140 mph; further shape revisions would take place in 1987.

The new 300ZX came in 1989 and was packed with hi-tech equipment, from variable valve timing on the 24-valve V-6 to HICAS rear steering on its multi-link independent suspension. In normally aspirated form the engine developed 222 bhp, which is enough for 143 mph and 0-60 mph in 6.7 seconds; but the twin turbo version developed 300 bhp (280 bhp for low octane Europe) and will reach 155 mph with a 0-60 mph time of 5.6 seconds. Americans can have two-seater versions but the European market has the 2+2 with an extra 4.7 inches in the wheelbase.

The 300ZX is an extremely effective sports coupé which has earned as passionate a following as did the old 240Z of twenty years earlier.

The 280ZX, pictured here, moved further in the comfort direction.

SPECIFICATION	240Z (1969)	280ZX TURBO (1986)	300ZX (1990)
ENGINE	6-cyl, 2393 cc	6-cyl, 2753 cc	V-6, dohc, 2960 cc
POWER	150 bhp @ 5600 rpm	180 bhp @ 5600 rpm	300 bhp @ 6400 rpm
TRANSMISSION	Manual 5-speed	Manual 5-speed	Manual 5-speed
CHASSIS	Unitary steel	Unitary steel	Unitary steel
BRAKES	Disc/drum	Discs	Discs with ABS
TOP SPEED	125 mph	129 mph	155 mph
0-60 MPH 0-100 MPH	8.3 sec 23.9 sec	7.9 sec 20.5 sec	5.6 sec 14.9 sec

While the 1983 300ZX was a recognisable descendant of the 240Z, the 1989 300ZX was full of the latest Nissan technology under a completely new skin.

PONTIAC GTO, FIREBIRD TRANS-AM, FIERO

'The youth market was all about performance.'

Pontiac always seems to retain more autonomy than most GM divisions, in style as well as fundamental engineering; high performance packs have been part of the option list since the division found its feet in the late 'fifties under Bunkie Knudsen. Knudsen recognised that the youth market was all about performance, whether on the race track or the drag-strip; they went racing. Between 1957 and 1963, Pontiac saloons won 69 top NASCAR races, including three Daytona 500s on the trot in 1957-9. In the showrooms every purchase form had a massive list of option boxes to convert a staid base model into a high-style road-racer.

However in 1963 GM put a stop to factory racing and option boxes seemed set to diminish rapidly. The Pontiac response was to follow the hot-rodders' dictum of dropping a large engine into a small car. The chosen recipient was the 1964 Tempest, a conventional car until you reached the end of the option list and found the GTO pack. Pontiac had already started down the route of race-evocative name tags like *Grand Prix* and *Le Mans*, so borrowing the Ferrari GT soubriquet caused no heartache in Detroit. The GTO pack was based on the 389 cu.in (6.4-litre) V-8 fitted to the bigger and heavier Catalina and Bonneville ranges; it came in 325 and 348 bhp forms with a stiffer suspension and the famous lettering set into the grille and on the flanks – Ferrari never did that!

While the car was technically a Tempest GTO and most were fitted to the Le Mans coupé and convertible, the GTO option was also available for the four-door and the estate. Despite GM management reservations, the GTO was an instant success; plans to produce just 5000 were swamped and 32,000 were sold in that first year. The muscle car had arrived, and option packs were back with a vengeance. For 1965, the base GTO was given 335 bhp with 360 bhp as the alternative using triple twin-choke carburetters. The following year saw a new style with a fast-back joining the convertible and hard-top, but the car was getting heavy; for 1967 the engine was bored out to 400 cu.in but still with 360 bhp on a single four-barrel carb – a 4-bolt-mains block came in mid-year as part of the ram-air package with scoops on the bonnet.

An innovative plastic bumper-less front end characterised the 1968 cars which also had disappearing headlights set into the grille; 1969 saw the arrival of the orange Judge, complete with 400 cu.in. 355 bhp engine with a rev counter on

Just a number on the Tempest option list, the GTO was the first of the auto-makers' muscle cars to follow hot-rod practice and put the biggest engine into the smallest car – this is a 1966 model.

Pontiac's attempt to make an American Fiat X1/9 as a personal commuter car met with little success.

the back of the bonnet. By 1970 the top engine was up to 455 cu.in (7.45-litres), still with 360 bhp. Ever more strangled by emission legislation, the GTO carried on until 1973, by which time the pony-car market was in full swing (see also Mustang – page 44).

Chevrolet had introduced the Camaro in autumn 1966 and Pontiac's Firebird, always the better looking, followed in early 1967. Pontiac didn't join in the pony programme until the beginning of 1966, so used the Camaro centre section with its own front and rear. The engine choice ran from the 230 cu.in (3.8-litre) six with 165 bhp, through the 250 cu.in 'six' and the 326 cu.in (5.3-litre) 250 bhp V-8, to the top of the range 400 cu.in (6.6-litres) developing 325 bhp. By 1966, Mustang lessons had been thoroughly absorbed, and there was a full list of options including manual boxes and the GM 2 and 3-speed automatics.

Despite Pontiac's sporting past, it was Chevrolet who went racing. Using the 5-litre 302 Z-28 option, Roger Penske took the Camaro to two consecutive Trans-Am championships in 1968/9, but it was Pontiac who took the model name and the Firebird Trans-Am has been top of the range ever since. While early Firebirds looked very European, the 'nineties range has had a global attraction that outshines most; paint a 1995 Trans-Am Ferrari red and Pininfarina would get the applause.

By the end of the 'seventies, Pontiac orders were not too strong and they were seeking to rejoin the youth market. Ever innovative, they came up with the mid-engined Fiero, similar in concept to the Fiat X1/9. To GM, sports cars meant Corvette, so the Fiero was only allowed to be called a commuter car and was initially given a basic four-cylinder 2.5-litre lump with a mere 92 bhp taken from a front-wheel-drive car. It used a basic steel sub-frame but every external panel was in some form of plastic. Launched in September 1983, it was given a 2.8-litre V-6 option with 140 bhp for 1985 which gave it the 125 mph performance its chassis deserved. It was probably too small for the American roads and never gained a great following, despite providing the basis for an IMSA race-derivative. In 1988 it was dropped, a sadly short run for an enterprising design.

Below: Pontiac's Firebird was the pair for the Chevrolet Camaro, but it was the Firebird that used the Trans-Am title for the top of the range. Plastic noses were well established by the time of this 1979 Trans-Am.

SPECIFICATION	GTO (1964)	FIREBIRD T-A (1969)	FIERO (1986)
ENGINE	Cast-iron V-8, 6377 cc	Cast-iron V-8, 6550 cc	Cast-iron V-6, 2837 cc
POWER	325 bhp @ 4800 rpm	335 bhp @ 5000 rpm	135 bhp @ 4900 rpm
TRANSMISSION	Manual 4-speed	Auto 3-speed	Manual 5-speed
CHASSIS	Perimeter frame	Unitary steel	Steel & plastic
BRAKES	Drums	Discs all round	Discs all round
TOP SPEED	122 mph	125 mph	125 mph
0-60 MPH	6.9 sec	5.8 sec	7.7 sec

Porsche Speedster, Super 75, 1600SC

'The tail happy handling had gradually been brought under reasonable control.'

Although Dr. Porsche had a remarkable reputation in the automotive engineering world for most of the first half of the century, the man in the street knew nothing of the name until the mid-'fifties, by which time a few of the aerodynamic coupés were spread around the world – the 5000th car emerged from the Zuffenhausen plant in March 1954. Ten years later, the 911 would commence the rise to iconic status.

Dr Porsche's first project at the turn of the century was the electric Lohner-Porsche in his native Austria. He then worked with Austro-Daimler before joining the parent company in Stuttgart for whom he developed the powerful open Mercedes-Benz sports cars. With his own consultancy during the 'thirties, he was the man behind the Auto-Union GP car and the designer of the Volkswagen Beetle. As competition was a Porsche watchword, he designed and built three VW coupés to take part in a Berlin-Rome road race which the war cancelled.

This design, using the characteristic rear-mounted air-cooled engine and Beetle suspension components, was to form the basis of Porsche production which started in 1948. While the first of these 356s was an open car, the rest would be coupés until the Cabriolet joined the range in 1951; by this time only 50 cars had been built during two years in Austria before the move to Stuttgart generated an increase to 60 cars per month. Those original 356s used an 1100 cc version of the Beetle's flat-four engine giving out all of 40 bhp; but the aerodynamic shape allowed a top speed over 80 mph.

In 1951 the engine was enlarged to 1300 cc and 44 bhp, while a new roller-bearing 1500 cc unit with aluminium heads became top of the range with 60 bhp and a 95 mph performance capability. Porsche was on the power ladder; while the cars changed little, extra power justified a model change. The 1300S came in 1953 and the 1500S with 70 bhp followed a year later.

Already Porsches were beginning to record

The Speedster, introduced in 1952, was a Cabriolet body with a shortened windscreen and simpler trim; this is a 1955 example.

Cabriolets joined the range in 1951 with a more substantial roof than the Speedster or later Roadster.

class victories in International motor sport; at Le Mans they won the 1100 cc class from 1951-55 and the 1500 cc class from 1953-55. Class wins from 1952-54 in the Mexican Carrera Panamericana justified the name Carrera being applied to the top of the Porsche range in 1955. Competition would always be used to promote the Porsche name.

While the Cabriolet had been offered in 1951, the American market wanted a cheaper open Porsche with a simpler folding roof; the result was the 1952 America model which led directly to the 1954 Speedster. Although this was still a cabriolet below the waistline, the windscreen was 3.5 inches shorter, which gave the car a much lower-looking appearance. The Speedster and the Roadster would become interchangeable with Convertible D through to 1963.

The first major change to the appearance of the 356 came in 1956 with the 356A featuring a curved windscreen, wider 15-inch wheels, a new painted bumper style and a 1600 cc engine option plus a few interior changes. This mixture of engineering and minor styling changes would produce the 356B in 1960 and the 356C in 1963. By then the rear window had been considerably enlarged, disc brakes were used on all four wheels and the engine choice was limited to 1600 cc in 75 bhp C and 95 bhp SC forms. The tail happy handling had gradually been brought under reasonable control. The final 1600SC was an impressive sporting car that had diverged a long way from its Beetle ancestor over the intervening 15 years.

The final 356C series came in 1963 with disc brakes all round, and engine options of 75 or 90 bhp.

SPECIFICATION	1500 SPEEDSTER (1956)	SUPER 75 (1960)	1600SC (1964)
ENGINE	Air-cooled flat-4 1488 cc or 1582 cc		
HORSEPOWER	66 bhp @ 4400 rpm	75 bhp @ 5000 rpm	95 bhp @ 5800 rpm
TRANSMISSION	Manual 4-speed (*all models*)		
CHASSIS	Steel unitary body/chassis (*all models*)		
BRAKES	Drums	Drums	Discs
TOP SPEED	100 mph	110 mph	115 mph
0-60 MPH	13.9 sec	14.6 sec	13.2 sec

PORSCHE 911, 911S 2.4, 911 TURBO 3.0

By the time the Porsche 911 arrived in 1963, the name had become as well known around the race-tracks of the world as it was in the high streets and over 76,000 had been produced in the 15-year life of the 356. The 911 was really an evolution from the 356 in that the rear-mounted air-cooled engine layout remained the same, and the basic design was laid out by the same people who had drawn up the original car.

But the Beetle no longer provided any parts. The new engine was an air-cooled flat-6 2-litre which developed 130 bhp; as before, the rear mounting allowed an aerodynamically clean front end, and the car would do 130 mph. The rear seats would take slightly older children than in a 356 and they still folded flat to increase the luggage capacity, which was already good with the whole of the front compartment available.

Thirty years ago, the 911 was a clean, lithe shape with no air dams, wheel-arch flares or rear wings. With 130 bhp from 2-litres giving 130 mph it was very efficient in every way. S-type wheels were an early option.

Maybe its heating and ventilation was primitive, maybe you had to drive with care in the wet, but this was a driver's car, and one that would keep going and going.

The Targa version, launched in 1965, has been with us almost as long; in design it appears to follow the Triumph TR4's Surrey top – a lift-out panel held between fixed front and rear screens – but Porsche made the vertical pillar into a safety roll-over bar, and it has been a model option ever since; a full folding-roof Cabriolet was only added in 1982.

First in the series of steady uprates came in 1967 with the 911S sporting the famous five-spoke alloy wheels; the 2-litre engine was uprated to 160 bhp. A year later, the wheelbase was stretched by 2.2 inches to improve the weight distribution, and the body flared to allow wider rear wheels. Three

While the roadholding characteristics of the 356 could easily catch out the unwary with a sudden tail-slide, just like the VW Beetle, the 911 design attempted to tame this with revised rear suspension, but this was only partially successful. The 911 would always be potentially tail-happy until the arrival of the four wheel drive versions. However, few people drive on the limit and the 911 was a success from the moment it arrived.

SPECIFICATION	911 (1963)	911S 2.4 (1972)	TURBO 3.0 (1975)
ENGINE	Flat-6 1991 cc	Flat-6 2341 cc	Turbo flat-6 2994 cc
HORSEPOWER	130 bhp @ 6100 rpm	190 bhp @ 6500 rpm	260 bhp @ 5500 rpm
TRANSMISSION	Manual 5-speed	Manual 5-speed	Manual 4-speed
CHASSIS	Unitary steel body/chassis with Targa-style option (*all models*)		
BRAKES	Disc brakes all round (*all models*)		
TOP SPEED	130 mph	147 mph	155 mph
0-60 MPH	8.3 sec	6.2 sec	6.1 sec
0-100 MPH	24.3 sec	17.1 sec	14.5 sec

different engine versions ranged from the 911T at 110 bhp through the 140 bhp 911E to the 911S, now with fuel injection and 170 bhp. In 1970 these three models remained the same, but all engines were now 2.2-litre, and two years later the capacity went to 2341 cc – nominal 2.4 – with the three outputs at 130 bhp, 165 bhp and 190 bhp, the last capable of 147 mph.

Some of this steady capacity increase was to offset the restrictions of exhaust emission legislation without losing performance. For 1974 Porsche introduced the American 5 mph bumpers across the range and increased the capacity to the 2.7-litres which the Carrera RS had sported the previous year. A considerable programme of refinement had been effected too, including a better heating system, more comfortable seats and headlamp washers. This all left the 911S 2.7 down on power at 167 bhp but improved torque from the latest Bosch injection system ensured this was hardly noticeable. Besides, there was the Carrera RS now with 3-litres, and in 1975 the Turbo would arrive to expand the range.

The 911s had always done well in GT classes in the hands of private racers, but new International racing rules for 1976 gave a chance of outright victory to derivatives of road cars. Porsche had gained considerable experience of turbocharging when racing the Can-Am 917/30; it was logical to put this to good effect and create a race-winning 911 with turbocharging. But you have to sell road-going versions of such GT racers, so the 3-litre Turbo was launched in 1975 with 260 bhp.

The 911 cult and engine capacity continued to grow and they will all be recognised as classics in time; our selection comes from 20 years back.

'This was a driver's car, and one that would keep going and going.'

Introduced in response to International racing rules, the 911 Turbo came in 1975; type-numbered 930, it was to sire the 934, 935 and 936 racing machinery.

PORSCHE 924, 944, 928

Creating an entry level Porsche has always been difficult; if you make them in volume to get the price down you devalue the marque's exclusivity; and if you don't make them in volume you won't build them cheaply. Porsche twice tried to undertake a joint venture which would satisfy both sets of dealers, a cheaper car for Porsche, a sporting car for Volkswagen or Audi; but neither time did it work out as planned.

'Like all Porsches they are classics in their own time.'

Porsche has always worked fairly closely with Volkswagen from the days of their common Beetle heritage. The Beetle and its off-spring were still going in the late 'sixties when Volkswagen wanted a sports car; the result was the mid-engined 914 which would be built by Karmann. Over the five years from 1970 some 120,000 of these VW-Porsches were built; Porsche preferred their own derivative, the 914/6 using the 911 engine, but that only lasted two years and neither car served the purpose as an entry level to the 911 world.

The VW-Audi group wanted Porsche to produce another sports car to follow the 914, although this would be an Audi, a more up-market name. Work started on the 924 as the 914 began production. It was to use a water-cooled 2-litre VW engine mounted in the front to allow 2+2 seating and reasonable luggage space. Part-way through the project, VW called a halt in 1974 in the wake of the world energy crisis. The 914 was coming to an end, so Porsche took the plunge to buy out Audi's interest, which they achieved on the basis that the car would be built at the Audi-NSU plant in Neckarsulm – that suited Porsche as their own factory was full with renewed demand for the 911 and preparation for the new 928.

Work had started on the 928, the nominal 911 replacement, in 1971 with a view to phasing it in after 12 years or so of the 911's life. The new car would be be front-engined with a big V-8 to appeal to the American market and it would have two real seats in the back. Then came the 1973 Yom Kippur war and big V8s ceased to have appeal. The market looked brighter by 1975 but the 911 refused to die, so Porsche resolved to produce both, as well as the new 924. The chosen layout of the 928 – front engine and rear gearbox – influenced the final choice for the 924 transmission. The little car was launched in 1976 with the 928 following a year later, initially with a 4.5-litre engine developing 240 bhp.

The 924's single cam 2-litre engine produced 125 bhp and was good for around 125 mph with its low drag Porsche designed body. As ever, Porsche kept up a steady model development programme on the 924; a five-speed gearbox was standard by 1979, a 170 bhp 924 Turbo came in 1980 along with a 210 bhp Carrera GT competition version of the Turbo. That Carrera bodywork, a 924 shape with bulging wheel arch pods was exactly how the 944 would look when it arrived in 1982.

The 944 would be the next level, a 924 equipped with a genuine Porsche engine. The new 2.5-litre, canted over at 45 degrees, was a four-cylinder unit which used a certain amount of the thinking that went into the 928's V-8, with the added refinement of a pair of balancer shafts to smooth the natural vibrations of a big 'four'. The 944 had immediate appeal as a genuine Porsche, rather than an Audi-Porsche; even inserting the 944 engine into the 924S didn't give any great boost to the 924 range but it continued in production until 1988. The 944 had a turbo version in 1985 which raised the output to 217 bhp

Initially an Audi joint development, the 924 used a 2-litre sohc VW engine with water cooling and front mounting being Porsche novelties. This 1978 car has had a competition career.

and the top speed to over 150 mph. The 16-valve 944S followed in 1987, the same year that big brother 928 appeared in 5-litre 32-valve form as the S4 having had interim S and S2 models with 4.7-litre engines.

The 944S went on to become the S2 with a 3-litre engine developing 211 bhp and a lot more torque, and then became the 968. The 928 meanwhile continues as the GTS and will soon be clocking up its first 20 years. Like all Porsches they are classics in their own time; even Porsche's nominal joint ventures, the 914 and 924, have classic status.

Above right: For the 944, Porsche used their own 2.5-litre 'four' with twin balancer shafts, and wide-wheel body restyling that had been used on the 924 Carrera GT. Shown is a 1986 944.

Below: Porsche had planned the 928 as a 911 replacement, but the 911 refused to die, so the four-seater 928 has continued alongside from 1978 with a regular programme of performance increases.

SPECIFICATION	**924** (1976)	**944** (1982)	**928** (1977)
ENGINE	4-cyl 1984 cc	4-cyl 2479 cc	V-8 4474 cc
HORSEPOWER	125 bhp @ 5800 rpm	163 bhp @ 5800 rpm	240 bhp @ 5500 rpm
TRANSMISSION	Manual 4-speed	Manual 5-speed	Manual 5-speed
CHASSIS	Unitary steel with steel body panels (*all models*)		
BRAKES	Disc/drum	All disc	All disc
TOP SPEED	125 mph	137 mph	143 mph
0-60 MPH 0-100 MPH	10.1 sec 24.5 sec	8.2 sec 20.9 sec	7.4 sec 18.6 sec

STUDEBAKER COMMANDER, SILVER HAWK, AVANTI

'Loewy coupés were world landmarks in modern elegant style.'

Studebaker's origins date from its 1852 establishment as horse-drawn carriage makers. They switched to cars in 1902 but long-term commercial success was to elude them throughout their existence until car production ceased in 1965, but during that time they produced some remarkable cars, memorable particularly for the advanced styling of the post-war years, the products of Raymond Loewy, Studebaker's consultant from 1936.

In the 'twenties, they produced six and eight-cylinder engined cars, publicising them with long distance runs such as 30,000 miles in under 30,000 minutes in 1928; when Indianapolis accepted touring car engines, Studebaker engined cars took a 4th in 1931 and a 3rd in 1932. But despite the promotion, the Depression bit and the company went under in 1933. Revived, they were back in force by 1939 reaching 100,000 production with the $700 Champion as the mainstay.

After profitable war work Studebaker were out with striking-looking new models for 1947, the work of Virgil Exner at the Loewy studios; with wings merged into the waistline they were well ahead of their time, particularly the Starlight Coupé with its four-piece wrap-round rear screen. The Champion used the pre-war 169 cu.in six and the bigger Commander a 226 cu.in (3.7-litre) version. For 1950 Loewy introduced the bullet-nose, a circular chromed intake flanked by head and sidelights arranged in a single vertical housing; in the same year the 1935-style transverse leaf independent front suspension was replaced by a coil spring system. Engineering kept up with style; a year later came the first overhead-valve V-8, a 232 cu.in. (3.8-litre) 120 bhp unit.

Striking though the previous models had been, the 1953 Loewy coupés were world landmarks in modern elegant style with minimal chromework, the best being the pillar-less Starliner; the four-door saloons were still striking but not as dramatic. Engines were the old Champion 'six' now at 185 cu.in and the 120 bhp V-8. These models continued with minor changes until 1956, to be replaced by the Hawks.

Low and sporting, these too were styled by

In an age when fins and chrome were infecting style, the Loewy-designed Commander was elegantly restrained; this is a 1954 model.

Loewy's final fling for Studebaker produced the legendary Avanti for 1962 with the coke-bottle styling for its glass-fibre bodywork. It failed to save the company but lived on through other owners.

Loewy; while the centre section was little changed, the rear began to grow fins and the front took on a more conventional grille shape. The range included the Power Hawk using a 4.7-litre version of the V-8 and the top Golden Hawk powered by a 5.8-litre Packard engine – Packard had been taken over by Studebaker but was to die by 1958. For 1957, the Packard unit was replaced by a supercharged version of the Studebaker 4.7-litre 289 and the Silver Hawk adopted the normal unit. In an age of excess, the Hawks' comparative restraint stood out – they were almost as impressive as the 1953 cars had been.

Interesting though the Studebaker models were, they were fighting a losing battle against the big three engaged in their own price-cutting wars – good for the consumer but bad for the smaller rivals; being based in Indiana, away from the mainstream suppliers didn't help. The company went for volume by leading into the Compact market – the 1959 Lark, a shortened saloon, was an immediate success in modest Studebaker terms and gave them some breathing space.

They now needed a new sports coupé and once more turned to Raymond Loewy, who came up with the fascinating Avanti for 1962; its exceptionally clean lines included a grille-less front with the air intake beneath the bumper, and the start of the renowned 'Coke-bottle' waist-line. With glass-fibre bodywork it had a steel chassis to carry the familiar 4.7-litre V-8 with supercharged options giving 240 and 290 bhp; it was also the first American chassis to carry front disc brakes as standard. Fewer than 4500 had been built by the time that Studebaker production ceased at Indiana in early 1964; although Larks continued to be made in Canada using Chevrolet engines until 1966, the Avanti was left behind. Its production was taken over by two South Bend dealers in 1965; using Chevrolet power, it was to continue in limited numbers until 1991, by which time it had new owners in Ohio. Along the way, a convertible and a four-door version were added. Even now, it is a striking looking car, the final tribute to the Loewy designs for Studebaker.

Arriving in 1956, the Hawks were recognisably evolutions of the Commander series with restrained period fins and a more normal grille shape; the powerful Golden Hawk was top of a range which included Power Hawk and Silver Hawk, 1958 version shown here.

SPECIFICATION	COMMANDER (1953)	SILVER HAWK (1961)	AVANTI (1963)
ENGINE	Iron V-8, 3813 cc	Iron V-8, 4735 cc	S/c V-8, 4735 cc
POWER	120 bhp @ 4000 rpm	210 bhp @ 4500 rpm	290 bhp @ 5200 rpm
TRANSMISSION	Manual 3-speed	Manual 4-speed	Manual 4-speed
CHASSIS	Steel frame	Steel frame	Steel, grp body
BRAKES	Drums	Drums	Disc/drum
TOP SPEED	95 mph	115 mph	125 mph
0-60 MPH	14.9 sec	10.2 sec	8.8 sec

SUNBEAM TALBOT ALPINE, ALPINE MK.II, TIGER

'It was attractive although the rear fins were too pronounced for some tastes.'

The Rootes Group had been assembled in the 'thirties with the merger of Humber and Hillman followed by the 1935 acquisitions of Sunbeam and Talbot. Despite their individual illustrious past histories, neither of the latter marques contributed to Rootes' design – they were just names to be used in badge engineering of the solid, dependable Hillman and Humber ranges. While there was initially a Talbot Ten, the Sunbeam name lay fallow until the 1938 arrival of a Sunbeam-Talbot range – double-barrelled names suggested class at the time – with a Ten and two short-lived six-cylinder cars, joined by a 2-litre as war broke out.

While the Ten and 2-litre were renewed after the war, both were replaced by the 80 and 90 in 1948. These used overhead valve versions of pre-war 1185 cc Minx and 1944 cc Hawk engines in pre-war beam-axled chassis, with their own attractive saloon and convertible models. The 80 didn't reach Mk.II form, but the 90 Mk.II came in 1950 with an all-new, but still separate, chassis with independent front suspension, and an engine increased to 2267 cc with 70 bhp. This model soon clocked up rally successes and formed the basis of the long-standing Rootes competition department; rally work led to the Mk.IIA in 1952 with bigger brakes, 77 bhp and a maximum speed around 82 mph. And it was rally success that led to the 1953 launch of a sporting two-seater version of the Mk.IIA – the Alpine; as this was essentially for export to the USA where Talbot meant little, it was marketed there as the Sunbeam Alpine although Sunbeam-Talbot was to remain the marque name in Europe for another year. The chassis was stiffened to compensate for the loss of the roof and the engine output was increased to 80 bhp which gave the sleek new model 95 mph performance. By then, though, Healeys and Triumphs were faster and cheaper, so the first Alpine died after just two years in 1955; the IIA's successor, the Sunbeam Mk.III continued from 1954 to 1957, taking advantage of the Alpine's 80 bhp engine.

The louvred bonnet and the long sloping tail gave the 1953-5 Alpine a very sporting appearance which was backed by rally successes.

Meanwhile the Rootes Group had launched a new range of unitary construction family saloons in 1955 with the Hillman Minx, Singer Gazelle and Sunbeam Rapier supplemented by the Husky van which used the same platform with 10 inches removed from the wheelbase. Initially the saloons had 1390 cc ohv engines, rising to 1494 cc in 1958; for the Rapier Mk.II this gave 68 bhp. For 1959 the Alpine name returned for a new two-seater built up on the Husky platform with uprated Rapier running gear including an aluminium head, disc front brakes and 13-inch wheels. With in-house styling once more mainly for the American market, it was attractive although the rear fins were too pronounced for some tastes. With 78 bhp, it wasn't quite a 100 mph car, and the extra 2 bhp from the 1594 cc Mk.II a year later made little difference.

Chassis improvements and a choice of GT (with detachable hard-top) or the more powerful 82 bhp Tourer denoted the Mk.III's arrival in 1960. The hard-top was square-rigged and spacious and justified the creation of small +2 seating. It was less than a year later that the Mk.IV arrived with its fins cut back to the vertical to make a much better balanced shape; an auto-box option was offered for the first time. After some 50,000 units of the 4 models in six years, the final Alpine Mk.V came in 1965 using the 1725 cc engine with 92.5 bhp; by the time the model was phased out in 1968, a total of nearly 70,000 had been built. The Alpines were always more comfortably trimmed and arguably better built than the rival MGs and TRs, but were never genuine 100 mph cars.

For those that liked the Alpine's style and comfort but also wanted genuine high performance, there was the sadly short-lived Tiger based on the

Series IV. Taking a leaf from the AC Cobra story, the same 4.2-litre (260 cu.in) Ford V-8 was successfully inserted by an American dealer and became a production reality in 1964. American gearbox, stronger back axle with Panhard rod location, and rack and pinion steering contributed to the Alpine's ability to accept a 137% increase in torque, while the 75% power increase brought the top speed to nearly 120 mph. Nearly 6500 were produced in two years before a mere 571 Tiger IIs were built with the 4.7-litre Ford V-8 in 1967. Meanwhile Chrysler had become shareholders in 1964 and taken over in 1967 – the Ford-powered Tiger was an inevitable casualty.

SPECIFICATION	ALPINE (1954)	ALPINE SERIES II (1960)	TIGER (1965)
ENGINE	4-cyl, 2267 cc	4-cyl, 1594 cc	V-8, 4261 cc
POWER	80 bhp @ 4200 rpm	80 bhp @ 5000 rpm	141 bhp @ 4400 rpm
TRANSMISSION	Manual 4-speed	Manual 4-speed + o/d	Manual 4-speed
CHASSIS	Steel frame and body	Unitary steel	Unitary steel
BRAKES	Drums	Disc/drum	Disc/drum
TOP SPEED	95 mph	99 mph	116 mph
0-60 MPH	18.9 sec	13.6 sec	9.4 sec
0-100 MPH	—	—	30.6 sec

Right: The second generation Alpines were based on the Hillman Husky van chassis, using the period best of the ohv 'four' range. Despite sports car looks they were never 100 mph cars. This is a 1966 Alpine Mk.V – with detachable hardtop.

Below: Putting the 4.2-litre Ford V-8 into a strengthened Alpine Series IV gave instant high performance and a strong basis for a successful rally car, this being an ex-works 1964 team car.

TOYOTA 2000GT, CELICA, MR2

'The MR2 would give 120 mph performance and superb roadholding in a neatly styled sporting package.'

Toyota was relatively late on the automotive scene. Although the Toyoda Automatic Loom works was founded in 1926, and an automobile section was set up in 1933, the plant wasn't completed until 1937 and few cars had been produced by the outbreak of war. Car production resumed in 1949; where other Japanese companies had initially built foreign cars under licence, Toyota developed their own range of saloons initially for the home market but with an eye to export. By the end of the 'fifties, production had gradually built up to 30,000 cars a year but was to accelerate rapidly from then. By 1965, it had reached 230,000 cars a year of which 20% were exported. As all these were family saloons, the announcement of such an overtly sporting coupé as the Toyota 2000GT was something of a surprise.

In fact, the 2000GT started life as the Goertz-styled car that Nissan sub-contracted Yamaha to produce in 1963. Yamaha Motor Company had been separately founded in 1955 to major on motor-cycles but to develop a general transport engineering ability, including the production of sporting engines for other manufacturers. Nissan didn't take up the project once the prototype was completed, so it was offered to Toyota with whom it was then co-developed; the 2000GT was launched at the 1965 Tokyo Motor Show but it was to be another two years before the car went into limited production at Yamaha's Yamamatsu Headquarters.

The design was very much European influenced. While Toyota's own cars were using a separate cruciform frame, the 2000GT copied the Lotus sheet steel backbone system, but then used a steel bodyshell to increase the torsional stiffness. Suspension front and rear used double wishbones and coil springs with rack and pinion steering, while Dunlop disc brakes were made under licence by Sumitomo. Using the Crown's 2-litre seven-bearing six-cylinder as a basis, Yamaha designed an aluminium twin-cam head to develop 150 bhp at 6600 rpm, while an extra gear was grafted onto the back of the Crown's four-speed box. With an E-type style two-seater coupé body, it was an attractive car and concept. During 1966, a lightweight version had won the Suzuka 1000 Km race and taken a number of International records in a 72-hour endurance run. It should have been a success, particularly in America, but only 351 were produced – virtually hand-made, they were too expensive to build and couldn't justify a higher price than the Jaguar. If it didn't work for Toyota, it did for Yamaha – they still build most of Toyota's multi-valve engines.

While Toyota produced two-door coupé models within most of their saloon ranges in the late 'sixties, it wasn't until 1970 that a sporting version received its own model name; the two door

With E-type looks and a twin-cam engine Toyota's first sports car was right up-to-date when first shown in 1965; although too expensive, it was a strong pointer to the future.

The second generation Celica came in 1977 including this neat 2000ST coupé.

Celica and the four-door Carina were developments of the previous Corona and shared the same chassis, but different body panels created entirely different styles. A neat 4-seater coupé with European appeal, the Celica was powered by a cross-flow 1600 cc 'four' with 105 bhp, enough to reach 104 mph; while its details showed a period Japanese fussiness with a nondescript full-width grille, the style showed promise. In competition trim, it made its mark in rallies while the twin-cam engine became the top F3 power unit. The 1977 replacements included a lift-back coupé with a choice of 2-litre engines including the twin-cam 2000GT with 118 bhp. The third generation came in 1981 with all-independent suspension and some 4-valve engines, with the front-drive fourth generation arriving in 1985. In ever more sophisticated forms the Celica is still with us and has been one of Toyota's best exports. Meanwhile a six-cylinder version had been added in 1981 as the Celica Supra, but this became a model name in its own right for 1985; it is still their supercar flagship.

Meanwhile Toyota's sporting successes had led to the introduction of the mid-engined MR2 in 1984; taking a leaf from the Fiat X1/9 book, it used a transverse front-drive power pack from the Corolla and set it amidships. With the 16-valve 120 bhp 'four', the MR2 would give 120 mph performance and superb roadholding in a neatly styled sporting package. A T-bar version – twin removable roof-halves – came in 1987; the first generation was phased out in 1990 to be replaced by faster models with even better roadholding. Despite a shaky sports car start with the 2000GT, Toyota's sporting machinery is now among the world's best.

Below: Arriving in 1984, the MR2 followed the simple formula of the Fiat X1/9 with a front-wheel-drive package reversed behind the cockpit. A T-bar roof came in 1987.

SPECIFICATION	2000GT (1967)	CELICA 1.6 (1971)	MR2 (1986)
ENGINE	Dohc 6-cyl, 1988 cc	Four-cyl, 1558 cc	Dohc 4-cyl, 1587 cc
POWER	150 bhp @ 6600 rpm	105 bhp @ 6000 rpm	135 bhp @ 6600 rpm
TRANSMISSION	Manual 5-speed	Manual 4-speed	Manual 5-speed
CHASSIS	Steel frame and body	Unitary steel	Unitary steel
BRAKES	Discs	Disc/drum	Discs
TOP SPEED	132 mph	104 mph	122 mph
0-60 MPH	9.8 sec	11.5 sec	8.0 sec
0-100 MPH	24.8 sec	—	21.6 sec

TRIUMPH TR2, TR4, TR6

'Originally a motor-cycle company, Triumph began to produce small cars from 1923.'

Now just another vanished name, Triumph, along with MG and Austin-Healey, was one of the star players in the economy sports car market that was such a British preserve through the 'fifties and 'sixties.

Originally a motor-cycle company, Triumph began to produce small cars from 1923; moving up-market for the 'thirties gave more prestige but the investment required for a new range of engines was to bring the company down before the outbreak of war; the motor-cycle business was another casualty, having been sold off in 1936. However some rally successes had been achieved in the hands of the Technical Director Donald Healey. Meanwhile Standard had been building sensible family cars for many years and had also supplied the pre-war SS Cars with chassis and engines; they at least had a feel for sports cars but no reputation. Standard thus absorbed the Triumph name, all that was left, in the latter part of the war to use as the up-market and sporting Standard, when post-war design could resume.

The first sporting Triumph came in 1946; the 1800 Roadster was built up on the pre-war Standard 14 chassis but it lacked the speed and style to be a real sports car. It was fortunate that Standard-Triumph's Sir John Black did a deal with tractor magnate Harry Ferguson to build tractors for him around a new power unit which could double as tractor and car power; modelled on the pre-war Citroen unit, this was the big ohv 'four' designed with wet liner cylinders for easy repair and simple capacity adjustment. While the new engine went into the hump-backed Standard Vanguard and the Triumph Roadster 2000 in 1948, Sir John Black still wanted a real sports car – preferably to sell at £500 – for the export market.

After two false starts, the definitive Triumph TR2 arrived at the Geneva Motor Show in March 1953; a short-tailed prototype had been seen at Earls Court in October 1952, but a lot of development work had gone on in between, including an increase in power for the 2-litre engine from 75 bhp to 90 bhp – enough for an easy 100 mph car. The TR2 had its own separate chassis frame but used front suspension and rear axle from the Mayflower saloon while its neat and modern body had been designed by Walter Belgrove, who had drawn up the pre-war Triumphs. Its pre-tax UK price was £555 against

Launched in definitive form at Geneva in March 1953, the TR2 was the best value 100 mph sports car and soon established the Triumph name in sporting circles. This 1954 TR2 has a later TR3A grille.

The TR6 proved a best-seller – this is a 1972 model.

the MG TF at £550 or the Austin-Healey 100 at £750 while the XK120 started at £1130; it was a good value performance package but production was slow to get under way. Only some 8600 TR2s had been built by the time the TR3 arrived in October 1955, but 30 per cent, remained in the United Kingdom.

The TR3 showed little change – an egg-box grille in the intake, sliding panel side-screens, and bigger carburetters to take the power up to 95 bhp – but it was to be produced in much greater numbers. Power rose to 100 bhp the following year and disc front brakes became standard at the end of 1956. A year later came the TR3A with a full-width grille with other detail changes.

With the help of Italian stylist Michelotti, the new-shaped TR4 arrived in September 1961; wind-up windows, an optional Surrey hard-top, face-level ventilation, and considerably more space made this a very civilised car. Under the skin the engine had been enlarged to 2138 cc while rack and pinion steering was fitted to a wider chassis. TR enthusiasts had to wait until March 1965 before criticism of the hard ride was countered with the TR4A and its all-new chassis with independent rear suspension.

Meanwhile the 4-cylinder engine was getting a little too old and unsuited to emission laws. Announced in late 1967, the bodily unchanged TR5 used a 2.5-litre version of the Triumph 6-cylinder engine in 142 bhp fuel-injection form, or for America as the TR250 with carburetters and a mere 104 bhp. This only had a brief run before the TR6 arrived in January 1969; front and rear panels revised by Karmann transformed its looks although there were few other changes. This final separate-chassis TR6 was actually the most popular TR with 91,850 models produced during its 8-year spell as part of a total of over a quarter-million real TRs - TR2 to TR6.

Below: While TR3, TR3A and TR4 followed the TR2 design with revised bodywork and a steady increase in power, it was not until 1965 that the TR4A came out with independent rear suspension.

SPECIFICATION	TR2 (1954)	TR4 (1962)	TR6 (1969)
ENGINE	4-cyl, 1991 cc	4-cyl, 2138 cc	6-cyl, 2498 cc
POWER	90 bhp @ 4800 rpm	100 bhp @ 4600 rpm	142 bhp @ 5500 rpm
TRANSMISSION	Manual 4-speed + optional overdrive (*all models*)		
CHASSIS	Separate steel frame chassis with steel body panels (*all models*)		
BRAKES	Drums	Disc/drum	Disc/drum
TOP SPEED	107 mph	109 mph	117 mph
0-60 MPH 0-100 MPH	12.0 sec —	10.9 sec 39.9 sec	8.5 sec 24.7 sec

TVR GRANTURA MK.II, TAIMAR, TASMIN

'All models have been pretty exclusive and arguably classics in their own time.'

For over 40 years now the unlikely venue of Blackpool has played host to the charismatic TVR. The company is the only one of the rash of 'fifties special-builders to have survived, although it too has had its share of ups and downs, receiverships and ownership changes. But throughout it all, the TVR has remained an enthusiast's car, right for the period; perhaps the early ones were not such good value in performance terms as in exclusivity, but for the last twenty years a TVR has been a fast car.

The basic principles of the TVR have remained unchanged. The chassis has always been a built up tubular frame which has become even stiffer over the years; the original Grantura Mk.I and II used the independent front suspension of a VW Beetle at both ends but from the 1962 Mk.III onwards full wishbone systems have been used, usually made by TVR but attached to a proprietary upright. The chassis was lengthened from the original overly short 7ft wheelbase to 7ft.6in many years back and the cars have always been two-seaters until the arrival of the current Cerbera. Fortunately there has been no reluctance to supply engines even from a major to a minor in the same market; TVR have used Coventry Climax, MG, Triumph, Ford's 4-cyl, V-6 and American V-8 engines, with modified Rover power most popular from the mid-'eighties.

Bodies have always been built within TVR in high-quality glassfibre. The original rounded dumpy look of the first 1958 cars gave way to the Manx tail in 1964. The similar but longer M-series body came on a new stiffer chassis in 1972. The hatchback Taimar came in 1976 and the Convertible in 1978, both using Ford V-6 3-litre power. New for the 'eighties was the sleeker, sharper Tasmin shape with a 7ft.10 in wheelbase which was to come in lift-back, 2+ (very little) 2 and convertible forms. Initially the engine was the German Ford V-6 2.8-litre, but the Pinto 2-litre was available from 1981; then 1983 saw the 3.5-litre Rover at which point the Tasmin name was dropped in favour of engine-related numbers.

By this time TVR prices had moved steadily upmarket and were looking overly expensive; the cars were always very well finished, with comfortable leather interiors, and took many hours to build with a lot of parts bought from outside. The 1986 Convertible S was a much simplified car modelled on the original convertible and, with the

While this Grantura Mk.III is virtually identical to the Mk.II, the chassis was all new and featured wishbone suspension instead of the VW-based trailing arms.

Ford V-6, was 25% cheaper; for 1988, 515 of the 701 cars produced were the S model. This paved the way for the new Griffith 4.3 in 1992 – sophisticated high performance in a nostalgic package.

TVR have never quite reached the 20 cars per week level, so all models have been pretty exclusive and arguably classics in their own time; until the current series, no single model has had 1000 examples. So what to feature, apart from one per decade? The cars that set TVR on the map were the original short-wheelbase VW-suspended Mk.II Granturas; around 400 were produced of which the MGA 1600 engined cars were the most popular and indeed formed the basis of TVR's attempts at International racing at the time. Being some 350 lb lighter than the MGA, the TVR was faster off the mark and would reach 60 mph in 12.0 sec against the MG's 13.3 sec – it was also 2 mph faster; but at £1184 inc taxes in 1961 it was also £157 more expensive than the MGA coupé, reflecting a small price for exclusivity.

While the Triumph-engined 2500M from 1972-77 was the most popular of that series, the majority of the 947 built went to America. The 3000M, with Ford V-6 power, was better known in Europe and was the basis for the Taimar/Convertible/Turbo models; there were 1370 variations on the 3000M theme of which 63 were the Broadspeed Turbos with 230 bhp rather than 140 bhp. The hatch-back Taimar was a truly practical TVR.

From the 'eighties, one can only choose a Tasmin shape. While the Ford V-6 2.8-litre was the mainstay in the first half of the 'eighties, the first of the Rover V-8 powered cars is the more significant – the 350i. The Tasmins were some 300 lb heavier than the preceding 3000M series, so needed the extra power to stay ahead. Both, however, had four-cylinder equivalents for those less interested in sporting acceleration. TVRs could be all things to all people.

Above: After years of evolution, the 1980 Tasmin was the start of a new style. This early model was powered by the German Ford V-6. By 1983, the Rover V-8 had been adopted for the 350i.

The hatch-back Taimar used the 3-litre Ford V-6 to give a practical 120 mph 2-seater sports coupé.

SPECIFICATION	**GRANTURA Mk.II** (1961)	**3000M** (1974)	**350i** (1984)
ENGINE	MG 4-cyl, 1588 cc	Ford V-6, 2994 cc	Rover V-8, 3528 cc
POWER	79 bhp @ 5600 rpm	138 bhp @ 5000 rpm	197 bhp @ 5300 rpm
TRANSMISSION	Manual 4-speed	Manual 4-speed	Manual 5-speed
CHASSIS	Tubular steel chassis, all-independent suspension, glassfibre bodywork		
BRAKES	Disc/drum	Disc/drum	Discs
TOP SPEED	98 mph	121 mph	136 mph
0-60 MPH	12.0 sec	7.7 sec	6.6 sec
0-100 MPH	—	25.6 sec	20.2 sec

CHIC SALOONS – VW BEETLE, CITROEN 2CV, MORRIS MINOR

'Cult status breeds longevity which increases the cult status.'

Classics don't have to be sporting cars to be appreciated, although it helps. There are, though, a handful of mass-production small saloons that became cult cars during their own lifetimes; they fulfilled the market need but they did it differently whether through particularly clever engineering or quirky styling, or a mixture of the two, and demand was such that production went on and on. Cult status breeds longevity which increases the cult status.

Our chosen trio all started production shortly after the war, although the designs had been under way for some time. First away was the Volkswagen designed by Professor Porsche in response to Hitler's demand for a people's car shortly after he became Chancellor in 1933; the contract was signed in June 1934 and the first car was shown in February 1936. After three sets of prototypes the final version evolved with a view to production starting at Wolfsburg in mid-1939 but war stopped that. Design novelties included the all-independent suspension whose torsion bar trailing arm and swing axle systems had been seen on the Auto Union GP car, and the air-cooled flat four engine mounted behind the rear axle; these were mounted within a platform chassis under the beetle-shaped skin that was to remain throughout a life that extends to the present day – swing axle Beetles are still made in Mexico with 44 bhp 1600 cc engines. Beetle production started slowly in 1945 with 1131 cc and a 65 mph maximum. Exports began in 1949. Over the years the engine was steadily enlarged through 1200, 1300 and 1500 cc while the body and windows had detail changes; the first design change came in 1970 with the 1302 when MacPherson struts and semi-trailing arm suspension made the handing considerably less wayward. By 1973 the Beetle had passed the American Model T Ford record of 16.5 million and ensured its place in history.

Opposite: This 1970 Beetle may have changed somewhat in detail, but the design is still that of Professor Porsche's pre-war Peoples' Car; more Beetles have been built than any other car.

Production of the 2CV from 1948-90 passed the 5-million mark but this was mostly confined to mainland Europe; it was never going to appeal to the US in any numbers. Design work started on this in 1936 using much the same team as had created the Light Fifteen, hence the front-wheel-drive; work was still under way at the outbreak of war and continued during it, although little was to change by the time the car was finally launched in 1948. It was intended to be totally reliable whatever the treatment it received from first-time motorists – like the Ford Model T. The air-cooled flat-twin engine was only 375 cc and developed all of 9 bhp which was enough to give a maximum of 40 mph. Interconnected front leading/rear trailing arm independent suspension with long wheel travel gave a remarkable ride that would allow easy carriage of eggs or people. Bodywork was extremely simple, thus repairable; the canvas roof would fold all the way back to provide fresh air and extra carrying capacity. It was odd in the extreme but very effective. In 1954 the engine was increased to 425 cc and 12 bhp which allowed 50 mph and in 1971 a 602 cc 26 bhp version was available as the 2CV6 – the new engine having come from the more upmarket Dyane.

Built to carry the goods and chattels of the French agricultural worker, the Deux Chevaux provided cheap and entertaining, if slow, motoring for many more.

Demand for the 2CV had picked up in the aftermath of the 1973 fuel crisis, but dwindled thereafter – it was, however, well established by then as a quirky classic.

Like the others, the Minor was conceived as a

universal people carrier but production only ever reached 1.2-million during its 1948-71 span. Much of it was fairly straightforward – a unitary platform chassis, leaf-sprung live rear axle, 918 cc side-valve engine from the pre-war Morris 8; but torsion bar front suspension with rack and pinion steering gave it remarkably sporting roadholding. Its styling was scaled-down American and it seated four in comfort – an extra four inches was added to its width at quite a late stage of development. Its appeal was based on a mixture of looks, small-car comfort and its sporting performance, whether in its 'woodie' Traveller, convertible or saloon forms. When BMC was formed in 1952, the side-valve engine was replaced by Austin's A-series and the Minor used most of its capacity variations over the years – 803, 948, 1098 cc – while maximum speeds went up from 60 mph to nearly 80 mph.

The Minor might have been replaced by what became the Riley 1.5/Wolseley 1500 in the late 'fifties, but the market wouldn't allow it to die; eventually it was replaced in 1971 by the unloved Marina. But it still stands out as a very good simple family four-seater.

Inset below: Universal UK motoring was provided by the Minor which combined style with sporting handling. This 1948 version has the split windscreen and low headlights that distinguished the early cars.

SPECIFICATION	VW 'BEETLE' (1952)	CITROEN 2CV (1950)	MORRIS MINOR (1948)
ENGINE	Flat-4, 1131 cc	Flat-twin, 375 cc	4-cyl, 918 cc
POWER	25 bhp @ 3300 rpm	9 bhp @ 3500 rpm	28 bhp @ 4400 rpm
TRANSMISSION	Manual 4-speed	Manual 4-speed	Manual 4-speed
CHASSIS	Steel platform	Steel platform	Unitary steel
BRAKES	Drums	Drums	Drums
TOP SPEED	64 mph	41 mph	62 mph
0-30 MPH	8.3 sec	19.6 sec	9.7 sec
0-50 MPH	22.1 sec	—	32.5 sec

SUPERCARS – PORSCHE 959, JAGUAR XJ220, McLAREN F1

'The 959 was the ultimate Porsche 911 with its twin-turbocharged 450 bhp engine.'

It is a long-trumpeted theme that motor sport improves the breed, the arrival of disc brakes being the most oft-cited example. But sometimes motor sport creates a new breed and few more exciting road cars have emerged than during the short-lived period of International Group B competition following a 1982 rule change.

International motor sport has always been largely based on developed road cars, although the outright racing cars have received greater promotion. Rules define the limits to which all must work, but the Group B rules just said that 200 must have been built within 12 months and laid down a few road car dimensions; the number is just big enough to ensure that the factory has to sell a reasonable number to the general public. The rally world responded with a mixture of purpose-built devices like the Ford RS200, purpose-built under a production shape – Metro 6R4 – and highly developed road cars like the Lancia Delta Integrale and Audis. There was also the Porsche 959 which was created for general Group B use, whether for race-track or the long-distance rally-raids.

The 959 was the ultimate Porsche 911 with its twin-turbocharged 450 bhp engine, electronically controlled four-wheel drive and composite body panels. It was first shown as a design study in 1981, getting into production in 1985 after further work; the 200 were not completed until 1986 at which point the rally rules changed to exclude the very fast specials although rally raids continued to accept them. In the end 250 959s were built; some ten years on, the latest Turbo embodies much of the same competition-proved technology.

While the 959 was the first of the new breed of 200 mph supercar to be shown, the Ferrari 288GTO was the first to get into production. Obviously not a rally car, the new GTO was based on the assumption that Group B racing would become a serious category; while there were group B classes, such events were dominated by the sports-racing Group C cars, so the 288GTO never took to the tracks, but some 260 were built. With this car, Ferrari had set a trend by taking large deposits against later delivery when the first car was shown at Geneva in 1984; Aston Martin did the same the following year with the Vantage Zagato – it wasn't a racer, so was made even more exclusive with just 50 to be built.

With deposits and premium prices everyone wanted to get into the supercar act; it seemed that whatever was available, fast and exclusive would be bought, whether by real enthusiasts or premium-price speculators. Jaguar's XJ220 was the next to be unveiled at the 1988 Motor Show as a technical wonder based on the recent V-12 Le Mans cars with the addition of four-wheel-drive; Jaguar couldn't produce it within their own system so it was given to JaguarSport to develop. They removed the four-wheel-drive and substituted the later racing 3.5-litre V-6 turbo for the traditional

Long, low and wide, the XJ220 is a big car in any company. While the original show car had a V-12 and 4WD, the production car used a turbo V-6 and 2WD to keep the size and weight down.

The McLaren F1 will probably remain the fastest ever production car – and the most expensive too.

V-12; it was still very fast but not exactly what every Jaguar enthusiast had been expecting. And it hit the downside of the 'eighties boom, so only 280 of the planned 350 were built .

While Lamborghini continued to produce their own brand of regular supercar – Countach followed by Diablo – another four-wheel-drive multi-turbo 3.5-litre race-technology device was being launched just down the road; the 200 mph Bugatti EB110 was first shown in September 1991. This is still in slow production.

Last of the 200 mph club to be revealed was the McLaren F1 which was launched at Monaco in May 1992, some 4 years after the project got under way. This too is full of race-technology with carbon fibre composites used extensively in chassis and body. Its 6.1-litre BMW V-12 produces a remarkable 627 bhp and the car is electrifyingly fast, faster than anything else sold for the road. And it carries racing design through to the central driving position; the driver sits ahead of two passengers who are staggered slightly behind. It is the ultimate *Grand Prix* car for the road; the plan was to build 350 over 7 years. Time will tell how many, but meanwhile the F1 has gained an extra dimension.

Group B racing had inspired the arrival of the Porsche 959 and Ferrari 288GTO, and then let them down. But now a similar formula has returned as the leading sports car series. The McLaren is currently one of the best suited for this and victory in the 1995 Le Mans 24-hour race can only increase its appeal.

Below: Recognisably Porsche 911 in parts, the 959 used many composite body panels.

SPECIFICATION	PORSCHE 959 (1988)	JAGUAR XJ220 (1993)	McLAREN F1 (1994)
ENGINE	Flat-6 turbo 2850 cc	V-6 turbo, 3498 cc	V-12, 6064 cc
POWER	450 bhp at 6500 rpm	549 bhp @ 7000 rpm	627 bhp @ 7400 rpm
TRANSMISSION	Manual 6-speed 4WD	Manual 5-speed	Manual 6-speed
CHASSIS	Steel and Kevlar	Ali composite	C/fibre composite
BRAKES	Discs with ABS	Discs all round	Discs all round
MAXIMUM SPEED	197 mph	217 mph	231 mph
0-60 MPH 0-100 MPH	3.7 sec 8.5 sec	3.6 sec 7.9 sec	3.2 sec 6.3 sec

Fastest Cars Database

Model	Year	Max speed	0-60 mph	0-100 mph
McLaren F1	1993	231	3.2	6.3
McLaren F1 LM	1995	220	3.0	5.9
Bugatti EB110S	1994	218	4.3	9.2
Jaguar XJ220	1993	217	3.6	7.9
Bugatti EB110 GT	1994	212	4.5	9.6
Lamborghini Diablo SE30	1995	207	4.2	9.3
Lamborghini Diablo	1991	205	4.4	9.7
Ferrari F50	1995	202	3.9	7.2
Lamborghini Diablo VT	1994	202	4.9	10.3
Lister Storm GTL	1997	200	4.0	8.0
Ferrari 550 Maranello	1996	199	4.6	10.1
Ferrari F40	1992	198	4.1	7.6
Porsche 959	1986	197	3.7	8.5
Ferrari F512M	1995	191	4.8	10.2
Porsche GT1	1997	190	3.7	–
Lamborghini Countach QV5000S	1986	190	4.9	11.0
Ferrari 288GTO	1986	189	5.0	11.0
Ferrari 512 TR	1992	188	5.0	10.2
Chrysler Viper Venom	1995	187	4.4	9.7
Ferrari 456GT	1994	187	5.1	11.6
Aston Martin Vantage Zagato	1986	186	4.8	11.3
Aston Martin Vantage	1993	184	4.6	10.1
Ferrari Testa Rossa	1985	182	5.7	11.9
Porsche 911 Carrera Turbo3.6	1995	181	3.7	9.2
Venturi 400GT	1995	180	4.7	10.4
Ferrari F355	1994	178	4.6	10.6
Isdera Imperator 108i	1987	176	5.0	10.8
Lamborghini Countach	1975	175	5.6	13.1
Ferrari 365GTB4 Daytona	1971	174	5.4	12.6
Porsche 911 Turbo 3.6	1993	174	4.6	10.6
Vauxhall Lotus Carlton	1990	173	5.3	10.9
Ferrari 365GT4BB	1975	172	6.5	13.5
Lamborghini Miura P400S	1970	172	6.7	15.1
Lotus Esprit V-8	1996	172	4.5	11.3
Aston Martin Vantage	1977	170	5.4	13.0
BMW 850CSi	1994	170	6.5	15.4
BMW M5 6-sp	1994	170	5.4	13.6
Chevrolet Corvette	1996	170	4.7	11.0
Marcos Mantis	1996	170	4.1	–
Porsche 928S4 GTS 5.4	1992	168	5.4	14.3
TVR Cerbera	1996	168	4.5	9.9
Chrysler Viper	1993	167	4.6	10.7
Porsche 911 Turbo 3.3	1991	167	4.7	11.4
Ferrari 250GTO	1963	165	6.1	12.6
Ferrari 410 Superamerica	1959	165	6.6	14.5
Porsche 928 GT	1991	165	5.6	13.4
Venturi 260	1994	165	5.5	14.8
Ford GT40 Mk III	1966	164	5.3	11.8
Ferrari 348 tb	1990	163	5.6	13.3
Ferrari 348GTS	1994	163	5.9	13.9
Ferrari 512BB	1978	163	6.2	13.6
Porsche 928 S4 5.0	1988	163	5.3	12.7

Model	Year	Max speed	0-60 mph	0-100 mph
Renault Alpine A610	1992	163	5.9	15.8
BMW M1	1979	162	5.4	13.5
BMW M3	1993	162	5.4	13.1
Jaguar D 3.4	1956	162	4.7	12.1
Marcos LM 500	1995	162	4.6	11.9
Monteverdi Hai 450SS	1970	162	5.0	11.8
Aston Martin DB7	1994	161	5.8	14.4
Iso Grifo A3L	1966	161	7.4	16.6
Lotus Sport 300	1993	161	4.7	11.7
TVR Griffith 4.3	1992	161	4.7	11.1
TVR Griffith 500	1993	161	4.2	10.3
AC Cobra 427	1965	160	4.6	10.1
Aston Martin DBS V-8	1971	160	5.9	13.8
Audi RS2 Estate	1994	160	4.8	13.1
Chevrolet Corvette 427	1968	160	6.3	14.3
De Tomaso Pantera GT5-S	1986	160	5.4	13.1
Honda NSX	1994	160	5.3	12.6
Lotus Esprit S4	1993	160	5.0	12.7
Maserati Bora	1973	160	6.5	14.7
Maserati Shamal	1994	160	5.4	13.0
Porsche Carrera 3.6	1994	160	5.2	12.9
BMW 850i	1991	159	7.1	17.3
Ferrari 275 GTB4	1966	159	6.4	12.5
Honda NSX	1990	159	5.8	13.7
Lotus Esprit Turbo SE	1989	159	4.9	12.4
Mercedes 600SEL (A)	1991	159	6.7	15.8
Mercedes 600SL (A)	1992	159	6.0	14.4
Porsche 911 Cabrio	1994	159	5.0	12.3
Chevrolet Corvette 5.7	1993	158	5.5	14.3
Ferrari 412	1986	158	6.5	15.2
Jaguar XK-8	1996	158	6.2	16.1
Lamborghini Urraco P300	1975	158	7.6	17.5
Maserati Khamsin	1978	158	6.5	16.8
Pontiac Firebird Trans-Am 5.7	1992	158	6.3	16.2
Porsche 928 S2 4.7	1984	158	6.2	15.8
Porsche Carrera 2	1989	158	5.1	12.7
TVR Chimaera 4.0	1993	158	5.2	13.2
Aston Martin Virage	1990	157	6.8	15.5
BMW M5	1990	157	6.4	15.6
Ferrari 308 GTB QV	1983	157	5.7	14.3
Jaguar XJR-S 6.0	1991	157	7.0	16.4
Lamborghini Islero 400GTS	1969	157	5.9	13.7
Lamborghini Jarama	1971	157	6.8	16.4
Mercedes 500 SL (A)	1989	157	5.9	14.0
Lamborghini 400 GT	1966	156	7.0	17.1
Maserati Indy 4.7	1971	156	7.7	17.6
Mazda RX-7	1992	156	6.0	15.8
Mercedes 500E	1991	156	6.3	14.7
Nissan 300ZX	1990	156	5.6	14.5
Porsche Carrera 4	1989	156	5.2	14.0
Toyota Supra 3.0	1993	156	5.1	12.3
Aston Martin V-8	1973	155	5.7	13.6

Model	Year	Max speed	0-60 mph	0-100 mph
Audi A8 4.2 Quattro	1994	155	8.3	19.1
Bentley Continental S	1994	155	5.5	17.2
BMW 740i (A)	1994	155	8.8	21.2
BMW 750iL (A)	1987	155	7.7	17.8
BMW M3 Cabrio	1994	155	5.7	14.3
Ferrari 250GT	1960	155	6.5	12.8
Jaguar XJR-S 6.0	1992	155	6.3	15.1
Jaguar XJS	1976	155	6.7	16.2
Lexus LS400	1995	155	8.5	20.8
Mercedes 500SE (A)	1993	155	6.8	17.2
Porsche 911 Turbo 3.0	1975	155	6.0	13.2
TVR Tuscan SE	1966	155	5.7	13.8
Ferrari 308 GT4	1976	154	6.9	18.1
Ferrari 308 GTB	1976	154	6.8	16.5
Ferrari Mondial t	1991	154	5.6	13.9
Ford Sierra RS500	1987	154	6.1	16.2
Monteverdi 375S	1970	154	7.2	15.5
Porsche 911 Carrera 3.2	1987	154	5.6	14.0
Renault Alpine GTA Turbo	1986	154	6.0	16.3
Bentley Continental R	1991	153	6.2	18.5
Ferrari 328 GTB	1987	153	5.5	13.8
Ferrari 400i	1985	153	6.7	15.6
Jaguar XJR	1994	153	5.7	15.1
Lamborghini Espada	1972	153	7.8	18.1
Maserati Ghibli	1994	153	5.6	13.6
Mercedes S500 Coupé (A)	1994	153	7.9	20.2
Mitsubishi 3000GT	1992	153	5.8	16.1
Porsche 911 Carrera RS 2.7	1973	153	5.5	15.0
Porsche 968	1992	153	6.1	15.7
Aston Martin DB4GT Zagato	1962	152	6.1	14.1
Aston Martin DB6	1966	152	6.0	14.9
BMW 750i (A)	1989	152	7.3	17.0
Chevrolet Corvette 427	1966	152	5.4	12.8
Chevrolet Corvette 427	1971	152	5.3	12.7
Jaguar XJS HE	1982	152	6.5	17.8
Porsche 944 Turbo SE	1988	152	5.7	14.2
Venturi 210	1987	152	6.7	17.9
Chevrolet Corvette 5.7	1985	151	6.0	16.5
Ferrari 365 GTC	1969	151	6.3	14.7
Porsche 928S 4.5 (A)	1985	151	6.7	17.3
BMW M635 CSi	1989	150	6.0	15.1
Ferrari 365GT4 2+2	1975	150	7.1	18.0
Ferrari 400GT (A)	1979	150	8.0	18.7
Jaguar E 3.8 fhc	1961	150	6.9	16.2
Jaguar E 4.2 fhc	1964	150	7.0	17.2
Lamborghini 350GT	1964	150	6.4	16.3
Lotus Esprit Turbo	1988	150	5.4	13.3
Porsche 911 SC	1983	150	5.4	14.8
Porsche 911S 2.4	1972	150	6.2	17.1
TVR 420 SEAC	1988	150	4.7	12.3
Vauxhall Calibra 2.0 Turbo	1992	150	6.2	16.9

Index